OUTLINE STUDIES IN LUKE

A Devotional Commentary

by
W. H. Griffith Thomas

Foreword by
J. I. Packer

Introduction by
Warren W. Wiersbe

KREGEL PUBLICATIONS
Grand Rapids, Michigan 49501

Outline Studies in Luke by W. H. Griffith Thomas.
Copyright © 1984 by Kregel Publications, a divi-
sion of Kregel, Inc. All rights reserved.

Library of Congress Cataloging in Publication Data

Thomas W. H. Griffith (William Henry Griffith),
    1861-1924.
    Outline Studies in Luke.

    Reprint. Originally published: Outline Studies
in the Gospel of Luke. Grand Rapids, Mich.: W. B.
Eerdmans, 1950.
    1. Bible. N.T. Luke—Sermons—Outlines,
syllabi, etc. I. Title.
BS2595.T46   1984   226'.407   84-784
ISBN 0-8254-3821-7 (pbk.)

Printed in the United States of America

OUTLINE STUDIES
IN LUKE

CONTENTS

Foreword by J.I. Packer 9
Introduction to the Author by Warren W. Wiersbe . . 11
Editor's Preface by Winifred G. T. Gillespie . . . 13
Introduction to the Gospel of Luke 15
1. Certainty (1:4) 25
2. The Forerunner Announced (1:5-25) 28
3. Mary, the Mother of Jesus (1:26—2:52) . . . 33
4. The Annunciation (1:26-38) 34
5. The Song of Zacharias (1:67-79) 37
6. Christ's Birth (2:1-16) 40
7. Christ: God's Revelation (2:1-10; 1:26-56; 2:21-52) . . 42
8. The Cradle of Civilization (2:8-20) 46
9. Good Tidings (2:8-20) 48
10. The Manger Scene (2:12) 50
11. Peace and War (2:14) 53
12. Simeon and the Marks of a True Life (2:25) . . . 55
13. Simeon and the Vision of Christ (2:25-35) . . . 57
14. Simeon and the Assurance of Christ (2:25-35) . . 59
15. Simeon and Anna (2:25-38) 61
16. The Youth of Jesus (2:39-52) 62
17. A Lost Boy Found (2:42-52) 66
18. Two Suppositions (2:44; John 20:15) 68
19. The Ministry of John the Baptist (3:1-20) . . . 70
20. Christ's Baptism and Temptation (3:21,22; 4:1-3) . . 75
21. Jesus in Nazareth (4:16-30) 83
22. Jesus in Capernaum (4:31-44) 89
23. Christ's Call to a Christian Life (5:1-11) 94
24. Christian Ministry (5:1-11) 99
25. The Christian Worker (5:1-11) 101
26. Christ's Call to Service (5:1-11) 103

6 / Contents

27. Fulness, Faith, Forgiveness (5:17-25) 105
28. Penetration, Pardon, Power (5:20-22) 109
29. Four Pictures of the Saviour (5:27—6:11) . . . 112
30. Christ Chooses His Twelve Apostles (6:13-16) . . 117
31. Healing of the Centurion's Servant (7:1-10) . . . 122
32. The Son of the Widow of Nain (7:11-16) 124
33. Christ and John the Baptist (7:18-35) 128
34. Two Sinners (7:36-50) 132
35. The Parable of the Soils (8:4-15) 137
36. The Raising of Jairus' Daughter (8:41,42,49-56) . . 140
37. A Woman Healed (8:43-48) 145
38. Enough and to Spare (9:10-17) 150
39. A Fully Yielded Life (9:12-17) 154
40. Confessing Christ (9:18-26) 158
41. The Transfiguration (9:28-36) 160
42. Three Spiritual Diagnoses (9:46-56) 166
43. Three Temperaments (9:57-62) 169
44. The Sending of the Seventy (10:1-24) 175
45. Kindness and Good Works (10:25-37) 182
46. Love in Action (10:25-37) 188
47. Practical Christianity (10:25-37) 190
48. Jesus with Martha and Mary (10:38-42) . . . 192
49. Vital Lessons on Prayer (11:1-13) 198
50. More Prayer, More Power (11:1-13) 202
51. The Lord's Prayer (11:2-4) 205
52. Greater Than Jonah (11:29,30,32) 206
53. Greater Than Solomon (11:31; 1 Kings 10:1-13) . . 209
54. The Parable of the Rich Fool (12:13-21) . . . 213
55. Solicitude (12:22-34) 219
56. A Miracle of Healing (13:10-13) 222
57. Christ and the Sabbath (13:14-17) 228
58. Salvation and Service (14:1-35) 232
59. Lost: Sheep, Silver, Son! (15:1-32) 240
60. The Parable of the Lost Sheep (15:1-7) 246
61. The Parable of the Lost Silver (15:8-10) . . . 248
62. The Parable of the Lost Son (15:11-32) 250

63. Brief Outlines of the Parable of the Lost Son (15:11-24) . 255
64. The Parable of the Unjust Steward (16:1-13) . . . 257
65. The Parable of the Rich Man and Lazarus (16:19-31) . 259
66. Character (16:19-31) 264
67. "Though One Rose From the Dead" (16:31) . . . 266
68. The Healing of the Ten Lepers (17:11-19) . . . 268
69. Two Parables on Prayer (18:1-14) 273
70. Childlike or Childish? (18:15-30) 277
71. A Blind Man Sees (18:35-43) 282
72. Jesus and Zacchaeus (19:1-10) 285
73. Life's Sycamores (19:4) 289
74. Sought and Saved (19:10) 292
75. The Parable of the Pounds (19:11-27) 295
76. Jesus Weeps Over Jerusalem (19:41-44) . . . 301
77. The Seven Days of the New Testament (19:42) . . 304
78. The Authority of Christ (20:1—21:38) 308
79. The Last Passover and the First Lord's Supper
    (22:7-20) 314
80. The Lord's Supper (22:19,20) 317
81. True Humility (22:25-27) 321
82. Selflessness (22:24-37) 323
83. Our Pattern of Service (22:27) 326
84. Friend and Foe (22:31,32) 330
85. The Agony and the Arrest (22:39-53) 332
86. The Trial of Jesus (22:54-71) 336
87. Two Signs of Discipleship (22:56,58) 342
88. The Touchstone of Human Character (23:1-12) . . 344
89. The Revealer of Human Nature (23:13-25) . . . 349
90. The Crucifixion and Death of Christ (23:33-49) . . 354
91. The Women at the Sepulchre (23:55—24:2) . . . 360
92. The Resurrection of Christ (24:1-12) 362
93. The Stone Rolled Away (24:2) 368
94. Living or Dead? (24:5) 375
95. The Witness of the Gospels to the Resurrection (24:6) . 377
96. A Personal Experience (24:13-32) 381
97. Christian Friendship (24:13-35) 387

98. Emmaus and After (24:28-43) 392
99. The Way to Faith (24:32) 396
100. The Ascension (24:44-53) 397
101. Divine Compulsions (24:46,47) 402
102. The Gift of the Holy Spirit (24:49) 406
    Devotional Summary of the Gospel of Luke . . . 409

FOREWORD

William Henry Griffith Thomas, who died in 1924, was a Bible teacher of the first rank. He was, as his friend, Dyson Hague, put it, "a prodigious toiler" and his books are all full of good matter, pressed down and running over, potent to clear the heads and warm the hearts of those who love the Bible and its Christ. His clear, crisp, straightforward style joined as it was with wisdom, both theological and devotional, gave his expository works classic status; and it is a pleasure to welcome this work on Luke back in print.

Dr. Ralph G. Turnbull says in volume 3 of *The History of Preaching:* "In Griffith Thomas was combined the skill of an expert homiletician and exegete with the theologians knowledge and the humility of the devout heart." *Outline Studies in Luke,* a write-up of sermon and Bible class material, shows how true that testimony is.

Welsh by birth, Griffith Thomas served as a pastor in London, principal of Wycliffe Hall, Oxford, and professor of Systematic Theology at Wycliffe College, Toronto, before he took up the itinerant teaching ministry which filled his last years. He would have been the first professor of Systematic Theology at Dallas Theological Seminary had not death intervened.

In days when popular liberalism was on the march in mainline churches and good if foolish men thought it important to tell ordinary believers not to trust all that their Bibles said; Griffith Thomas was a doughty defender of the "old-paths" of evangelical faith. He was learned, but not academic, and much of the learning was concealed; to build up ordinary folk in the faith of Christ was his goal, and the fruit of his learning was plain, forceful instruction to that end. He was a man of vast competence in his chosen craft: and the later books on portions of Scripture about which he wrote no more eclipse his contribution than later music turns Haydn and Mozart into back numbers.

Griffith Thomas' writing radiates a kind of sunny confidence —not the bluster of aggressiveness or conceit, but the vigorous certainty of one who has read up his subject fully, explored all the options, decided between them by analysis and argument, and now knows what he knows, knows that he knows it, and wants to share it. This present book is no exception. Bible students seeking refreshment and teachers seeking resources will both be delighted with it.

Professor of Systematic Theology   J. I. PACKER
Regent College
Vancouver, B.C. Canada

INTRODUCTION TO THE AUTHOR

His advice to young preachers was, "Think yourself empty, read yourself full, write yourself clear, pray yourself keen — then enter the pulpit and let yourself go!"

William Henry Griffith Thomas (1861-1924) followed that counsel himself, and in so doing, he became one of the spiritual giants of his day. As a preacher and a teacher of preachers, he excelled in spiritual depth, practicality, and a simplicity of expression that made the most profound truths come alive with excitement.

His mother was widowed before he was born, and family financial demands forced him to leave school when he was fourteen. He was converted to Christ through the witness of some friends on March 23, 1878. The next year, he moved to London to work in an uncle's office.

But Griffith Thomas was determined to get an education, so from 10:30 P.M. until 2:30 A.M. each night, he gave himself to serious study. He became a lay curate in 1882, while attending lectures at King's College, London; and was ordained in 1885. Griffith Thomas belonged to that early fellowship in the Anglican Church that was unashamed to be called "Evangelical."

The day he was ordained, Griffith Thomas was admonished by the Bishop of London, William Temple, not to neglect his Greek New Testament. The young minister took that word to heart and, for the rest of his life, read one chapter a day from the Greek New Testament! This kind of devotion to God's Word shows up in his writings.

He ministered at St. Aldate's, Oxford, and St. Paul's, Portman Square (London), and in 1905 was named principal of Wycliffe Hall, Oxford, the Evangelical center for Anglicans studying for ministry. He taught there for five years, then moved to Toronto to join the faculty of Wycliffe College, where he taught for nine years. He and has family then moved to Philadelphia and Griffith Thomas entered a wider ministry of writing and Bible conference work. He was associated with some of the leading preachers and conference speakers of his day and often spoke at the large Bible conferences.

He joined with Lewis Sperry Chafer and others to found the Dallas Theological Seminary and was to have taught there; but his death on June 2, 1924, interrupted those plans.

Associate Teacher   WARREN W. WIERSBE
Back to the Bible Broadcast
Lincoln, Nebraska

EDITOR'S PREFACE

This book contains but a small part of the voluminous notes on Bible passages left behind by my father. It is not intended as a commentary. As will be readily seen, the notes do not by any means treat of every passage in the Gospel of Luke, and those passages which are included are sometimes outlined in more than one way, representing the author's study at various times. The volume is simply a collection of the outlines resulting from his private meditations which he expanded into sermons, addresses, or articles, as occasion arose. Indeed, I have used, for the purpose of amplification, some of the lesson helps on Luke which were based on these notes and published in *The Sunday School Times*. For this privilege I am greatly indebted to the Editors, and I wish also to acknowledge with gratitude the co-operation given me by my mother and my husband.

I send this little volume forth with the earnest hope and prayer that it may bring a blessing to each of its readers, as it has to its editor, and that the contents may be of particular use to young students of the Word.

Lafayette, Louisiana   WINIFRED G. T. GILLESPIE

INTRODUCTION TO THE GOSPEL OF LUKE

I. *Its Relation to Other Three Gospels*

    A. Grouped with first two as Synoptics. Each is a conspectus, or general survey, based on outlook common to authors. Within limits, can be arranged in tabulated form and harmonized.

    B. Relation of Synoptics to Fourth Gospel.

        1. All have in common:

            a. Backgrounds—Galilee and Judaea.

            b. Certain miracles and external events in life of Christ.

            c. Offer and rejection of Christ as King, in greatest detail.

            d. Resurrection and promise of Second Coming.

            e. Spiritual meaning of utterances to disciples.

            f. Contrast between world and church.

        2. Differing characteristics:

            a. Four Gospels and one Christ, but varying phases of His life and ministry.

            b. Early Church saw parallel with

                (1) Four heads of rivers of Eden (Gen. 2:10).

                (2) Cherubic symbolism of Ezekiel 1:10 and Revelation 4:7

                    (a) Matthew—Lion (Kingship)

                    (b) Mark—Ox or Calf (Service)

                    (c) Luke—Man (Humanity)

                    (d) John—Eagle (Deity)

            c. Matthew emphasized Judaea and Jews; Past and its Fulfilment. Mark, Rome and Romans; Present and its Works. Luke, Greece and Greeks; Future and its

Progress. John, Universe and Church; Eternity and its Spiritual Values.

d. Matthew may be said to demonstrate; Mark to depict; Luke to declare; John to describe.

e. Matthew is concerned with the coming of a Promised Saviour; Mark with the life of a Powerful Saviour, Luke with the grace of a Perfect Saviour, John with the possession of a Personal Saviour.

f. There are omissions and incidental variations in Luke's Gospel; and of 100 additions 59 are peculiar to it and characteristic of its purpose.

g. There are traces of Pauline influence, as of Peter on Mark—but no definite use of doctrines and none whatever of Epistles—striking proof of inspiration—faithful post-Pentecost record of Christ's earthly life.

II. *Its Author*

A. Never names self or uses first personal singular beyond prefaces (1:1-4; Acts 1:1,2); but universally accepted as author of this Gospel which has always borne his name, and of the Acts of the Apostles which is its sequel.

B. Mentioned by name in three New Testament passages, all in Pauline Epistles:
   1. Colossians 4:14—"Luke the beloved physician."
   2. 2 Timothy 4:11—"Only Luke is with me."
   3. Philemon 24—"Lucas, my fellowlabourer."

C. Companion of Paul in work and in prison:
   1. Acts 16:10—Joined him at Troas (perhaps because of Apostle's malady) —beginning of first "we" section.
   2. Acts 16:7; 17:1—Probably left at Philippi for seven years.
   3. Acts 20:5,6—Rejoined Paul's party there—indicated by resumption of word "we." Accompanied Paul to Jerusalem (Acts 21:15), and later to Rome (Acts 27:1; 28:16; 2 Tim. 4:11).

D. Nationality uncertain—possibly of Palestinian ancestry—a Jew of the Dispersion. Tradition has him native of Antioch. However, it is argued from Colossians 4:14 that his name is placed among Gentile Christians. If so, only non-Jewish writer of New Testament books. Godet suggests Luke was one of Emmaus disciples, accounting for very full account of incident (24:13-35) also, but briefly, mentioned by Mark (Mark 16:12,13); also substantiating Luke's claim to have had "perfect understanding of all things from the very first" (1:3). Note:—

1. References to geography of Palestine strikingly accurate throughout (e.g., 8:26; 19:1, 24:13).

2. Use of Jewish history full and correct (e.g., 1:5; 2:1-3; 19:43,44).

3. Use of Old Testament—Chapters 1-3 full of Old Testament language and genealogy, yet elsewhere less than other Gospels.

4. Clear references to political situation of Palestine (e.g., 1:15; 7:2; 20:22,24), especially in chapters 2 and 3, related to Christ's life.

5. References to social life in notable conformity with Palestinian usage.

6. Language of Gospel in three types of Greek:
    a. 1:1-4—Idiomatic.
    b. 1:5 to 2:52—Hebraic.
    c. Remainder—Less Hebraic, and with distinctive characteristics of its own.

7. Religious attitude—Christian, cosmopolitan, probably Pauline.

E. Luke an accomplished personality.
    1. Close observer—"perfect understanding" (1:3).
    2. Excellent writer—pure Greek.
    3. Painstaking historian—fullness, accuracy, continuity.
    4. Self-effacing chronicler—no mention of self beyond preface.

  5. Well-trained physician.
  6. Earnest Christian worker.
  7. Faithful friend.
F. Evidence as to authorship.
  1. Inherent in preface (1:1-4).
  2. All early MSS. headed *"kata Loukan,"* "according to Luke."
  3. Acceptance by earliest writers, from Irenaeus on.
  4. Cf. references under I-B.
G. Readers.
  1. "Theophilus," Gr., "lover of God" (1:3 as in Acts 1:1), otherwise unknown but evidently representative of Greek-speaking world—therefore, Gospel directed towards Gentiles.
  2. There are genealogical notes for their benefit.
  3. Sermon in chapter 6 summary for them of teaching of Matthew 5 to 8.

III. *Its Purpose*
A. Statement in preface not so argumentative as Matthew's, but more definitely historical in character.
B. Scope universal (cf. 2:31,32; 9:52), hence portrait of Christ also.
C. Human relationship to God emphasized (cf. chap. 15).
D. Also men's universal relationships to each other (6:27ff.; 10:30-37; 16:19-31).
E. Special reference to Greek needs, with three characteristics kept prominent:
  1. Reason—intellectuality.
  2. Culture—perfection in man.
  3. Humanity—crown of creation—deification, not God. Hence, subject of Gospel may be said to be The Universal Grace of the Divine Man Christ Jesus.

IV. *Its Analysis*
A. The Coming of the Divine Man (1:1 to 4:13).
  1. Introduction (1:1-4).

2. Origin, birth and early days (1:5 to 2:20).

3. Development under law, human and Divine (2:21-52).

4. Special preparation for work (3:1 to 4:13).
   a. His forerunner.
   b. His baptism.
   c. His descent.
   d. His temptation.

B. The Ministry of the Divine Man in Galilee—to the Jews (4:14 to 9:50).

1. Teaching leading to rejection (4:14 to 6:11).
   a. In Nazareth (4:14-30).
   b. In Capernaum (4:31 to 6:11).
2. Teaching as to Kingdom of God (6:12 to 9:50).
   a. Its constitution (6:12 to 8:3).
   b. Its development (8:4-56).
   c. Its claims (9:1-50).

C. The Ministry of the Divine Man in Samaria and Peraea —to the Gentiles (9:51 to 18:30).

1. Beginning of last journey and mission of Seventy (9:51 to 11:13).
2. Condemnation of age (11:14 to 13:21).
3. Tidings of salvation (13:22 to 15:32).
4. Life in Kingdom of God (16:1 to 18:30).

D. The Ministry of the Divine Man in Jerusalem—as Sacrafice for salvation of both Jew and Gentile (18:31 to 24:53).

1. Preparation for death (18:31 to 22:38).
   a. Triumphal entry.
   b. Last teaching.
   c. Predictions.
   d. Plot.

2. Death (22:39 to 23:56).
  a. Trial.
  b. Crucifixion.
  c. Burial.
3. Triumph (24:1-53).
  a. Resurrection.
  b. Manifestation.

OR

Luke's Thesis to Win Theophilus to Christ—through Greek ideal of Perfection personified in Him:

1:5 to 3:38—By Birth: youth, development and consecration.

4:1 to 9:36—By Life: testing, teaching and transfiguration.

9:37 to 24:53—By Death: preparation, accomplishment and culmination.

V. *Its Outstanding Characteristics—*

Spring from circumstances of writer's own life. It is a Gospel—

A. *Of Praise*
  1. Begins (1:14, 19, 42, 44, 58, 64) and ends (24:41, 52, 53) with joy: first, of meek—last, of faithful.
  2. Many instances throughout (2:10, 13, 20, 28, 38; 6:23; 8:13; 9:6; 10:17; 5:7, 10).
  3. First hymns of Christian Church here—songs of the New Covenant linked it with the Old—still in constant use, viz.; Magnificat (1:46-55); Benedictus (1:68-80); Gloria in Excelsis (2:14); Nunc Dimittis (2:29-32); and the only true form of Ave Maria (1:28, 42-45).

B. *Of Prayer*
  1. Christ's own prayers emphasized (6:12; 9:28, 29; 11:1; 22:41-46; 23:34, etc.).
  2. One of two Gospels which contain Lord's Prayer (11:2-4).

3. Other instructions as to prayer (e.g., 21:36).

4. Three parables on prayer found here only (11:5-8; 18:1-14).

C. *Of Childhood*

Fullness of detail in regard to early days of John the Baptist and of Christ peculiar to this Gospel. Chapters 1 and 2 so full of Aramaisms that they seem to have been translated from Palestinian documents the substance of which may have come from the Virgin Mary herself, or from Zacharias, or both.

D. *Of Womanhood*

Record of Elisabeth (ch. 1); the Virgin Mary (chs.1, 2); Anna (2:36-38); Mary and Martha (10:38-42); the widow of Nain (7:12-15); the woman with the infirmity (13:11-16); the women who ministered to Christ (8:2,3; 23:55; 24:10); the weeping women on way to Cross (23:27-31); and the woman a sinner (7:35-50).

E. *Of Tolerance*

Teaching of 9:52-56 exemplified in 10:33, 17:16 (re Samaritans) and in 17:12 (re lepers).

F. *Of Humility*

Teaching of 6:20-25 exemplified by Mary (1:48); the shepherds (2:8-20); poor at great supper (14:21); Lazarus the beggar (16:20).

G. *Of the Outcast*

References to the sinning woman (7:37-50); the maniac of Gadara (8:26-39); the prodigal (15:11-32); the publican (18:9-14); Mary Magdalene (8:2; 24:10).

H. *Of the Humanity of Christ*

1. Emphasized at each stage of His life (ch. 2; 4:1-13; 6:1-5; 10:30-42; 14:1-6; 19:5, 41; 22:8,15,41-44; 24:28-30, 39-43).

2. Named "Son of man" predominantly (e.g., 5:24; 9:22; 11:30; 17:22; 18:8; 22:22; 24:7).

I. *Of Sin*

Mankind pictured throughout as lost and sunk in sin, and Christ offering Himself as Saviour (19:10). It has been said that this is key verse of Luke's Gospel.

J. *Of Grace*
1. Word "grace" Pauline—primary meaning "beauty." This Gospel called "the most beautiful book ever written."
2. Grace in full New Testament sense means "unmerited favor"—includes pardon and pity—exemplified, e.g., in 7:1-15,36-50; chapter 15.

K. *Of Universality*
1. Most prominent feature of all—Gospel seen to extend far beyond confines of Jewish nation.
2. Christ shown as Son of Adam (3:38) rather than as Son of Abraham (Matt. 1:1).
3. References throughout to Gentiles: e.g., Samaritans, Romans. Luke thought to have written more especially for Greeks, as Matthew for Jews and Mark for Romans.
4. Even two Hebrew prophets, Elijah and Elisha, mentioned in relation to experiences outside covenant people (4:25-27).
5. Notable absence of Hebrew words after first two chapters.
6. Of two Gospels that mention languages of superscription, Luke's puts Greek and Latin before Hebrew (cf. John 19:20.)

VI. *The Preface* (1:1-4)
1. Only two of four Gospels begin with preface, and Luke's is only personal one stating purpose of work (cf. John 1:1-14).

2. Greek style purer than in remainder of Gospel, for body of book contains Hebrew features since materials drawn from Jewish sources.

3. Pauline influence thought to be shown in words used.

4. Key to Luke's standpoint.

   a. Makes three claims (v.3):

      (1) Full acquaintance with facts of Christ's life—"all things from the very first"—or "from above" (Gr. *anothen*). If latter, Luke claims, like Paul 1 Cor. 11:23), confirmation by direct revelation.

      (2) Accurate interpretation of records—"perfect understanding"—implies diligent research.

      (3) Orderly presentation of materials—"in order"—chronological, methodical.

   b. These claims borne out by contents:

      (1) Luke has three-fourths of materials found in Synoptics in general.

      (2) Narratives marked by historical connections and other probabilities.

      (3) Has well-marked historical progression, depicting gradual development of Christ's work.

5. Contains purpose of Gospel—"certainty" (v.4). Narrative one of facts coming from eyewitnesses.

6. Many attempts had been made (v.1), but must have failed, since only four remain and are incorporated in New Testament. Luke feels his sources adequate enough to qualify him as historian.

7. Secret of his Gospel's development.

   a. Cycle of oral teaching recorded (v.1).

   b. Account of "eyewitnesses and ministers of the word" (v.2). Greek (*hoi ap'*, etc.) relates descriptive clause to "they," i.e., the "many" of verse 1, the actual disciples—not to "us," as English usage might imply. Note example of precision of Greek as New Testament vehicle.

c. These records, as far as authentic, used by all four Evangelists, but especially by Luke, who was not one of the Twelve.

d. Development thus natural, and yet God overruling.

8. Summary of preface:
   a. Nature of Gospel—narrative of facts.
   b. Nature of Apostleship—eyewitnesses, ministers.
   c. Nature of Luke's qualifications—knowledge exact and sources adequate.
   d. Nature of Luke's purpose—to emphasize certainty.

1

CERTAINTY
(Luke 1:1,4)

Having definitely in mind "those things which are most surely believed among us" (v.1), it is both important and necessary to find out *why* we believe them. Luke, as both physician and scientist, valued knowledge and the dissemination of it. The one great desire which he had for Theophilus, certainty, is our need today.

It is often said that "mystery envelops all spiritual truths," yet it is a mystery not vague nor confused, but one of depth and glory; a marvel not of fog, but of sunshine.

Why can we be quite certain of Christianity? Because facts are its foundation. Here are four of them, starting nearest to our daily life and leading up to the Great Cause of it all.

I. *The Fact of Christian Experience—Unique Life*
   1. *It is Real.*

      There is a true consciousness—

      a. Of Peace—quiet conscience—no longer any burden of sin.

      b. Of Fellowship—sense of nearness, of speaking, of presence of God.

      c. Of Hope—expectation and anticipation make fearless and joyful.

   2. *It is Universal.*

      a. In different classes—rich and poor, educated and illiterate.

      b. In different churches—essentially and fundamentally the same.

  c. In different races—white and black, brown and red and yellow. Cf. missions the world over.

 3. *It is Satisfying.*

  a. Delivers from sin.

  b. Upholds in sorrow.

  c. Suffices in perplexity.

II. *The Fact of the Church—Unique Organization*

 1. *Its Commencement*

  a. Here and now is effect. Trace back for cause.

  b. A few who believed in their Master and were united in faith and service.

 2. *Its Continuance*

  a. Three links common to all branches:

   (1) Baptism

   (2) The Lord's Supper

   (3) The Lord's Day

  b. Links impossible to break, or account for in any other way.

III. *The Fact of the Bible—Unique Book*

 1. *Its Message*

  a. Salvation from sin—free, full, permanent.

  b. Satisfaction in life—perfect, increasing, perpetual.

 2. *Its Power*

  a. In Development—the Holy Spirit of God.

  b. In Life—Missions.

  c. In Thought—influence on books, criticism of men.

 3. *Its Preservation*

  a. By Persecution—"blood of martyrs seed of Church"

  b. By Opposition—Higher Criticism, etc.

IV. *The Fact of Christ—Unique Person*

 1. *His Life*

  a. Its Sinlessness—testified to by friend and foe.

  b. Its Self-consciousness—Son of man, Son of God.

2. *His Work*
   a. By Death
   b. By Resurrection
3. *His Influence*
   a. Contrast between Christ and others.
   b. Name and memory down ages.

Conclusion

1. Dwell in region of fact.
2. Test facts fairly.
3. Compare results of faith with those of unbelief.

2

THE FORERUNNER ANNOUNCED
(Luke 1:5-25)

IN face of the universality of this Gospel, and the fact that so much of its later development was Gentile in nature and Pauline in expression, it is significant that at its inception it was so completely Jewish—"to the Jew first" (Rom. 1:16) .This was because the offer of the Saviour was God's vindication to Israel. All the promises of the Old Testament were made good in Christ. Hence the Jewish background of this passage.

I. *Zacharias at Home* (vs. 5-7)

1. After Luke's elaborately worded preface comes this simple, direct section possibly in words of the Virgin Mary, who would be in best position to "deliver" (v.2) this first part of Gospel to writer; or else of Zacharias himself, penned during his months of silence perhaps.

2. Herod was usurper of throne, placed there by Roman conquerors—cruel, clever (cf. Matt. 2:1-12) .

3. Zacharias means "remembered by Jehovah" (see v. 11) ; Elisabeth means "God of the oath" (see v.13) .

4. Of the "course of Abia" (cf. 1 Chron. 20:10; Neh. 12:4) .

5. "Righteous before God"—upright, sincere—probably in same group with Simeon (2:25) and Anna (2:36, 37) , and others (2:38) , belonging to godly "remnant" (Isa. 1:9; 10:22; Rom. 11:5) , referred to also in Mal. 3:16-18.

6. "Commandments and ordinances"—moral law and prescribed ritual—Exodus and Leviticus.

7. Having, "no child" was heavy misfortune in Orient—counted among Jews reproach, even sin—no chance to

bring forth Messiah. But this pair had resigned themselves—they were "blameless."

II. *Zacharias at the Temple* (vs. 8-10)

1. The "lot" to burn incense came perhaps only once in
priest's lifetime and was considered highest function. Said
to have been 20,000 priests at this time (cf. only 3 in time
of Eli, 1 Sam. 2:12,13; 4:4). Divided 24 hours by retain-
ing four priests to serve six hours daily for eight days.

2. "Incense" symbol of prayer—fragrant, valuable, warm, ascending—offered possibly with words of Psa. 41:2.

3. Beautiful picture of priest and people worshipping:
   a. People in court of Temple—silent, waiting.
   b. Priest in spotless robe at altar of burnt offering—bells
   on robe showing movements.
   c. Priest in Holy Place—burning incense at golden altar.
   Now, clergyman and people minister together, through
   Sacrifice of Christ once for all. Gospel of Luke begins
   with priest executing priest's office before God, and
   ends with our High Priest Jesus Christ, entering heavenly Holy of Holies.

III. *Zacharias and Gabriel* (vs. 11-13)

1. "Right side"—favorable side (cf. Acts 7:56; Psa. 110:1).
Left was side of doom (cf. Matt. 25:34, 41) but "everlasting fire" was prepared for "devil and his angels,"
not for men.

2. "Fear not"—Divine assurance opens dispensation of grace,
after four centuries of silence following "curse" (Mal.
4:6) which was God's last word in dispensation of law.

3. "Thy prayer"—especially for son, but also for Messiah—
shows God's answers, though delayed, are sure to come.

IV. *Zacharias and John* (vs. 14-17)

1. "Joy . . . gladness . . . rejoice"—strange prophecy, joy
not characteristic of life of John the Baptist but of Messiah—yet fulfilled before and after birth (vs. 44,58).

    2. "Great" because of high office of forerunner and Nazarite character.

    3. "Turn"—keynote of John's ministry—best definition of conversion—turn with, together, i.e., turn with or to "the Lord their God" from former life. But man by nature is otherwise.

    4. "Spirit" of Elijah—righteousness and fearlessness. "Power" of Elijah—not by miracles but in sincerity and influence (John 10:41). No finer encomium—coupled with Christ's own (7:28).

V. *Zacharias and God* (vs. 18-20)

    1. "Whereby . . . ?" Zacharias looks at circumstances and cannot believe.

    2. "These things"—Gabriel—
        a. Refers to own name and position in presence of God.
        b. Declares accomplishment of Divine purpose, and
        c. Pronounces dumbness of Zacharias as proof because of unbelief.

VI. *Zacharias and the People* (vs. 21-23)

    1. Smoke of incense ascending would indicate completion of sacrifice. First, delay and, then, dumbness of their priest would mark some special occurrence—"a vision in the temple."

    2. How strange the accomplishment of "the days of his ministration" without voice, before his departure "to his own house"!

VII. *Zacharias at Home Again* (vs. 24,25)

    1. Return in faith even if weak.
    2. In due course God's Word fulfilled.

Conclusion

    Some applications:
    1. *The wisdom of delay.*
        a. Delay, not denial, in answering prayer (vs.7,13,25).
        b. Cf. ways of God and of world—God's is best!

    c. Discipline of waiting brings—
      (1) Added strength.
      (2) Deeper knowledge.
      (3) Richer answers.
    d. Cf. preparation of Christ—picture of gentleness coming out of Jewish formalism.
    e. If before God's time, never approved—other people and circumstances to be considered.

2. *The blessedness of duty.*
    a. Zacharias spiritual, faithful in ordinary life.
    b. God met him there and promised reward—such revelations best, along line of humble loyalty (cf.16:10).

3. *The keynote of the Gospel.*
    a. "Fear not" (v. 13) —removing curse of sin. Cf.—
      (1) Angel and Mary (v. 30).
      (2) Angel and Joseph (Matt. 1:20).
      (3) Angel and Shepherds (2:10).
      (4) Angel at Resurrection (Matt. 28:5).

    b. What is formerly feared often blesses and leads to repentance.
    c. Unbelief often followed by true faith. But did Elisabeth believe throughout (vs. 25,41-45,60), as contrasted with her husband's initial lack of faith (v. 20)?

4. *The strength of goodness.*
    a. Its influence—true joy and transparent virtue are catching.

    b. Its standard:
      (1) "In the sight of the Lord" (v.15).
      (2) In the sight of men (v.16).
      (3) "In the spirit and power of Elias" (v. 17).

    c. Its elements:
- (1) First character, then conduct (vs. 15-17).
- (2) John to be forerunner, reconciler, reformer, preacher.
- (3) Through Holy Spirit for both positive and negative virtues.

    d. Its consequences:

Infinite possibilities, e.g., here: Pentecost traceable to this episode!—viz., Peter to Andrew to John the Baptist to Zacharias and Elisabeth—through power of Holy Spirit and union with Christ.

3

MARY, THE MOTHER OF JESUS
(Luke 1:26—2:52)

Contrast the following outline of the Virgin Mary's life as given in Scripture with the claims which Roman Catholicism makes in order to justify worshipping her. Nowhere is she called "the Mother of God," but usually "the mother of Jesus," related as she is only to His human nature. "The young Child and His mother" is the Divine order, and our Lord even rebuked her (John 2:4), and placed His true followers on a level with her (Matt. 12:48-50). Notice her, then, in the four periods of her experience:

I. *Through Surrender to Obedience*
1. At Nazareth (Luke 1:26-56).
2. At Bethlehem (Luke 2:1-20).
3. At Jerusalem (Luke 2:21-38).
4. In Egypt (Matt. 2:13-23).
5. At Nazareth again (Luke 2:29,40,51,52).

II. *Through Uncertainty to Knowledge*
1. At Jerusalem again (Luke 2:41-50).
2. At Cana (John 2:1-12).
3. At the Lake of Galilee (Matt. 12:46-50; Mark 3:31; Luke 8:19).

III. *Through Darkness to Light*
1. At the Cross (John 19:25-27).
2. In the Upper Room (Acts 1:14).

Conclusion
Yield—Trust—Obey

4

THE ANNUNCIATION
(Luke 1:26-38)

"B<small>Y THE</small> mystery of Thy holy Incarnation," says the Anglican Litany, "good Lord, deliver us." Here we tread on holy ground and we do well to walk reverently and with godly fear. God had spoken to the fathers by the prophets, and after four centuries of silence He was now about to speak to all mankind in His Son.

I. *The Revelation*
   1. It came quietly.
      People in Palestine at that time utterly unconscious of events of permanent and universal influence.
   2. It came to woman of humble position.
      Mary lived in city of dubious repute, and yet was of priestly or Pharasaic line, with royal blood in veins.
   3. It came as announcement of God's special interest.
      Every woman desired to become mother of long-expected Messiah.
   4. It came not for merit of Mary's own.
      However, her very excellence of character was result of God's grace.

II. *The Redeemer*
   1. His Name (v. 31).
      "Jesus" means "Jehovah-Saviour," revealing Divine purpose, for He saves from sin (Matt. 1:21).
   2. His Character (v. 32).
      "Great"—
      a. In His heavenly origin as "Son of the Most High."

b. In His earthly life—in mercy, love, sympathy, blessing and power.

3. His Work (vs. 32,33).

   a. As King—which He will yet be.

   b. As King "over the house of Jacob"—implying rulership over Jews who rejected Him.

   c. As King "for ever"—when as "blessed and only Potentate, the King of Kings, and Lord of lords" (1 Tim. 6:15), He shall rule over universe (cf. Rev. 11:15), and "of His kingdom there shall be no end."

III. *The Reponse*

Mary's attitude to angelic message passed through four stages:

1. Perturbation (v.29)—perplexed at greeting from superior being.

2. Consideration (v.29)—exercised her mind as to meaning of what was evidently Divine message.

3. Investigation (v.34)—inquired further with childlike simplicity, but with no hint of unbelief (cf. Zacharias, v. 18).

4. Submission (v. 38)—responded with absolute, unquestioning confidence in God.

IV. *The Realization*

This included:

1. Evidently instantaneous thought of kinswoman in comparable case, followed by hasty departure to visit her (vs. 39, 40).

2. Immediate and Spirit-inspired response of Elisabeth to Mary's salutation (v. 41).

3. Comforting assurance of Mary's blessedness, being called the mother of the *Lord* for first time—and only time in Scripture (vs. 42.43).

4. Deserved commendation of her faith and reassurance as to "performance" of promise (v. 45).
5. Miraculous prenatal testimony of John the Baptist to Christ (vs. 41,44).

Conclusion

1. The angel brought the remarkable message.
2. Mary received it as a Divine revelation.
3. Elisabeth confirmed the promise through the Holy Spirit.

Thus the response of faith—

1. Takes God at His word.
2. Rests entirely on what God says because it is He who says it.
3. Finds in His revelation the great secret of strength, comfort and blessing.

5

THE SONG OF ZACHARIAS
(Luke 1:67-79)

Zacharias had "remained speechless" all those months. Corroborating his wife's declaration, "He (the child) shall be called John" (v. 60), by a flat statement in writing, "His name is John" (v. 63), "his mouth was opened immediately and his tongue loosed." What the months of silence must have done for Zacharias in contemplation of the Messianic idea! Faith, not learning, was the substance of its development in his mind, and when faith was shown speech came again, Zacharias quickly used it in praising God for remembering His promises after four centuries of silence. Then he foretold what John the Baptist would be and do.

Here is the beautiful song known to the Church as the Benedictus (from the Latin of its initial word). The mind of its author was full of Scripture, almost every verse containing some allusion. It was first used in public worship during the sixth century. In verse 67 it is called a prophecy, or inspired utterance, and it has been referred to as the last prophecy of the old dispensation and the first prophecy of the new. Thus it forms a link between the two. God had "visited" (v. 68) his people Israel, and had "raised up an horn of salvation" (v. 69) in fulfilment of Hannah's prophecy (1 Sam. 2:10). the horn being a symbol of power and glory.

I. *The Jewish Conception of Messiah*

1. Cf. their idea of king.

2. Note Maccabbean influence (Apocrypha).

3. Yet Roman yoke heavy—hence their rejection of Christ.

4. But Zacharias and others had glimpses at times of true situation.

II. *The Holy Spirit before Pentecost*

1. Cf. Him in Old Testament and note continuity.
2. Here (v. 67) is instance of such inspiration.
3. After Pentecost, difference in both form and degree.

III. *The Influence of Holy Scripture*

1. Authority of Old Testament—to New Testament as foundation to roof.
2. Cf. Paul's words to Timothy (2 Tim. 3:14-17).
3. Hebrews influenced by Leviticus—Matthew by Old Testament prophecy.

IV. *The Redemption of Christ*

1. Its order—remission, salvation, deliverance, light, guidance (vs. 76-79).
2. Its source—tender mercy of God (v. 78).
3. Its result—service—fearless, holy, righteous, continual (vs. 74,75).
4. Its Author.

   a. A Horn of Salvation (v. 69).
   b. The Highest (v. 76).
   c. The Lord (v. 76).
   d. The Dayspring—margin, Sunrising (v. 78).

V. *The Faithfulness of God*

1. Visited—had not forgotten (v. 68).
2. Kept His promise, covenant and oath (vs. 72, 73). Note progression here.
3. In His wisdom, this was the time, though Israel had wandered far from His purpose. "I am the Lord, I change not" (Mal. 3:6).

Conclusion

1. *A Backward Look*

   Compare what is to what might have been:

   1. Character crude, badly developed.
   2. Work poorly done, opportunities lost. But God is the same, so we take heart, and return to Him.

2. *A Forward Look*

   1. Conditions.
      a. Worthy object.
      b. Fitting energy.
      c. Earnest movement.
      d. Real progress.
      e. Divine guidance.

   2. Nature.
      a. Increase of manhood.
      b. Holiness.
      c. Truth.
      d. Service.

   3. Motives.
      a. God's call.
      b. God's help.
      c. God's blessing.

6

CHRIST'S BIRTH
(Luke 2:1-16)

THE "fulness of time," "the hour," had come. With the Augustan Era, pagan culture had reached its zenith, pagan crime its lowest depths. When Jesus Christ was born, the world's outlook was one of unparalleled sorrow and sin.

I. *The Birth*

1. A Mystery.

   Every cradle holds the mystery of life, this one more than all others.

2. A Miracle.

   Physical and moral—"that holy thing" (1:35).

3. A Marvel.

   Consider who He is who came: "Before Abraham was, I am" (John 8:58); "was rich, yet for your sakes became poor" (2 Cor. 8:9); "being in the form of God . . . took upon him the form of a servant" (Phil. 2:7).

II. *The Angel*

A Model Preacher—of highest order of God's messengers—his sermon short, pointed, comprehensive, effective.

III. *The Shepherds*

Model Hearers—eager listeners, instant seekers, ardent believers, reverent worshippers, earnest preachers. "They came with haste" (v. 16); "they made known abroad the saying" (v. 17).

Conclusion

1. *Look into the Cradle*—a Virgin's Child, Israel's Messiah, the world's Saviour, God's own Son. It conceals His power and majesty; it reveals His grace and love.

2. *Listen to the Message*—the Gospel summed up: A Saviour—is born—unto you—this day—for all people.

3. *Learn the Angels' Hymn*—"that glorious song of old"—its keynote joy.

4. *Love the Saviour*—"I love Thee, Lord Jesus"—His love begets love.

5. Be *Like the Shepherds*—make Him known "till each remotest nation has learned Messiah's Name."

7

CHRIST: GOD'S REVELATION
(Luke 2:1-10; 1:26-56; 2:21-52)

I. *Jesus Born of Woman* (vs. 1-7)
   1. The Time (vs. 1-3)
   2. The Place (v. 4)
   3. The Parent (v. 5)
   4. The Circumstances (vs. 6,7)

   Lessons from Mary
   1. Her Privilege—mother of Messiah (1:31-33,43).
   2. Her Proving—as to faith and courage (1:38). Cf. her first question with that of Zacharias (vs. 34,18).
   3. Her Patience—Cf. Mic. 5:2, and yet she lived at Nazareth. 70 miles from Bethlehem—circumstances all against her (1:39-56).
   4. Her Praise—heart filled with joy (1:46-55).
   5. Her Peace—caused by faith (1:48).
   6. Her Pondering—intelligence (2:19,51).
   7. Her Piety—kept the Law (2:21-24, 39, 41-43).

II. *Jesus Announced of Angels* (vs. 8-14)
   1. The Shepherds (v. 8)
   2. The Angel (v. 9)
   3. The Message (vs. 10-12)
   4. The Song (vs. 13,14)

   Lessons from the Angels
   1. The Time of God's Revelation (v. 8)
      a. Night—symbol of world's ignorance, sorrow, sin, death. Heathenism and Judaism had alike failed.
      b. Yet unobtrusive as light.

2. The Method of God's Revelation (v. 9)
   a. Angel—as if most natural (cf. 1:11, 26).
   b. Glory—Shekinah, absent for years.

3. The Progress of God's Revelation (vs. 10-14)
   a. First reassures, then arrests attention.
   b. Develops fully—born man, Christ is revealed as needed Saviour as well as Lord Jehovah of Old Testament.

4. The Character of God's Revelation (vs. 10,11)
   a. Good. Not merely re-enactment of Law, but good news to those breaking Law.
   b. Joyful. Cf. (1) world then; (2) early Church; (3) Middle Ages; (4) now.
   c. Universal. "All"—cf. "you" (v. 11), not "us," for angels excluded, but "all people" included.

5. The Proofs of God's Revelation (v. 12)
   a. Strange mark of divinity—sign a babe in a manger—human, yet having Divine majesty.
   b. Note "Alps" of Revelation.
      (1) The heavens—power and wisdom.
      (2) Mineral kingdom—form and color.
      (3) Plant kingdom—life and growth.
      (4) Animal kingdom—instinct, impulse, affection.
      (5) Man—highest peak of creation, yet sinful as others are not, they being only influenced by man's sin.
      (6) Christ—greatest of them all—necessary in order fully to realize God—added new character to volume of God's love.

6. The Results of Revelation (vs. 13,14)
   a. "Glory to God" realized at once.
   b. "On earth peace" fulfilled gradually—individual, family, national, universal.

III. *Jesus Seen of Shepherds* (vs. 15-20)
   1. Faith (v. 15)
   2. Reward (v. 16)
   3. Testimony (v. 17)
   4. Outcome (vs. 18-20)

Lessons from the Shepherds
   1. Revelation to Humble
      a. They were poor, weak, unlearned men. Cf. 1 Cor. 1:26-29—"not many wise . . . mighty . . . noble are called."
      b. Do we, therefore, want revelation?

   2. Revelation in Path of Duty
      a. At work when angel came. Cf. Moses, Joshua, Gideon, Zacharias.
      b. "Do ye nexte thynge"—old English motto.

   3. Revelation causing Momentary Fear
      a. Because of gulf between God and man. Cf. angelic appearances to Manoah, Zacharias, Mary.
      b. Because of sin—feeling of unworthiness.

   4. Revelation Received
      a. Accepted at once.
      b. Acted upon at once.

   5. Revelation Verified
      a. Go—see—know.
      b. Live truth and know more and more.

   6. Revelation Shared
      a. Testify—Divine compulsion.
      b. Cf. Acts 4:20—"cannot but speak."

   7. Revelation Retained
      a. Returned to daily life—Sunday to Monday—has been called "the glory of the commonplace."
      b. Praising because revelation real—result abiding.

Conclusion

1. What is Christ to us?
   a. Familiar story? Or one ever fresh?
   b. A test for us: Are we like the shepherds, who received, rejoiced, recounted, and returned?

2. How may Christ be all in all to us?
   a. "Let us now go" to Bethlehem—Calvary—Olivet!
   b. Let us yield to Him as center of life now as then.

8

THE CRADLE OF CHRISTIANITY
(Luke 2:8-20)

I. *The Event*

The birth of Christ was the Hinge of History, the Cradle of Christianity, but—

1. Mark its Lowliness. In a manger was the beginning of a life of sorrow, of poverty, of rejection. A little Stranger. His own received Him not—a great mystery when we think who He was: a Saviour—the Christ—the Lord—the Eternal Word made flesh to dwell among us, full of grace and truth.

2. *Mark its Quietness.* An entire absence of pomp, display, earth's fireworks—the secret told to a few shepherds, hinted to a few wise men. But this is intelligible when we consider what kind of work He came to do. A Saviour—that word holds all His history, explains it, makes it beautiful and fitting.

3. *Mark its Apparent Weakness.* A babe, a child, a grain of mustard seed, a tiny rill of the river of the water of life, a tiny ray of the Light that was to lighten the Gentiles and give light to them that sat in darkness.

II. *The Event Announced*

1. *The Message Delivered.* Its keynote was joy—great, lasting, holy.

2. *The Song Sung.* Its dominant note was glory to God— God coming very near in the Person of His Son Emmanuel—"God with us"—God coming down to men, not to condemn but to save.

3. *The Marvel Revealed.* Greatest of wonders, of miracles, because He is the "Wonderful" (Isa. 9:6).

4. *The Recipients Indicated.* Throughout the New Testament:

   a. "Unto you is born this day a Saviour" (2:11).

   b. "Unto you, first God, having raised up His Son Jesus, sent Him to bless you" (Acts 3:26).

   c. "Unto you is this salvation sent" (Acts 13:26).

   d. "Unto you which believe He is precious" (2 Pet. 2:7).

III. *The Event Acclaimed*

The shepherds were:

1. *The first hearers of the Gospel.* What attention! At night, yet they were wide awake. What reverence! In that temple, the sky above for roof, the flowery sward beneath for floor, and the glorious light around for walls!

2. *The first believers of the Gospel.* Faith led their steps to Bethlehem, to the stable, to the manger.

3. *The first preachers of the Gospel.* They "made known abroad" (v. 17). "Let him that heareth say, Come" (Rev. 22:27).

Conclusion

1. Is the purpose of Christ's birth being fulfilled in *me*? If it is not, why not?

2. Has the Gospel become good news to *me*? If it has not, why not?

3. What am *I* doing to "spread the blessed tidings all the world around?" If nothing, why not?

9

GOOD TIDINGS
(Luke 2:8-20)

I. *What the Angel Said* (vs. 8-14)

His message was given—

1. To quiet fear—"fear not"—assurance.
2. To awaken joy—"good tidings of great joy"—announcement.
3. To indicate universality—"to all people"—application.
4. To dispel doubt—"city of David"—fulfilment.
5. To reveal threefold Name:
   a. "Saviour"—Redeemer.
   b. "Christ"—Messiah.
   c. "Lord"—God Himself.

N. B. Angels—

1. Know what is going on upon earth (2 Sam. 14:20; 1 Cor. 4:9).
2. Have borne special messages (Judg. 13:2-23; Luke 1:11-20,26-38).
3. Especially watch over children (Matt. 18:10).
4. Especially minister to believers (Heb. 1:14).
5. Especially care for spirits of blessed dead (Luke 16:22).
6. Will be active in end of age (Matt. 13:39).
7. Will be active in Second Coming of the Lord (Matt. 16:27; 2 Thess. 1:7).
8. Will be our companions for eternity (Rev. 22:9).

II. *What the Shepherds Did* (vs. 15-20)

1. Spoke.
2. Went.

3. Saw.

4. Told.

5. Rejoiced.

Conclusion—

1. The Gospel meant "great joy" to—
   a. Mary
   b. Messengers
   c. Men
   d. Me

2. Let me, therefore—
   a. Seek the Saviour
   b. Spread the Story
   c. Swell the Song

> What can I give Him,
>   Poor as I am?
> If I were a shepherd
>   I would bring a lamb;
> If I were a wise man
>   I would do my part;
> Yet what can I give Him?
>   Give Him my heart!

10

THE MANGER SCENE
(Luke 2:12)

T HERE are two incidents, one at the commencement and the other near the close of Christ's life, which are very familiar and yet contain one of the great mysteries of Christ and of Christianity. In Luke 2:11,12, we find One who is called "Saviour" and "Lord" and yet is referred to also as "the babe." In John 13:3-5, this same Person is shown as fully conscious of His unique relationship to God the Father, and yet He actually washed human feet, one of the lowliest and most distasteful of occupations. But these were no accidents—His manger birth, His feet-washing. They are symbolic of Himself, of His Gospel, and of His Church. Note the elements of Divine power in the manger scene:

I. *Naturalness*

1. Sight simple and natural—Babe yet Saviour. Jewish leaders desired "signs" but shepherds rejoiced because they could see Divine in ordinary.

2. Christ's life one with ours—makes Bible a different book—sacraments, though both are human in form of institution, take on new significance.

3. Gospel along lines of nature and of human temptation. Assimilation therefore true and intensifies with time—no eccentricities in it. Relationship parallels need—perfectly natural to see Christ as babe, child, and youth—not mature man all His earthly life.

II. *Quietness*

1. Picture scene—simple, quiet, unpretentious, unknown to world—absence of adventitious interest or awe-inspiring circumstance. Like air and light—unobtrusive, yet permeating.

2. Christ's life—"Not shout nor cry"—like His Gospel—like His Church.

3. World ignorant—yet testifies to revelation by date on every letter and document. All seemed as before, yet new era had dawned. Silently, quietly, world changed.

III. *Meekness*

1. Humility—so through life, attitude of servant (Matt. 11: 29; John 13:3-5). Sign and source of greatness.

2. World scornful—yet Galilean has conquered.

IV. *Unselfishness*

1. Christ descends—within limits of Phil. 2:5-8. "Not to be ministered unto, but to minister, and to give His life a ransom for many" (Mark 10:45).

2. World scorns such attitude. Men soar but God stoops. Ambition human, unselfishness Divine.

3. Christ-like life the self-sacrificing life—selfless, therefore helpful.

Conclusion

1. Ask yourself:

   a. Is this Christ yours?

   b. Have you room for Him?

   c. Are you among His own?

2. Submit and imitate—strive to be—
   a. Natural yet spiritual.
   b. Quiet yet powerful.
   c. Meek yet noble.
   d. Unselfish yet God-like.
   So Christ will be manifest in your life.

"Holy Lord, we now surrender to Thy loving, glad dominion;
We will welcome Thee as Saviour, as our Master, Guide, and Friend;
We will henceforth only glory in Thy Gospel's wondrous story,
And will be Thy willing servants for a life that knows no end."

11

PEACE AND WAR
(Luke 2:14)

T HE Christmas message is one of peace; and yet Christ Himself said, "I came not to send peace, but a sword" (Matt. 10:34). However, peace is a great word in the Bible (e.g., Isa. 11), and always a complete contrast to war. We read, "Peace, good will to men"—what do these words mean? The change of one letter in the original marks the difference of translation between the King James and the American Standard Versions, the latter reading: "Peace among men in whom he is well pleased." There are high authorities on both sides. If the reading of the Standard Version is correct it must mean that peace will be found only among those who through their acceptance of Christ are "men of God's good pleasure."

But war is a factor grim and terrible in our world of today, and we must take it into account.

I. *When War is Unjustifiable*

When it is war of aggression. There have been war-loving nations all through history: Assyria, Egypt, France under Napoleon, Germany. We ourselves have not been guiltless.

II. *When War is Justified*

Only on ground of righteous cause:

1. Self-defense—e.g., England vs. Spanish Armada, France in 1870.

2. Relief of downtrodden—e.g., Soudan, Cuba, Philippines, Belgium.

III. *How War may be Prevented*

Even justifiable war is a curse. How may we end war of all sorts?

1. By acceptance of Gospel of Peace by the individual:

   a. First, peace with God (Rom. 5:1).

   b. Then, the peace of God, between man and man (Eph. 2:14).

2. By acknowledgment of Gospel of Peace by the nation:

   a. Christianity only religion which emphasizes brotherhood between man and man. Hinduism, Confucianism, Buddhism, Imperial Rome, Judaism, not favorable and never missionary. But basis must always be the Fatherhood of God, not by generation but by regeneration.

   b. Christianity always urges good international relations, as free as possible. e.g., in education, art, literature, trade. God has been called "Great Free Trader"— air, sun, rain, etc., all free for all. Cf. preferential trade of nation with nation—colonies only, mother-country only, similar currency only, etc. What is morally wrong—opposite of brotherhood, freedom of movement—never politically right.

Conclusion

Acceptance of the Gospel will inevitably lead to support of and participation in foreign missionary work. Cf. Paul's constant emphasis on Christian character and holiness, of which soul-winning will be natural outcome (e.g., 2 Tim. 4:5). This is best method of paving way to true world peace which will have its complete fulfilment only in coming of Prince of Peace, our Lord Jesus Christ Himself.

12

SIMEON AND THE MARKS OF A TRUE LIFE*
(Luke 2:25)

THERE are few more interesting subjects for study than the group of choice souls associated with our Lord's birth and early days—Zacharias, Elisabeth, Mary, Joseph, Simeon, Anna. Of each something commendatory and distinctive is said, indicating the reality of his or her life and relation to God. Here it is Simeon who illustrates the marks of a true Christian experience.

I. *The Elements of a True Life*

    1. In relation to the past—"righteous"
       a. Sin forgiven and covered.
       b. Guilt removed for ever.
       c. Acceptance with God assured.

    2. In relation to the present—"devout"
       a. The saved sinner as a worshipper.
       b. A true attitude to an almighty, gracious God.
       c. Dependence—Delight—Demonstration.

    3. In relation to the future—"looking for the consolation of Israel"
       a. The forward look of hope.
       b. Not to death but to Christ's coming (v. 26)—so we to His Second Advent.
       c. To look forward thus was "consolation," not dread—so to us now.

---

* Also in Sermon Outlines, p. 98

II. *The Secret of a True Life*—"the Holy Spirit was upon him"

1. The Spirit brings the soul to Christ (v. 27) who is our salvation (v. 30), and applies His righteousness (1 Tim. 3:16).

2. The Spirit makes us truly devout and inspires our devotion (v. 28), sonship (Gal. 4:6), and holiness (2 Thess. 2:13).

3. The Spirit inspires our hope by glorifying Christ (v. 32) and bringing His words to our remembrance (John 14:26).

Therefore, all is by the Holy Spirit, in Him and through Him.

Conclusion

1. The True Christian Life
   a. Means of its commencement—faith.
   b. Secret of its retention—love.
   c. Anticipation of its fulfilment—hope.

2. The Holy Spirit of God
   a. Rests on the soul in conversion.
   b. Reveals to the mind in consecration.
   c. Replenishes the life in anticipation.

13

SIMEON AND THE VISION OF CHRIST
(Luke 2:25-35)

THE circumcision of Christ and the ceremonial purifi-
cation of His Mother (vs. 21-24) had to be exactly as directed
to Abraham (Gen. 17:9-14) and in the Mosaic Law (Lev. 12:
1-8). Mary's offering was a pair of the birds designated for a
poor woman's gift, and this sacrifice was in effect to "redeem"
(Exod. 13:13-15) the Child—her firstborn (Num. 8:17)—from
the Temple. The little Family is met by Simeon (vs. 27, 28),
in a scene of strong contrast between infancy and old age.

I. *His Character*—"just and devout" (v. 25)
   Stood out from low state of morals of time—yet many such,
   especially in quiet places.

II. *His Attitude*—"waiting" (v. 25)
   Not as majority who waited for a Conqueror with temporal
   power, but had special conception of Christ as Consolation
   of Israel with spiritual power—and this by both prophecy
   and promise. Simeon was like a sentinel keeping watch—
   antithesis of his times—taking part, with Old Testament
   prophets and John the Baptist, in moral preparation for
   Christ.

III. *His Secret*—"the Holy Ghost was upon him" (v. 25)
   The Holy Spirit—
   1. Brings the soul to Christ (v. 26) —dealing with the past;
   2. Calls forth the soul's devotion (v. 27) —commanding the
      present;
   3. Inspires the soul's hope (v. 25) —making the future
      bright.

IV. *His Satisfaction*—"blessed God" (v. 28)

His assurance (v. 26) and his leading (v. 27) coincided with preparation of Child Jesus (v. 27) in this result of his waiting (v. 25). No wonder Simeon rejoiced!

V. *His Song*—*"Nunc dimittis servum tuum, Domine"* (v. 29)

The fifth and last of our Divinely inspired canticles recorded by St. Luke:

1. Dismissal of Simeon's spirit requested (v. 29).
2. Cause—sight of God's Salvation (v. 30).
3. Characteristics of this Salvation:
   a. Prepared by God Himself (v. 31). Cf. Rev. 13:8.
   b. For Gentiles as well as Jews—"all people" (vs. 31,32).
   c. To be "glory" of Israel (v. 32)—full realization still future.

VI. *His Prophecy*—"behold, . . ." (vs. 34,35)

1. Concerning Mary—a shadow, a sword.
2. Concerning Christ—a touchstone, a sign, to reveal the very thoughts of those who would—
   a. Fall and not rise again—into eternal death;
   b. Fall but rise again—into and out of grave of self.
   All world affected in one way or another by Mary's Son.

VII. *His Anticipation*—"depart in peace" (v. 29)

1. To "depart," according to God's promise (v. 26) Cf. Phil. 1:23.
2. To go "in peace," because he had seen Christ (v. 29).

Conclusion

In Simeon's vision of Christ, His life and His death were like the two points of a crescent moon. Our vision of Christ should be fuller and more abiding than was his—like the sun shining in its strength. Is it?

14

SIMEON AND THE ASSURANCE OF CHRIST
(Luke 2:25-35)

T̲ʜ̲ᴇ̲ time was favorable for the coming of the Messiah. Religion was powerless to "heal the tainted fountains of the blood." Heathen systems had confessedly failed, and Judaism had become formal and lacking in spirituality. Rome bound a great portion of the civilized world together under one government with fine roads to facilitate travel stretching from the capital to the most distant parts of the Empire. Greek, as never before, was the one great language of cultured and intellectual life. The Jews were dispersed over many lands and had carried everywhere their national hope of a Deliverer.

This hope was shared by Simeon—in fact, he had assurance of Him. Note in this incident:

I. *Simeon*

1. The Revelation he had of Christ (v. 26).
"The Lord's Christ—God's Messiah—through study of Scriptures, prayer, waiting, and witness of the Holy Spirit.

2. The Recognition he made of Christ (v. 27).

Common occurrence to see infants brought into Temple—but this Child thrilled his heart with unwonted excitement.

3. The Reception he gave to Christ (v. 28).

Took Him in his arms—arms of faith stretched out. Early illustration of saving faith, "whereby we receive and rest on Him alone for salvation."

4. The Rest he obtained in Christ (v. 29).

Ready to "depart in peace"—satisfied. Those who welcome Christ may also welcome death if and when it comes. Terror and darkness flee before presence of Him who is Light and Life.

II. *Jesus Christ*

In this incident, He is seen to be:

1. The Consolation of Israel, of Gentiles, of sinners, of saints (v. 25).

2. The Light of men—dispelling darkness, showing way back to God (v. 32).

3. The Revealer of thoughts of mind, tendencies of heart (v. 35).

4. The Touchstone of many: to some the Stepping-Stone to higher things; to others the Stone of Stumbling to deeper depths (v. 34; 1 Pet. 2:8).

Conclusion

1. Jesus resting in Simeon's arms—Service.

2. Simeon resting on Jesus' breast—Salvation.

15

SIMEON AND ANNA
(Luke 2:25-38)

I. *They Were Competent Witnesses*

   1. Honest (v. 25)
   2. Alert (vs. 25,28,38)
   3. Inspired (vs. 25,26,27,38)
   4. Enlightened (vs. 26,34,35,36)
   5. Guided (vs. 27,38)
   6. Consecrated (vs. 29,37)

II. *Theirs Was A Conclusive Testimony*

   1. Satisfaction acknowledged (v. 29)
   2. Saviour recognized (v. 30)
   3. Source attributed (v. 31)
   4. Service outlined (v. 32)
   5. Sign described (v. 34)
   6. Sorrows anticipated (v. 35)
   7. Salvation proclaimed (v. 38)

16

THE YOUTH OF JESUS
(Luke 2:39-52)

THE silence of the New Testament concerning this period of our Lord's life is broken only by this passage. Many strange and improbable stories of His youth are narrated in the Apocryphal "Gospels," but this is the only authentic record of nearly thirty years. It is a fragment, but it is also a sample, and therefore adequate and valuable.

I. *A Child Grew in Nazareth* (v. 40)

"Fair as a beauteous, tender flower amid the desert grows."

1. Growth was complete and balanced, being threefold: physical, spiritual, mental. Cf. order here with that of v. 52. Child needs growth, strength, knowledge; youth needs wisdom, stature, Divine favor, and human favor, or good social relationship.

2. Nazareth (vs. 4, 39) was village in Galilee—quiet, insignificant, rural, beautifully situated, yet, we do not know why, notorious for rudeness and wickedness (4:29; John 1:46). Hence suitable as scene of early life on earth of the Saviour—mingling of restraint and license—for children are plants that do better in shelter than in conservatory. Mother and foster-father Joseph doubtless of stalwart, decent working class, but poor (Cf. 2:24; Lev. 12:8).

3. Home was godly one—Scripture training doubtless (Deut. 6:6,7). Jesus would attend village school connected with synagogue. We know He could read (4:16), and write (John 8:6). Languages were Syrian, or Aramaic, and Greek.

II. *A Boy was Found in the House of God*

1. *The Great Event to the Boy Jesus.*

   a. Annual visit of parents to Jerusalem was in obedience to law (Deut. 16:1), for Passover was most important feast (Exod. 12:2, 25). "The days" (v. 43) would be seven, as required in Deut. 16:3ff.

   b. At age of twelve, Jewish boy became a "son of the law" and commenced life on own responsibility—life developing earlier in East. Local synagogue first, then Temple at Jerusalem. Fact of personal responsibility of Boy Jesus may account for parents leaving Him to Himself (vs. 43,44).

2. *The Great Anxiety about Jesus*

   a. For three days, Jesus was "lost" in Temple—there by inclination (Cf. Psa. 27:4; 69:9). Further, imperative of duty indicated—"I must" (v. 49).

   b. "Doctors" (v. 46) from Latin *doctores,* those who teach. Pictures of this episode are entitled "Child Jesus Disputing . . ." but not so. Attitude was perfectly natural and in keeping with intelligent youth: listened first, then asked questions (v. 46). Learned men were astonished at His mental powers (v. 47).

   c. Mary and Joseph also amazed—mother's expostulation suggests forgetfulness for time being of uniqueness of her Son. May not have discussed with Him circumstances of His birth.

3. *The Great Answer from Jesus*

   a. But note contrast between Mary's words, "thy father" (v. 18) and the Boy's words, "my Father" (v. 49). Clearly He knew Who and What He was.

   b. Reply first recorded words of Christ. Literally, "in the things of my Father" and can include "business" (Authorized) and "house" (American Revised). Word "must" very striking and often used by and of Christ (Cf. 22:37; Matt. 26:54; Mark 8:31; John 3:30; 4:4; 9:4). Suggests He lived in obligation to Father's will. Indicated to Mary and Joseph He knew what they did not think He knew—and even yet they did not understand (v. 50). But we do not know *how* He became conscious of His special relationship to God.

   c. Note therefore Christ's assumption of obligation:
     (1) His relationship to His Father.
     (2) His communion in His Father's House.
     (3) His service in behalf of His Father's business.

III. *A Youth was Trained in a Godly Home*
Notwithstanding His self-knowledge, His "Messianic consciousness," Jesus ready to return to Nazareth. Note His life there for eighteen more years:

1. *In Relation to Man*
   a. Subjection. God's mode of training often involves obedience to authority and acceptance of obscurity. In all Nature, great results from secret processes, e.g., rocks, coal, seed.

   b. Jesus knew seclusion, confinement, routine, but made no complaints of narrow life. Did not measure work by magnitude or conspicuousness.

   c. Growth natural, and yet consciousness of supernatural vocation was deepening.

   d. Development did not mean imperfection at any stage, as with us—from error to truth, out of greater deficiency into less. But Jesus grew as plant does ("a rod out of the stem of Jesse," Isa. 11:1)—from shoot to bud to flower to fruit, perfect at each stage. Thus Jesus was perfect as babe, boy, youth, man.

   e. Favor includes widening opportunity—life testifying to qualities in sight of others.

2. *In Relation to God*
   a. Devotion. "Father's business" at twelve and throughout life—yet meanwhile, according to tradition, worked as carpenter.
   b. Patience. So necessary in important work. In spite of consciousness of Sonship and mission, did not rebel or chafe as young often do. "Hurry enfeebles."
   c. Worship. Communion with His Father and attendance on services in sanctuary.
   d. Learning. Ready to receive instruction of others and yet use His own mental powers.

Conclusion

There should be:

1. Growth—constant progress and development.
2. Complete Growth—no part lacking.
3. Proportionate Growth—toward a fourfold life:
   a. Physical—body needs development in strength, purity, and capacity.
   b. Intellectual—mind requires information (knowledge) and power to use it (wisdom).
   c. Spiritual—relation to God essential for contrast and communion. Growth in the direction requires:
      (1) Knowledge of His Word—He speaking to us.
      (2) Power in prayer—we speaking to Him.
   d. Social—relation to fellow men must be right. Character is what we are—reputation is what others think us to be. Both must be in line with Christian profession. Cf. Acts 6:3; 1 Tim. 3:7.

"The length and the breadth and the height of it are equal" was written of the Bride of Christ, the New Jerusalem (Rev. 21:16). Christ Himself grew in personal power (length), social influence (breadth), and spiritual attitude (height), and every part was proportioned.

"What is *your* life?"

17

A LOST BOY FOUND
(Luke 2:42-52)

IT IS a truism that like seeks like. "Birds of a feather flock together" is another way of putting it. Someone has expressed the same principle thus: "Let me see where you go and I will show you what you are!"

I. *Lost in the City* (vs. 42-45)

1. Perhaps Mary and Joseph were not really neglectful, for they supposed Jesus to be with kinsfolk or friends. They may have actually left Him with them.

2. Not finding Him, they turned back to seek Him. What were their feelings? Did they recall circumstances of birth, including Herod's enmity, and become prey to panic?

II. *Found in the House of God* (vs. 46-52)

1. The Boy Jesus—

   a. Sinned not.
   b. Studied Word of God.
   c. Sought wisdom.
   d. Submitted Himself.

2. For true development of body, there must be food and exercise. Spiritually, these mean the Word of God and service. We find Jesus—

   a. Loving and being in God's House.
   b. Loving and knowing God's Word.
   c. Loving and finding out God's Will.

d. Loving and doing God's Work. All of which gave Him, and will give us.

e. Loveliness of Life.

Conclusion

We, too, shall be found often in God's House, whenever we find that—

1. The Word of God is truly taught there, and
2. The people of God there are mutually helpful.

18

TWO SUPPOSITIONS
(Luke 2:44; John 20:15)

Two suppositions concerning Christ have been recorded for us. In the first passage, He was supposed to be—

I. *In the Company*
   A. *The Error*

   It was due to the following:
   1. Haste. Hurried departure from Jerusalem put Mary and Joseph out of touch with Jesus. So neglect of communion with God often comes through haste.
   2. Preoccupation. They omitted to watch over Jesus because occupied with other matters. So ceasing to "keep your eyes upon Jesus," with its necessary verification of leading, may bring disaster. Cf. 1 Kings 20:40.
   3. Substitution. Busy with conversation with kinsfolk perhaps seldom met. So talk with Christians, and reading of other books, though often good and legitimate, may exclude Bible-reading or make it merely second-hand.

   B. *The Test*

   If communion with Christ be true and real, there will be:
   1. Peace (John 20:19; Rom. 15:33)
   2. Purity (Hos. 11:9; 1 Cor. 3:16)
   3. Power (Zeph. 3:17; 2 Cor. 13:3)
   4. Courage (Josh. 1:9; Psa. 42:5)

5. Wisdom (Eph. 1:17; Col. 2:3)
6. Unity (John 17:22,23; Eph. 4:3)
7. Satisfaction (Joel 2:26f; Psa. 36:8)
8. Expectation (Col. 1:27; Titus 2:13)

In our second passage, Christ was supposed to be—

II. *The Gardener*

A. *The Error*

It included the following:

1. A Low Estimate of Christ. Mary Magdalene was occupied with merely human Master. So we shall find this conception of Him insufficient to salvation or communion.

2. The Thought of Christ as Dead. She did not expect Him to rise again. So Roman Catholic crucifix as symbol of faith, instead of empty tomb (Cf. 2 Cor. 5:16).

B. *The Test*

If knowledge of Christ be true to facts, there will be:

1. Sorrow for sin.
2. Deliverance from fear.
3. Relief from responsibility.
4. Assurance of individual care.
5. Desire for God's glory.
6. Expectation of fruit-bearing.
7. Concern over others.

Conclusion

Don't "suppose"—say, "I know!"—I know *where* He is; I know *what* He is. My *knowledge* of Him will lead me to *union* and *communion* with Him, the end and object of all God's dealings with man. Christ's work on the Cross had two aspects: It was for sin (Rom. 8:3); and that we might dwell in Him and He in us (Col. 1:27—"in us;" Phil. 3:9—"in Him"). "For" was in order to "in." Let us be able to say with the Apostle, "I know *whom* I have believed."

19

THE MINISTRY OF JOHN THE BAPTIST
(Luke 3:1-20)

G<small>ENERAL</small> preparation for Christ's coming had been made by means of, first, Prophecy and, second, Providence. Now comes the special preparation, the Precursor. It was the ministry of John the Baptist that showed the real need of man, a Saviour from sin.

In this chapter, too, we are given four metaphors to describe the influence and activity of the Holy Spirit in preparation for the coming of Christ: axe (v.9), wind and fire (vs.16,17), and dove (v.22). All were necessary, and still are, in connection with both individual and corporate life.

I. *The Setting* (vs. 1,2)

1. When? A. D. 27, a date arrived at by means of Luke's historical exactness combined with secular records. "The Word of God came unto John"—old prophetic formula (Jer. 2:1, *inter alia*), showing John sent by God at proper time and stage of history.

   a. Herod was also known as Antipas, son of Herod the Great.

   b. Two high priests because Annas, being old, continued office in family by appointing son-in-law, Caiphas, Cf. John 11:49; 18:13; Acts 4:6.

2. How?
   a. From heaven.
   b. In God's own time.
   c. After thorough preparation.

3. Where?

In the wilderness, north of Dead Sea. This desert country has been called "the hottest and deepest chasm in the world." There John found, in further preparation for his ministry—

a. Solitude—developing courage.
b. Abstemiousness—developing self-denial.
c. Ruggedness—developing humility.

II. *The Message* (v. 3)

1. Repentance.

a. Announcement already made (1:16,17,77).
b. Action new—not fanaticism, not superstition, but change of course, as of ship nearing rock.

(1) Two Greek words translated repentance:

(a) "After-thought"—change of mind.

(b) "After-feeling"—change of emotion.

These two, intellect and heart, should influence will and lead to change of conduct (2 Cor. 7:10, 11).

(2) Sorrow for sin, or penitence, not enough. Must prove itself by repentance, "whereby we forsake sin" (Prayer Book), including:

(a) Recognition of sin in life.

(b) Restitution of wrong done to others.

(c) Renewal of obedience to God.

(3) All this possible through receiving Christ (Cf. Acts 5:31).

(4) Repentance is gateway to kingdom of heaven, which means rule of God over man's life, present and future.

   2. Baptism.
      a. Sign of repentance—"the outward and visible sign of an inward and spiritual grace" (Prayer Book).
      b. Testimony to need of cleansing, even of Jews, God's chosen people.
   3. Remission.
      a. Gr., sending away, or passing by, of sin.
      b. Cf. Matt. 26:28; Acts 10:43; Heb. 9:20.

III. *The Prophecy* (vs. 4-6)

Isaiah's predictive words (v. 5; Isa. 40:3-5), as applied by John the Baptist to himself, present the Forerunner as a road-builder and strikingly represent the four classes of his listeners:

   1. "Valley"—penitent souls receiving pardon—being "filled."
   2. "Mountain and hill"—Pharisees and Sadducees rebuked for highhandedness and pride—"brought low."
   3. "Crooked"—publicans convicted of dishonesty—"made straight."
   4. "Rough ways"—soldiers, often rude and violent—"made smooth."

These four included in "all flesh" who should "see the salvation of God" (v. 6), the only requirement being true repentance.

IV. *The Influence* (vs. 7-9)

Showed by multitude who came to be baptized:

   1. Some insincere:
      a. Thought natural privilege sufficient—displayed false confidence—God able to provide spiritual children apart from them—judgment already commencing.
      b. Like many present-day church-goers—had wrong motives, so derived no good.
      c. Thought they conferred honor on God—but no one can lay Him under obligation.

2. Others definitely antagonistic:
   a. Calling reputable people "vipers" was plain speaking; but it has been said that nowadays many could truthfully be called "generation of butterflies."
   b. Now, ministers must be milder or churches are empty.
   c. Many true men of God would like to be comforting instead of plain-spoken, but all His real messengers have been fearless.

V. *The Application* (vs. 10-14)

Questioning a healthy sign:
   1. People in general warned—
      a. Negatively, against luxury, as illustrated by owning two coats and eating meat, and—
      b. Positively, to practice sharing with those in need.
   2. Publicans enjoined to be honest. Cf. Zaccheus (19:8).
   3. Soldiers urged to avoid—
      a. Violence.
      b. False accusation.
      c. Discontent.

In all this John showed himself, in spite of asceticism, to be cognizant of his life and times, of "exceeding sinfulness of sin," and of inclination of human nature towards it.

VI. *The Testimony* (vs. 15-18)

   1. John's moral greatness in pointing to his greater Successor.
   2. Reality of Christ's future work, including:
      a. Holy Ghost baptism.
      b. Judgment.
   3. "Many other things"—how we wish we could know them, but no doubt all pointed to Christ.

VII. *The Result* (vs. 19, 20)

Apparent failure after unusual circumstances of birth and early life—e.g., no visible foundation laid for Christian Church. But—

1. All held John to be prophet.
2. Conscience of Herod Antipas stricken (Mark 6:14).
3. Even as late as A.D. 70, Josephus wrote of John with awe.

Conclusion

John the Baptist was—

1. *Only a Voice*—His Humility
   a. Cf. voice and person—latter usually more important.
   b. But consider purpose of voice — message more important than messenger.
   c. Self-effacement enchances reputation—but how much we enjoy notice!
   d. Christ was still hidden, so John His only voice.

2. *Yet a Voice*—His Power
   a. Much depends on what sort of tone.
   b. As the voice, so the person.
   c. Manner of speaking important — voice of Christian must be seemly and sanctified, appropriate and real.
   d. Sometimes necessary to use stern language: e.g., vipers—tree hewn down and cast into fire—fan and fire of threshing-floor.
   e. Voice silent finally—no word from Herod's dungeon —but broken hearts of disciples turned to "Lamb of God" (John 1:36).

So our voices should point to Christ. May I, while *only* a voice, *yet be* a voice—one that shall be at once so faithful and so tender that men shall hear, shall heed, and shall find Christ as their All in all.

20

CHRIST'S BAPTISM AND TEMPTATION
(Luke 3:21,22; 4:1-13)

THERE is a sequence here—first baptism, then temptation. The first is the key to the second.

I. *The Baptism*

It was—

1. Christ's inauguration or consecration to office.
2. The Father's attestation of the Son.
   Note words "Thou art"—not "This is My beloved Son," as at Transfiguration. So evidently for Christ Himself rather than for benefit of others. Thus every true baptism.
3. The endowment of Christ with power for His work through descent of Holy Spirit. Cf. Acts 11:16.
4. The Temptation of Christ should not be considered apart from His Baptism.

For fuller accounts of latter, see Matt. 3:13-17, Mark 1:9-11, and John 1:29-34.

II. *The Temptation*

1. When Tempted?
   Immediately after Baptism (4:1 follows 3:22 chronologically, with genealogy in 3:23-38 as parenthesis). True Holy Spirit baptism fortifies against temptation.

2. Where Tempted?
   In the wilderness—i.e., in solitude. Temptation highly individual.

    a. Now, after thirty years of waiting (3:23), Christ is called and empowered.

    b. Thoughts crowd in and so time needed to reflect on what lay before Him.

    c. Testimony of Father at baptism might well be overpowering and cause desire for instant action. Yet quiet time first. Cf. Paul in Arabia (Gal. 1:17).

3. By Whom Tempted?

    a. The Devil, Satan—evil power, ever adversary of Christ, full of malignity—unseen yet real. But not likely to have form such as traditionally pictured: horned head, cloven hoof, tail, etc. *Illus.*: Old Scotsman, seeing such picture in gallery, gave knowing smile and said, "Yon devil would never tempt *me!*"—meaning too hideous and obvious to deceive anyone. No, more likely as "angel of light" (2 Cor. 11:14) he came to tempt our Lord.

    b. Temptation of Christ striking proof of Satan's identity and sin's reality.

4. How Tempted?

    a. The Nature of the Temptation
    Note following steps in reasoning:

      (1) No temptation if no desire to respond.

      (2) Some things wrong *per se;* others wrong only under certain circumstances.

      (3) Desire for things wrong *per se* proof of sinful nature.

      (4) Therefore, no sinless being could be tempted to desire such.

      (5) Christ was sinless, therefore temptation was also (Heb. 4:15). Two sides to this truth:

        (a) If He could have sinned, He could not have been our Redeemer;

(b) But if He could not have been tempted, He could not have been Man and one with us.

Both must be held without ability to reconcile them fully under present conditions of human knowledge. Thus, our Lord was both not able to sin and able not to sin.

(6) In every sinless temptation, object desired is right but circumstances wrong as means to obtaining it, so surrendered will says No, and waits for light or change.

(7) Now see Satan's temptations of Christ were harmless as to objects but wrong as to means.

b. The Stages of the Temptation
Let us substitute, as many prefer to do, Matthew's order for that of Luke—viz., personal, national, universal; or, as affecting body, mind, spirit. Action was not entirely bodily or seen, but second and third stages were spiritual and in the mind's eye (see especially v. 5), unless Satan was permitted to work a miracle. Narrative appears to indicate Christ was in wilderness all through. Says Plummer: "The change of scene is mental . . . the glory of all the kingdoms of the world could be suggested to the mind . . . What these words do imply is that the temptations came to Him from the outside." Says Sanday: "The meaning and essence of the temptation is wholly spiritual." None the less, it was real temptation, from real devil, and concerned with definite realities. Our Lord manifestly believed in existence of devil and his power to tempt. He, innocent, felt force and suffering far more than do we with sinful nature.

(1) Personal temptation—as Son of God (vs. 3, 4; Cf. Matt. 4:2-4)

(a) Christ very conscious of spiritual power (e.g., Holy Spirit at baptism). Therefore He might well have questioned extent of its use—right or wrong—e.g., should He employ it to supply natural needs? Satan thus throws doubt on testimony at baptism by suggesting Christ make stone into bread.

(b) But Christ rejects temptation, not because bread wrong *per se,* but because making it thus would have been forsaking that reliance on God which was primary condition of His assumption of humanity.

(c) So answers Son of man, *"Man* shall not, etc."— taking place of man and meeting temptation as such, not claiming use of right and power as Son of God.

(d) Note this was not temptation to distrust. Any such tendency would have proved Him not sinless.

(e) It was temptation to forsake position of man in which He had come to live and die—so rejected.

(2) National temptation—as Jewish Messiah (vs. 9-12; Cf. Matt. 4:5-7)

(a) Mention of temple significant—heart and center of Jewish life instead of some mountain in wilderness.

(b) Therefore, work some miracle in sight of all Jews and they will follow You as Messiah, implied Satan. Remember John's preparation for You!

(c) But Christ rejects temptation, not because His leadership of God's people wrong *per se,* but because establishing it thus would have been by—strange paradox—material and supernatural means instead of spiritual and (temporarily) human. Spiritual results come only through keeping spiritual laws.

(d) Note this was not temptation to pride. Any such tendency would have proved Him not sinless.

(e) It was temptation to take easy way of winning His own people: first by attracting from outside, then by influencing from within, instead of reverse order, which was Divine one—so rejected.

(3) Universal temptation—as Divine Saviour (vs. 5-8; Cf. Matt. 4:8-10)

(a) "The kingdoms of the world in a moment of time"—what a vision to One who yearned to save and bless!

(b) You want world, said Satan, and to be its Ruler; here is short cut, avoiding Cross! Worship the one who owns it!

(c) But Christ rejects temptation, not because His rulership over world wrong *per se,* but because long way, though hard, was right way, and way of world's salvation.

(d) Note this was not temptation to ambition. Any such tendency would have proved Him not sinless.

(e) It was temptation to lower standard of spiritual work by spiritual means—so rejected.

5. Why Tempted?

a. To Prove Qualifications of Messiahship

(1) Not so much as Man but as Messiah, officially not personally. Hence so soon after baptism, as test of gift of Holy Spirit.

      (2) Not whether He, as good Man, would yield to sin, but whether, as part of His qualification for office, Christ would realize and carry out spiritual ideal of Messiah, or fall below that high level.

      (3) Not so much leading into sin on part of devil as of undermining principles of Kingdom and avoiding Cross which Satan knew would draw all away from him.

      (4) Not so much rude assault on holy Man as struggle in consciousness of His mission and between judgment and misjudgment of means to good end.

      (5) These constitute key to temptation of Christ: i.e., would He carry on imposed form of Servant (Phil. 2:3-5), or use inherent power of Son?

  b. To Establish Character through Victory

      (1) No inclination to sin—Cf. "nothing in Me" (John 14:30).

      (2) But in resisting officially was strengthened personally—Cf. "perfect through suffering" (Heb. 2:10).

      (3) Innocence (purity untempted) developed into virtue (purity tempted and kept).

      (4) Will never swerved from God, so temptation had no power—thus "more than conqueror."

Conclusion

  1. *Life's Epitome*

    a. "Led" (v.1), "tempted" (v.2)—both. Leading and testing—good combination for character-building.

    b. Adam had innocence but fell. Character only formed by either resistance or response to evil.

    c. Our word "character" comes from Greek word meaning exact expression—we are what we do. Note abiding results in Christ's immediate work (vs. 14-30)—wonderful blessing and power in testimony.

d. Note order: led first, then tempted. No inversion—if "led by the Spirit," no fear where, foundation not touched—e.g., oak need not fear tempest if roots firm.

e. Adam had liability, but not tendency; our Lord had neither liability nor tendency; we have both—hence all the more need to "watch and pray, that" we "enter not into temptation" (Matt. 26:41).

2. *Life's Danger*

We must not yield either to wrong objects or to wrong methods:

a. As in First Temptation, of using means for self-life not justified by circumstances or leading.

b. As in Second Temptation, of reforming from without and *en masse* instead of from within and individually.

c. As in Third Temptation, of employing carnal weapons in spiritual warfare, of descending to level of expediency, or of lowering standard of morality in view of human misery.

3. *Life's Power*

a. Living in God's will as revealed in His Word.

b. Being saturated in Scripture which will show—

(1) Principles involved in given situation;

(2) Speciousness of temptation, whether of self or of Satan;

(3) Shallowness of life resulting from yielding.

c. Discovering what Christ knew all the time, i.e., that—

(1) First type of temptation was really to turn "bread" into "stones";

(2) Second type of temptation was really to risk God's plan under pretense of great work: and

(3) Third type of temptation was really to admit that whoever demands "worship" owns "kingdom" also.

Cf. Psa. 119:11; 27:31; Isa. 8:20; 30:21; Josh. 5:14.

d. Trusting in Christ as Priest—sympathetic, tested, triumphant:

   (1) His qualifications—oneness with man and authority from God.

   (2) His work—Author of eternal salvation and Mediator between God and man.

   Cf. Heb. 4:14 to 5:10.

e. Overcoming because Christ has overcome—in union with Him (John 15:5).

21

JESUS IN NAZARETH
(Luke 4:16-30)

Between verses 13 and 14 of this chapter comes chronologically the section John 2 to 5. Jesus was in Judaea for fourteen months, eight of which were spent in obscurity, perhaps because the people were unprepared and needed first the ministry of John the Baptist. Jerusalem was the natural center, but when John was put into prison Jesus chose a different locale, at least temporarily, viz., Galilee. This region, 70 miles north of Jerusalem, and an area of about 60 by 30 miles bounded on the east by the River Jordan and the Lake of Galilee. Fertile and thickly populated, it lay on the highway of trade between Egypt and Damascus. Reports from Jerusalem of Christ's doings proceded Him (vs. 14,15,23; John 4:45), as He came back to Nazareth, home of His boyhood.

Our Lord is referred to as Jesus of Nazareth by the Evangelists and, in the Acts of the Apostles, by Paul (e.g., 26:9), and by Peter (e.g., 10:38), never as Jesus of Bethlehem. Paul's missionary work brought him the false accusation of being a "ringleader of the Nazarenes" (Acts 24:5). To this day, tradition has professed to identify the holy places of Nazareth (now Nazirah), such as the pillar where the Angel Gabriel sat (which is now marked by the Church of the Annunciation), the workshop of Joseph, and a certain rock where Christ and His disciples are said to have dined. But there are no details about Nazareth in the New Testament, so that all we know is from external sources.

I. *The Place*

A. *The Village*

1. Its Situation. Lay in cup-shaped hollow surrounded by 14 hills. Approaching from Carmel, one can see Nazareth only when close. White walls surrounded by cactus hedges and olive trees—magnificent view thirty miles in three directions: north, to plain of Esdraelon (Barak, Saul, John the Baptist); east, to valley of Jordan and Mount Gilgal; and west to Mediterranean. Besides being on trade route to Egypt, it was stopping-place for pilgrims on way to Jerusalem and for Roman legions en route for Acre. Village small, with inhabitants known to each other.

> "Dear Nazareth! despised and mean,
> Exalted by the Nazarene;
> Himself despised—enthroned now,
> Before whose face the angels bow." (T.R.)

2. Its Influence. Christ's ripening powers as Perfect Man needed place for long preparation. In Nazareth He must have found:

a. The value of waiting. Thirty years' training for three years' service would be influence against impatience.

b. The power of home life. Love, work, worship.

c. The dignity of work. Considered common evil, but in reality common good that glorifies life.

d. The responsibility of privilege. Called Himself "prophet" (v. 24; and Mark 6:4, when there again).

e. The possibility of blessing. "Jesus of Nazareth passeth by" (18:37).

B. *The Synagogue*

1. Went "as His custom was"—value of regular church attendance. "The temple should be the centre of thy circumference" (Nehemiah Rogers).

2. Platform for elders—two lessons, from Law and from Prophets, read from scrolls—visitors often invited to take part (Cf. Acts 13:15).

3. Christ would read first lesson, then would mount to desk for second. Would see many familiar faces, and His mother doubtless present in women's gallery.

II. *The Lesson*

Taken from Isaiah 61:1,2.

A. *The Messiah's Work.*

1. What were to be its characteristics?

a. No glory or earthly power.

b. Sounding keynote of Gospel—seeds germinate in appropriate soil, so Gospel in hearts needing God's love.

c. Average life not mighty—Christ welcomes such. *Illus.*: Lincoln's remark about God preferring common people or He would not have made so many of them.

d. Science shows survival of fittest, with weakest going to wall. Christianity very different.

2. Why did Christ stop where He did in His reading?

a. Only comma separates phrases in verse 2.

b. It was because words—"and the day of the vengeance of our God" referred to future. Today is always "acceptable year of the Lord"; "day" of God's vengeance has yet to dawn.

c. Sermon was applicable, therefore, only to our Lord's first coming and present dispensation of grace.

B. *The Messiah's Power*

1. Anointed by Spirit.

2. Led step by step through Spirit.

So we in our lives for Him.

III. *The Sermon*

A. *The Substance*

1. Fulfilment of prophecy claimed (v. 21).

2. Objections anticipated—proof needed (v.23). But value of miracles depends on state of mind—Christ could not work in Nazareth—had not come to satisfy mere curiosity of fellow-townsmen. Cf. other miracles when any true disposition.

3. Truth stated (vs. 24-27).

a. Acceptance of message neither in Israel in days of Elijah nor here in Nazareth now.

b. Yet others accepted—viz., widow of Sarepta, Naaman the Syrian, and people of Capernaum—no favorites with God.

B. *The Secret*

1. Relation between Himself and Word.

a. Teaching was Person and Person teaching.

b. Jesus Himself subject and center.

2. Consciousness of Himself and Truth.

a. Gave Him authority and power.

b. Spoke definitely and unmistakably.

c. Had clear vision of purpose of coming.

3. Consistency of Idea through Life.

a. Never swerved whatever happened.

b. Note His faithfulness here, in "home town."

IV. *The Effect*

A. *The Reactions*

1. Rapt attention (v. 20).

2. Unanimous identification (v. 22).

3. Great surprise (v. 22).

4. Envious doubt (v. 22).

5. Angry opposition (v. 28).

6. Ugly action (v. 29).

B. *The Reasons*

1. People of Nazareth did not consider themselves those mentioned in verse 18.

2. Objected to Christ's high claims—hard to accept from one presumably on same level.

3. Required miraculous power as proof.

4. Abominated reference to Gentiles.

5. Jealous of Capernaum—self-esteem wounded, civic pride hurt.

6. So personal pique prevented reception of Christ, who departed, to return only once more and find same attitude (Matt. 13:54-58; Mark 6:1-6).

Conclusion

This narrative is found only in Luke's Gospel. Why? Perhaps it is a sort of frontispiece of the universal Gospel and of Christianity. It illustrates:

A. *Christ's Mission*

It was to bring grace—

1. Free (v.18)—to poor, broken-hearted, captives, blind, bruised. Cf. Rev. 22:17.

2. Present (v. 21)—"now" because it is "acceptable year of the Lord" (v.19), "accepted" time (2 Cor. 6:2), and Christ is worthy of all "acceptation" (1 Tim. 1:15).

3. Universal, yet limited (vs. 25-27). The Gospel that effects such changes is for all, yet it must be received and appropriated (cf. Christ's own illustrations).

B. *Christ's Method*

1. Systematic (v.16).

2. Scriptural (vs.17,21).

3. Spiritual (v.18).

4. Sympathetic (v.22).

5. Searching (vs.23-27).

C. *Christ's Reception*

There is shown:

1. Curiosity and interest (vs.20,22), yet—
2. Rejection, because of prejudice and pride (v.28). *Illus.*: Lady who refused to be saved in same way as her footman. Blossoms not always sign of fruit— these people of Nazareth shrank from application of lesson to selves.

D. *Christ's Action*

1. He departs—never forces. If a man won't, he won't!
2. Yet He is never far away and His ministry is never wholly in vain:
   a. "A few sick folk" were healed on a subsequent visit (Mark 6:5).
   b. His mother and brethren came to Him later (8:19-21).

Let us, therefore, go on with God and be faithful. He knows all, and we have His promise that His Word shall not return unto Him void.

22

JESUS IN CAPERNAUM
(Luke 4:31-44)

Jesus, we are told, having left Nazareth, "came down to Capernaum, a city of Galilee" (v.31, and for eighteen months this was "His own city" (Matt. 9:1), where He paid tribute. Capernaum has vanished, even its site being unknown. We may well wonder why Jesus is not associated in our minds with Capernaum as He is with Bethlehem, Nazareth, and Jerusalem. Perhaps it is because Capernaum, together with the neighboring cities of Chorazin and Bethsaida, was associated in judgment with Tyre and Sidon (10:13-15). Its position was central and important, on roads running east, west, and south, and there were good opportunities of visiting surrounding villages, by boat on the lake of Galilee, or on foot.

This passage contains not only an account of our Lord as a powerful Teacher, and of the first miracle recorded by Luke, but also more numerous and more varied cases of healing than any other. It continues the story of Christ's first circuit of Galilee which ends at 5:16. See in it four pictures of our Saviour:

I. *The Supreme Lord* (vs. 33-37)

  1. The Distress of the Man with the Unclean Devil.

    a. Demon possession not lunacy, but distinct and extraordinary manifestation of demonic power during Christ's lifetime on earth.

    b. Devil in synagogue—not first time or last he has possessed a pew-holder!

  2. The Rage and Terror of the Demon.

    a. How there? Sacred precincts attract and yet repel powers of evil.

b. "What have we to do with Thee?" What in common? How true! Feared interference.

3. The Knowledge and Testimony of the Demon.
   a. Knew all about Jesus of Nazareth—holy, divine, tested.
   b. Hell watched heaven and was baffled.
   c. Knew much and talked well.

4. The Sternness and Authority of Christ.
   a. Cf. His treatment of spirits and of men—severity and pity.
   b. Evokes and accepts imperfect recognition by man.
   c. Silences clear knowledge of demon.
   d. Confession of head belief rejected—only heart love accepted.

5. The Control and Power of Christ
   a. Unclean spirit tore man (Mark 1:26), but no use—eyewitnesses testified, "They come out" (v.36).
   b. It is always darkest before dawn—sometimes love is sufficient, but at other times there must be action.
   c. Therefore, possibility of alienation till stage is reached where subject is incapable of improvement.
   d. Then God's pity steps in.

6. The Astonished Report of the People
   a. His authority.
   b. His fame.

II. *The Gentle Healer* (vs. 38, 39)
   1. Loving Presence.
      a. Jesus in house—disciple's abode sanctified.
      b. Service in home as well as in church, but not always as easy.

2. Domestic Sorrow.

   a. "Great fever"—may have been either chronic or acute.

   b. Affliction unites—"they."

3. Anxious Inquiry.

   a. "Besought" strong word in Greek: to beseech, to pray fervently—not milder equivalents of our words ask or summon.

   b. Parallel word in Mark's account means to tell—probably true of early stage of illness, or merely layman's expression as against physician's.

   c. In either case, family felt free to apply to Jesus and to pour out hearts.

4. Tender Sympathy.

   a. In synagogue rebuke was for demon; here it is for fever.

   b. No sternness or abhorrence here.

   c. God moves great forces and yet lets us move Him.

5. Complete Cure.

   a. Immediate.

   b. Thorough.

6. Grateful Service.

   a. Prompt.

   b. Necessary.

   c. Quiet.

   d. Real.

III. *The All-Sufficient Helper* (vs. 40, 41)

   1. The Time of Coming.

      a. After morning in synagogue and midday in Peter's house.

      b. Crowds gathered at sunset, and probably stayed into the night.

2. The Sense of Need.
   a. Jews had little knowledge of medicine. Thought sickness came from sin and evil spirits.
   b. Therefore expulsion emphasized. Competent man was not best educated but most religious.

3. The Expectation of Help.
   a. Thought what they believed they got—if one believed more, he got more.
   b. Crowds thought more of bodies than of Redeemer—so now, scramble to be healed.

4. The Feeling of Pity.
   a. This Luke's strong point—misery spoke to his heart, even at second hand.
   b. Heart that feels is never callous; how much more Christ's heart!

5. The Fulness of Power.
   a. This also typical of Luke—"all"—"every one of them."
   b. Christ never baffled by disease or demons.

6. The Reality of Joy.
   a. It suited His love thus to bless.
   b. As faces lit up in relief of pain and weakness, how happy He in bliss of doing good!

IV. *The Unselfish Worker* (vs. 42-44)
   1. The Need of Rest.
      a. After work, rest in proportion.
      b. But here, according to Mark (1:35), it was short.

   2. The Power of Prayer.
      a. Cf. Mark's account again.
      b. Christ's dependence on prayer proof of reality of His manhood.

3. The Request of Gratitude.
   a. Seeking.
   b. Finding.
   c. Cleaving.

4. The Testimony of Fame.
   a. Cf. Mark (1:36,37) —disciples also followed and found Him.
   b. Glowed with pride as they declared, "All men seek Thee."

5. The Sacrifice of Self.
   a. Humanity to be considered and sensationalism repelled.
   b. Others, not self, His care.

6. The Reminder of Love.
   a. "Also"—extension of blessings to others.
   b. Work necessary — "must"; message — "kingdom of God"; sphere — "other cities"; bond — "therefore . . . sent."

Conclusion

1. This Christ is our Saviour.
2. This Christ is our Pattern.
3. This Christ is our Power.

Therefore—"Go thou and do likewise."

23

CHRIST'S CALL TO A CHRISTIAN LIFE
(Luke 5:1-11)

W E may well inquire as to the purpose of this miracle. It is not difficult, as a rule, to discover a reason for each of Christ's miracles. They are generally beneficent and in response to a serious, expressed need. Yet that is not entirely the case here. There was no appeal and, evidently, no acute need, so we must look further. It would seem that the miracle was a means to an end and formed the turning-point in the lives of four men—James and John, their father Zebedee, and Peter—especially Peter. Christ's dealings with the young men were in three stages: (a) Discipleship (John 1:35, etc.); (b) Ministry (Luke 5:1-11; and Apostleship (Luke 6:13). After (a) the disciples had returned to their work (Cf. Matt. 4:18; Mark 1:16). This miracle indicates the means and the symbol of the definite service they were to render. Gradual progress was made and all was subservient to the main issue.

I. *The Preparation* (vs. 1-5)

1. The Suitable Circumstance (vs. 1-3).

   a. Pressing of people on Jesus.
   b. Preaching the "word of God."
   c. Putting out of boat from shore.
   N.B. Note word "lake" used of Sea of Galilee—characteristic of Luke who had seen the Mediterranean.

2. The Simple Command (v.4)

   a. Cf. "launch out" (v.4) with "thrust out" (v.3).
   b. Whence and where? "From the land"—"into the deep."
   c. Note gradual character—so simple, yet natural.

3. The Significant Response (v.5)

    a. What was Peter's tone?

    b. How strong was his faith?

    c. Note his use of singular pronoun "I"—also singular noun "net" though Christ had used plural, "nets" (v. 4).

    d. Indication of untrustful response because only partial.

    e. To paraphrase: "The idea of telling us fishermen, who know the lake so well, to toil in morning! Unreasonable, so I'm unwilling—yet just as you say—but I know it will do no good!"

II. *The Progress* (vs. 6-9)

    1. The Unexpected Success (vs. 6,7).

        a. Multitude of fishes.

        b. Breaking of net.

        c. Call to partners.

        d. Risk of sinking both ships.

    2. The Great Surprise (v. 9).

        a. Because of quantity.

        b. Because of time of day.

        c. Because of evident lordship of Christ over forces of Nature:

            (1) Knowledge of fish—superior to that of fishermen.

            (2) Power over fish—in spite of circumstances.

    3. The Realized Sinfulness (v. 8)

    Fish occasion of Peter's declaration rather than cause of it. Why?

        a. Cf. account in John 21:1-14, when another miraculous draft of fishes followed Peter's denial of his Lord.

        b. Had seen other miracles (e.g., chap. 4 and John 2: 1-12), which did not have same result. Why this?

  c. Some say, dread and astonishment in presence of holy Lord—not worship.

  d. But deeper—Peter realized own distrust and disobedience—net would not have been broken if he had been obedient.

 N. B. 1. Higher conception of Christ — cf. "Master" (v.5) with "Lord" (v. 8). This needed—Jewish idea of mere Rabbi to be eradicated from disciples' minds.

   2. Lower conception of self—again cf. v.5, "nevertheless . . . I will" with v.8, "I am a sinful man." This also needed—Jews in their sin and blindness could not recognize spiritual aspects of Messiah.

III. *The Purpose* (vs. 10, 11)

 1. The Loving Assurance (v. 10)

  a. "Fear not" and "henceforth"—this twofold revelation necessary.

  b. "Depart"? Not so—lack of faith all the more reason for staying. Little knowledge vs. greater knowledge.

 2. The Higher Work (v. 10)

  a. Of catching men from sin, from waters of death.

  b. Of taking men alive—cf. difference between two occupations. This one of two instances in New Testament of use of word—other in 2 Tim. 2:26 and translated "snare." Thus every soul to be "taken alive" by someone:

   (1) By Christ to eternal life, or—

   (2) By Satan to eternal death.

  c. To be continuous and permanent—"from henceforth."

 3. The Full Consecration (v. 11)

  a. Old life abandoned—"forsook all"

  b. New life begun—"followed"

  c. Life transformed—step never regretted.

Conclusion

A. *Christ's Purpose with Us*

Call to higher stage of Christian life—more of Him.

a. Growth in grace—"excelsior!"

b. Yet not for ourselves alone, but for others. God's call always to ministry of some kind.

B. *Christ's Plan for Us*

1. Approaches us in daily round.

a. Perfectly simple and natural—nothing startling—"pulpit of boat."

b. Therefore, often unconscious in influence.

2. Gives us simple command.

a. Test is unquestioning, prompt obedience--and only that.

b. Purpose not often revealed—only tests.

C. *Christ's Purpose Endangered*

We miss both blessing and honor—

1. Through our "wisdom"

a. Questioning.

b. Reasoning.

2. Through our disobedience or partial obedience.

a. Shoals of fish outside lost because one net only used.

b. So same dead level for years—cf. Moses (Num. 20:12; Deut. 52:51).

D. *Christ's Plan Accepted*

1. By full trust.

2. By complete surrender.

a. Faithful loyalty in that which is least.

b. Acceptance of Christ as Lord.

c. Close walk with Him.

d. Instant and complete obedience—"whatsoever."

E. Christ's Purpose Realized

1. Fishermen appropriate for His work.
2. Qualities of fishermen needed:
   a. Tact, gentleness.
   b. Watchfulness, observation.
   c. Patience, earnestness.
   d. Perseverance, sincerity.
   e. Courage, readiness.
   f. Strength, power.
   g. Skill, prudence.

Soul-winning to be disciples' constant business—and ours.

24

CHRISTIAN MINISTRY
(Luke 5:1-11)

Our Lord was still in Capernaum, or rather in Bethsaida, the "fisher-row" of the city by the lake (Gr., "place of nets") and the home of Simon, Andrew, and Philip. It was a busy place then, but is one of desolation now. Christ's Galilean ministry was different from His Judaean ministry. He neither went from place to place nor used the synagogues. Capernaum was His center and from there He travelled around about, commencing in a western direction, with His disciples. Only an outline of the circuits is given, but there were four of these and four journeys up to the time of John the Baptist's death. At first, our Lord made no open avowal of His Messianic claim, but left the people to infer it from His words and works. These were all the proof necessary to those with discernment.

The Forerunner's imprisonment had, indeed, determined the character of Christ's ministry. After His stay in Judaea, His disciples had returned to their homes, leaving Him alone (cf. John 5 and His visit to Nazareth). After Nazareth, Christ spent some time teaching on the shore of the lake, and then proceeded to gather around Him believers, disciples or ministers, and apostles.

I. *His Words—Instruction Given* (vs. 1-3)

Introductory to account of miracle:

1. The People—seeking, learning.
2. The Pulpit—first the shore, then a boat.
3. The Preacher—gave "the Word of God," then "taught."

II. *His Works—Reward Bestowed* (vs. 4-7)

    The miracle performed:

    1. Obligation required.

    2. Obedience rendered.

    3. Outcome rewarded.

III. *His Ways—Vocation Announced* (vs. 8-11)

    The call interpreted:

    1. Confession made.

    2. Consolation ministered.

    3. Consecration manifested.

Conclusion

1. The Christian ministry was at that time a new social function in the world. It was to be analagous to Christ's own ministry to men: e.g.,

    a. The shepherd—the sheep—foresight.

    b. The husbandman—the field—diligence.

    c. The fisherman—the fish—hopefulness.

2. Men, like fish, were astray, were to be sought, and were to be caught.

3. He whom the disciples followed was infinitely greater than all whom they left; that which they found was superior to all the things they lost.

4. Christ cares for our work and will bless our obedience.

5. Here we may take our first steps to fulness of life, love and joy.

25

THE CHRISTIAN WORKER
(Luke 5:1-11)

A miracle was Christ's great symbol of truth, while a parable was its forceful expression in words of His choosing. This particular miracle may be considered in its application to the Christian worker. Let him consider, first—

I. *The Men*

    A. *They were Fishermen.*

        1. Apt illustration of Christian worker.
        2. Attributes should be:
            a. Tact
            b. Watchfulness
            c. Readiness
            d. Patience
            e. Perseverance
            f. Courage
            g. Strength
            h. Skill

    B. *They were Disappointed Fishermen.*

        1. Faithfulness—had labored long.

        2. Failure—their labors fruitless—yet failure may have advantages. Examination of case:
            a. Was it their fault? Was care taken? Were nets right?
            b. What other hindrances were there? Were other fishermen there first? Was it the absence of fish?

   C. *They were Persevering Fishermen.*
     1. Faith not deterred by failure—"washing their nets" (v.2).
     2. Faith providing for possible emergencies — "mending their nets" (Matt. 4:21).

II. *The Master*
   A. *His Presence.*
     1. "Into one of the ships" (v. 3). Cf. "Except the Lord . . ." (Psa. 127:1).
     2. The cheer of knowing He is interested in us.
   B. *His Perception.*
     1. Command.
     2. Knowledge.
   C. *His Power*
     1. Almighty.
     2. Inspiring.

III. *The Miracle*
   A. *Success*
     1. After long effort (Cf. Psa. 126:6).
     2. No true work lost (Cf. Gal. 6:9).
   B. *Strength*
     1. Divine power in human weakness (Cf. 2 Cor. 12:9).
     2. This the invariable condition.
   C. *Satisfaction*
     1. Time unfavorable and unexpected.
     2. God delights in this.

Conclusion
   1. Be patient.
   2. Be prayerful.
   3. Be persevering.
   4. Be peaceful.
     —and your work for God shall be rewarded.

26

CHRIST'S CALL TO SERVICE
(Luke 5:1-11)

Jᴇsᴜs is here found calling His disciples to service.

I. *By Words* (vs. 1-3)
   1. Anywhere—but not anyhow. Cf. places, e.g.,: by a well, in the temple, in a dwelling, in a synagogue.
   2. Any text—but always the truth. Cf. quotation from Old Testament, a child, a lily, seed, leaven.

II. *By Works* (vs. 4-7)
   1. Miracles such as this.
   2. His own death and resurrection.

III. *By Ways* (vs. 8-11)
   1. Behind both words and works are God's ways.
   2. Threefold cord:
      a. Obey Jesus (vs. 3,5,6) for Success.
      b. Confess Jesus (v.8) for Self-knowledge.
      c. Follow Jesus (v.11) for Soul-winning.

   3. Jesus in our work:
      a. Influencing us to Forsake Sin.
      b. Helping us to Follow the Saviour.
      c. Guiding us to Fish for Souls.

   4. Without Jesus:
      a. Night of toil.
      b. Nothing taken.
      c. Nets empty.

   With Jesus:
      a. Full nets.
      b. Full ship.
      c. Full hearts.

5. The people that day had—
    a. The Shore for Pews.
    b. The Ship for Pulpit.
    c. The Saviour for Preacher.

Conclusion

1. Give All For Jesus.
   Get All from Jesus.

2. As nets, let us use church, Sunday School, Bible texts, prayers, hymns, etc.

3. For bait, let us use loving words and deeds

> Launch out into the deep (v.4)
> Let down the nets (v.4)
> Answering (v.5)
> Astonished (v.9)
> Kneeling at Jesus' feet (v.8)
> Knowing our own sinfulness (v.8)
> Everything forsaken (v.11)
> Entering service of Christ (v.11)

27

FULNESS, FAITH, FORGIVENESS
(Luke 5:17-25)

AFTER the miracles of 4:31 to 5:11, Christ made a tour during which a leper's sad plight elicited His pity and power (5:12-15). Then "He withdrew Himself into the wilderness, and prayed" (v.16), and returned to Capernaum, where were manifested—

I. *Fulness* (vs.17,18)

   1. Of Wisdom
      a. Part of everyday life of Jesus.
      b. Days of splendid opportunity for hearers—Pharisees, doctors of law—people from every town and even from Jerusalem—what a conference!

   2. *Of Enmity*
      a. Christ unauthorized teacher, intruder—so here was test.
      b. Intolerable to be drawing people—so must be watched.
      c. "Heresy"—hurt because of low level of spiritual life.

   3. *Of Power*
      a. Its Source—"the Lord"
      b. Its Place—"was present"
      c. Its Effectiveness—"to heal"

   4. *Of Need*
      a. Living death.
      b. Two symptoms:
         (1) Sin.
         (2) Disease.

II. *Faith* (vs. 19,20)
1. Manifested
    a. Love of four men for friend.
    b. Confidence in Jesus.

2. Hindered
    a. Good desires often obstructed.
    b. New expedients necessary.

3. Determined
    a. The desired presence.
    b. The obstructing crowd.
    c. The unique method.

    When we cannot find a way, that is the very time to—
    find a way.

4. Recognized
    a. Christ's discerning eye.
    b. Christ's gracious word.

III. *Forgiveness* (vs. 20-25)
1. Pronounced
    a. Forgiveness man's deepest need—true religion calls for God.
    b. Declaration necessary—no silent God will suffice.
    c. Sin often source of need, so forgiveness must precede healing.

2. Questioned
    a. Logical premise of scribes correct but conclusion wrong.
    b. Forgiveness Divine act—person sinned against can only forgive.
    c. Cf. sin, vice, crime—three stages of evil.

3. Claimed

   a. Divine prerogative exercised.

   b. Not simply declaring Himself God, which would have been easier for an impostor.

4. Proved

   a. Would have been easy also to say merely, and not do —cf. many today.

   b. Power always sign of authority.

   c. Sin offense against Divine authority.

5. Enjoyed

   a. Possessed.

   b. Manifested.

   c. Acknowledged.

N. B. Doubtless room made for man to go, even though not for him to come! No wonder amazement possessed all beholders.

Conclusion

   A. *Christ's Power to Forgive Sin*

   1. Man's great need, because of sin.

   2. God's great love, because of the sinner.

   3. Christ's great gift, because of His Cross.

Idea of forgiveness often ignored by modern writers, but it has been called "Christ's most striking innovation in morality." J. B. Waddington wrote: " 'Man, thy sins are forgiven thee'—This is God's own true word to me, and to every lost and guilty sinner, who has been taught his ruined condition by the Holy Spirit; and, who, putting himself in the place of the poor palsied man to whom these words were first spoken, really believes in his heart that Jesus paid his great debt, once for all, by His death upon the cross—The Apostles always wrote to

believers as pardoned through faith in Christ's blood."
Forgiveness removes sin and thereby makes holiness
possible—only Christianity can do this.

B. *Christ's Example to His Children*

1. Ministry to body, mind and soul.

2. Methods were:

   a. Truthfulness—showing true nature of sin and need
   of forgiveness—not emphasizing culture, intelligence, social polish.

   b. Tenderness—dealing with sinner a delicate adjustment to his need—giving him God's Word.

   c. Thoroughness—leading to restoration, always His
   object.

   These will all test our evangelistic effort.

28

PENETRATION, PARDON, POWER
(Luke 5:20-22)

T HIS story, generally thought of as describing one miracle of our Lord, really records three miracles—each as remarkable and important as the other two. They provide three pictures of Christ which are for us as well as for those mentioned in the Gospel narrative. Note—

I. *His Penetration—The First Miracle*

1. He saw their faith (v. 20) .

   a. Crowd could see some things, i.e., love, earnestness, perseverance of friends, but Christ looked deeper and saw spring of these virtues, i.e., faith. They believed He could and would bless, and therefore made the great effort on behalf of their friend.

   b. Does Christ see faith in us now? He still peers into souls and penetrates defenses.

   c. How may we know we have true faith? By proofs in our lives of love, earnestness, perseverance. Do we ever labor to bring others to Christ as these men did?

2. He saw the man's need (v.20) .

   a. Friends brought him for healing of disease—Christ saw deeper and primary malady—sin.

   b. Forgiveness greater need than healing.

   c. So now He sees our need, which is the same.

3. He saw the Pharisees' thoughts (vs. 21-23).

   a. What they said.

      (1) Note their faulty logic (v.21)—syllogism with correct major and minor premises, but with wrong conclusion, may be paraphrased thus: "This man says he can forgive sins; but only God can forgive sins; therefore, this man is a blasphemer."

      (2) Cf. what would have been syllogism true to facts: "This Man forgives sin; only God can forgive sin; therefore, this Man is God." But Jesus also knew—

   b. What they thought.

      (1) Note sneering scepticism: "Easy enough to speak of forgiving sins—no visible result. But will he dare to tell man to rise up and walk—when all will see whether or not physical consequence follows?"

      (2) All this in silence, but Christ saw all.

So now Christ "perceives" unspoken thoughts. What does He see in our minds?

II. *His Pardon — The Second Miracle*

   1. He forgave the man's sin (v.20).

      a. Forgiveness is supernatural—never found—

      (1) In nature—"red in tooth and claw"—". . . in the raw is seldom kind."

      (2) In any religious or philosophical system—may enjoin severe penances, etc., but never gives assurance of favorable result.

      b. Every new birth a spiritual miracle.

   2. This forgiveness is—

      a. Immediate.

      b. Assured.

      c. Complete.

d. Permanent.

Cf. Christ's words to the paralytic (v.20).

III. *His Power — The Third Miracle*

He healed the paralytic (v.22.) This miracle was—

1. Proof of Christ's claim.
2. Parable of Christian life.

Conclusion

Christ still waits to do three miracles. He—

1. Sees our faith, our need, and our thoughts.
2. Forgives our sins.
3. Saves our souls, and often heals our bodies.

"Thy touch has still its ancient power."

Do we believe this?

29

FOUR PICTURES OF THE SAVIOUR
(Luke 5:27—6:11)

THERE are two methods of studying nature—special and general. These may be symbolized by the flower and the landscape, the moth and the mountain, the microscope and the telescope. There are the same two methods of Bible study—special and general, the individual passage or chapter or book, and the whole Book. It is possible in both instances to lose the general view in the special details, as one may watch a moth and miss a mountain, emphasizing a particular text and losing the drift of the whole section in which it is found.

Actions in Scripture are often grouped with an underlying connection, and so it is here. There are four distinct episodes and yet one single thought. Instead, therefore, of dwelling on minutiae, let us gain an idea of the whole passage in relation to this one thought—namely, the growing opposition of Christ's enemies. Out of this situation emerges a four-fold picture of our Lord. See Him as—

I. *The Great Physician* (vs. 27-32)

A. *The Murmuring*

1. Because Christ received Matthew, a publican—evidence of class hatred. Only "discrimination" shown by Christ was to choose Matthew because He saw potentiality for apostleship.

2. Because Christ mingled with such people—attracted by Him who inspired hope like medicine.

N. B. Easy to find fault—anyone can—and many feel education imcomplete without!

B. *The Answer*

1. Justified by results.

   a. Healing accomplished where there is sickness.

   b. Would go anywhere to do good—but only for that.

2. Implied claim.

   a. Healing part of Messianic work—cf. Hosea 5:13 to 6:3.

   b. God only Healer—therefore Christ is Messiah.

N. B. Resolute defiance of Pharisaic judgment—independence as to care of destitute—rebuke to slaves of expediency—shows fear mars usefulness by compromising, and so whole life is compromise.

C. *The Self-Revelation*

As the Great Physician, Christ reveals—

1. Tenderness and skill.

2. Efficacy of remedy.

3. Hope for worst patients—Christ drawn to very ones who repel cultured.

He is also—

II. *The Divine Bridegroom* (vs. 33-39)

A. *The Inquiry*

1. Why did John's disciples imitate their master's asceticism?

2. Why did Pharisees' own disciples also fast?

3. Why did not Christ's followers likewise?

B. *The Reply*

1. Presence of Master dispensed with fasting.

   a. Fasting right under certain circumstances, but wrong if done from formal Jewish motive.

   b. Christ brought joy and happiness unless obscured by sin—then search for trouble should be made.

   c. But no mechanical rule of time or method given.

2. Principle of fasting laid down by means of parable.
   a. Value of rites and ceremonies—garments and skins do hold.
   b. Emotions held and guided by external forms, or they may be lost.
   c. But if forms are outworn or unsuitable, strong feelings break through and are equally lost—therefore new forms necessary.
   d. Cf. church history: struggles between stiff formalism and new zeal—old phases and new experiences—icy precision of age and innocent warmth and freshness of youth.
   e. So Christ revealed new spirit of Gospel—not patch on old garment of Judaism.

   N. B. There must be adaptation to new times, places and circumstances.

C. *The Self-Revelation*
   1. Claim to be Divine Bridegroom immense one—Jews familiar with metaphor. Cf. Hosea 2, Isaiah 54, Jeremiah 2, where husband is Jehovah Himself.
   2. This title higher than that of Teacher. He not only revealed duty but modified it by His very presence —Jewish customs not wrong, but must be altered by His coming.

   But Christ is—

III. *The Ideal Teacher* (6:1-5)
   A. *The Question*
   1. Jesus still pestered with unimportant matters.
   2. Sabbath law very strict one with Jews, and opposition to Him on this subject may well have aroused murderous designs.
   3. Here and in vs. 6-11 are two incidents relating to it.

B. *The Answer*

   1. Often misunderstood—not throwing off Fourth Commandment:

     a. Christ was Jewish and honored Law.

     b. But Pharisees' strictness refuted by Old Testament example, David—proving freedom even in Hebrew discipline. So Christ not afraid of fact.

     c. Circumstances justified practice—larger obligation overruled lesser—ceremonial observance less important than meeting human needs.

     d. When principle of "mercy and not sacrifice" recognized, Fourth Commandment resumed and revitalized.

   2. In short, Sabbath for man, and Christ Lord of both.

C. *The Self-Revelation*

   1. Incisive to discern and show crucial point.

   2. Careless of small pedantries.

   3. Armed with principles going to heart of subject.

   4. Able to give immediate reply—not obliged to retire for consideration.

Christ is, lastly,—

IV. *The Supreme Lord* (6:6-11)

A. *The Malicious Desire*

   1. Leaders believed in Christ's power, but it had no effect on them.

   2. They wanted miracle, but only to accuse Him.

   3. Wished to push Him to extremity and to cavil no longer.

B. *The Complete Exposure*

   1. Christ makes their intention public and whets expectation.

2. Relieves man's suffering and yet exposes foes' malice.
3. Then by one word He eludes their grasp:
   a. To touch on Sabbath was profanation, so Christ spoke only.
   b. Man stretching forth hand no profanation either.
   c. Thus scribes and Pharisees were baffled and "filled with madness" (v.11).

C. *The Self-Revelation*
1. Christ competent both in theory (as in III) and in fact.

2. Encounter showed:
   a. Tact.
   b. Decision.
   c. Self-control.

3. Miracle wrought purposely on Sabbath (one of seven such) —
   a. Without means of any kind.
   b. As direct challenge to enemies.

Conclusion
1. What is Christ to "those that oppose themselves?"
2. What is Christ to "them that love Him?"
3. What is Christ to you?

30

CHRIST CHOOSES HIS TWELVE APOSTLES
(Luke 6:13-16)

J ESUS Christ while on earth followed three methods of work. The first was the performing of miracles, the second was teaching, and the third was through His apostolate. The establishment of this last was a necessity because the work was extending and pressing, and Jesus, in the limitations of His humanity, was unable to do it alone. Also, His aims were so far-reaching that it was essential to provide not only for the present, but for the future. Thus a landmark in Christ's earthly ministry was reached. But the important task of choosing twelve apostles was undertaken only after night-long prayer to God the Father. It was also in face of the fierce and calculated opposition so evident in the preceding chapter.

I. *Christ Entrusts Special Work to Special Disciples*

    1. Three stages with these men:

        a. Individual discipleship (e.g., 5:10,11,27,28) .

        b. Ministry (e.g., 5:29) .

        c. Apostleship (6:13-16; 9:1-6) .

    2. Apostleship flowering of discipleship in ministry.

        a. Disciple is learner, minister is servant, apostle is missionary.

        b. Like plant growing quietly, and lo! flowers appear.

        c. Long supply of nourishment at length displays results.

3. Yet apostles are disciples still—"also . . . apostles" (v.13) .
   a. Learners still, as plant ceases not feeding because it flowers.
   b. All the more need of nourishment during flowering.

4. Apostleship out of heart of discipleship.
   a. Very best—those who listened longest, most intelligently, and most lovingly.
   b. Christ used only such.

II. *Christ Calls for Thoroughness rather than Magnitude*

1. At first, His disciples seemed rude, with no apparent promise.
   a. Did they appreciate designs of His mind—that they should inherit His work, possess His exquisite spirit, transmit His character to others?
   b. No, but He carried on their education with infinite patience, bearing with their worldly hopes and clumsy mistakes.
   c. Their training was His constant care—they were also with Him, often His only audience.
   d. Above all, He was intent upon influencing their characters for His service.

2. He worked inward rather than outward.
   a. Intensively, not extensively—preferred to perfect some rather than partially train many.
   b. Stamped Himself on few, then sent out to reach many.
   c. Wrote not a line that endured, but much on tables of their hearts.

III. *Christ Does Not Despise Lowly Instruments*

1. His servants do not come from—
   a. Influential or powerful ranks—these unworthy.
   b. Learned or wise ones—human power and wisdom not wanted.

2. His servants are men of character. The twelve were—
   a. Good men.
   b. Simple men.
   c. Impressible men.

3. But His servants often men of superior though hidden gifts.
   a. Note His insight—e.g., Peter and John.
   b. Marvellous what He can do, if there is yieldedness.

IV. *Christ Uses Every Sort of Individuality*
   1. No man exact counterpart of others.
   2. Cf. differences—all available to Christ:
      a. Are we resolute, adventurous, original, born leaders? Christ chastens us and makes us steadfast (Peter).
      b. Are we keen observers and deep thinkers, but with no special gift of leadership? Christ utilizes facilities for insight, and for teaching others (John).
      c. Is our thought "sicklied o'er with doubt?" Christ can train intellectual questioners and use them in blessing to others (Thomas, Bartholomew or Nathanael).
      d. Are we practical men, conversant with public affairs? Christ will avail Himself of our administrative ability (Matthew, Judas).
      e. Have we directness and self-reliance? Christ will take these and enable us to give certitude to others (James, Andrew).
      f. Are we of unimaginative, prosaic and sluggish temperament? Christ will utilize our good points and energize us in His service (Philip).
      g. Are we unknown, inconspicuous, unimportant? Christ can use us—"you in your small corner, and I in mine" (the other James, the other Simon, the other Judas— N.B., not even bearing an exclusive name).

3. Therefore, let each be himself and do his best.

   a. Not pine to be another.

   b. But be all he is and do all he can.

4. Let each respect individuality of others.

   a. The Twelve walked with Christ, in much the same way, yet cf. Peter with John, Andrew with Matthew, etc.

   b. Christ's grace was to them as bodily food, giving them power to think, to go, to do, to speak.

   Illus.: Minister complains of young assistant's daring and novelty of method; let him alone, says older man, if root of matter be in him.

V. *Christ Honors Ties of Kindred and Friendship among His Servants*

1. Note the facts: two pairs of brothers, two friends, four partners in trade.

2. Note mutual help and pleasure—"two better than one"— natural relations channels through which higher elements can flow.

3. Note, e.g., influence of home on children if father and mother are one in Christ—office where two clerks are friends and Christians—two sisters, mother and daughter at one with father, with brothers.

VI. *Christ Utilizes in Best Way All that is Valuable in Our Past*

1. Same energies and characteristics transformed and newly directed.

2. Cf. Paul the faithful Apostle who had been a zealous religionist, John Calvin the theologian who had been a lawyer, etc.

Conclusion

There may, however, be formal enrollment in Christ's service without one's being truly His, e.g., Judas Iscariot.

1. Nominal connection no guarantee of character.

2. Habits may be so bad that best opportunities of reform do no good.

Let us, therefore, make sure that our discipleship is genuine, sincere, and true, based on a personal relationship to our Lord and Saviour.

31

HEALING OF THE CENTURION'S SERVANT
(Luke 7:1-10)

THIS chapter shows Jesus Christ as the Great Healer. In these opening verses He is shown helping a centurion, a soldier of Rome. Later, He helped a widow, His Forerunner, and a woman "who was a sinner."

I. *Receiving the Delegation—the Blessing Sought* (vs. 1-8)

    1. The centurion's character.

        a. Loving.

        b. Thoughtful.

        c. Benevolent.

    2. The centurion's faith.

        a. Strong.

        b. Humble.

        c. Intelligent.

II. *Restoring the Dying—the Blessing Brought* (vs. 9,10)

    1. The centurion's reward.

        a. Praise.

        b. Healing.

    2. The Master's response.

        a. Universal.

        b. Instant.

        c. With or without request (cf. vs. 11-16) .

Conclusion

1. Christ had power to help against (see v.2) —
   a. Despair—"dear unto him"
   b. Disease—"sick"
   c. Death—"ready to die"

2. It is the same power today, and we should therefore glorify God by—

   a. Thinking.
   b. Thanking.
   c. Trusting.
   d. Telling.

32

THE SON OF THE WIDOW OF NAIN
(Luke 7:11-16)

THE miracles of Christ were parables in action. They not only manifested acts of Deity, but also taught truths of eternal worth. They were visible actions but they also set forth underlying principles. They were at the same time proofs of Christ's power and symbols of Christian truth. Miracles were thus acted parables of His work for souls, symbolic of His triumph over their misery and sin, and typical of their spiritual deliverance and blessing.

The story of the raising of the widow's son is not merely a record of historical fact which might or might not be of practical significance today; it contains Gospel truth and Christian principle, and therefore comes home to our hearts.

I. *A Picture—Christ the Sympathizing One* (vs. 11-13)

  A. *The Story*

    1. Here are two processions face to face:

      a. Life and death.

      b. Order and disorder.

      c. Ministry and mourning.

    2. Here is one of the women of Luke's Gospel (see Introduction, p. 15).

      a. Loneliness of widow in spite of "much people" with her.

      b. Sorrow of mother—young life cut off.

3. Here is one of Luke's three stories of "only" children. Cf.—
   a. Daughter of Jairus (8:42).
   b. Child possessed of demon (9:38).

4. Here are Christ's reactions to situation:
   a. He saw.
   b. He felt.
   c. He spoke.
   d. He acted.

B. *The Suggestions*
   1. The shadows of life.
      a. Sorrow a fact of daily life—scarcely one individual escapes.
      b. Home as well as heart—trials, poverty, loneliness, sickness, death.

   2. The sympathy of Christ.
      a. Word from two Greek ones—"with" and "suffering" —includes feeling *with* as well as feeling *for*.
      b. Conscious human power often prevents true sympathy with the powerless—Christ's power did not freeze His compassion.
      c. We are often absorbed in self—Christ's perfect Manhood gave Him "heart at leisure from itself to soothe and sympathize."
      d. We have Him still—if His sympathy manifested in Nain only, we "of all men most miserable."
      e. His aid, though unasked, was instantly forthcoming, as always.
      f. His feeling was delicate:
         (1) Words few and simple, as all words of comfort should be—too much talk spoils.
         (2) Touch tender.

g. Sympathy soon put into action—deep lesson—feelings must become touch or soon evaporate.

II. *A Parable—Christ the Living One* (v.14)
A. *The Story*
1. The attitude of Christ—calmness.
   a. Of self-control—no surprise at emergencies.
   b. Of self-confidence—knew power to be grappled with.
   c. Of supreme authority—needed only touch to banish death.
2. The word of Christ—"Arise!"
   a. Cf. other miracles—means used to help faith.
   b. But in three of raising dead—bare word—cf. 8:54; John 11:43.

B. *The Suggestions*
1. Progress of death stopped.
   a. Christ's hand arrested not only departure of physical life, but onset of spiritual death.
   b. Power shown in regions of death, presaging final mission to abolish death for ever.
2. Progress of life established.
   a. Against sin, sorrow, and death.
   b. Christ still says to us, here and now, "Arise!"

III. *A Prophecy—Christ the Powerful One* (v.15)
A. *The Story*
1. Obedience—proof.
2. "Delivered him to his mother"—beautiful touch, chiefly for her sake.
3. Imagine her joy, and effect on crowd:

"And while the mourners hung about his neck,
Jesus went calmly on His way to Nain."

B. *The Suggestions*

1. Resurrection—hour coming.
2. Reunion—earthly ties renewed.
3. Recognition—shall we know each other? Of course, impossible otherwise. Cf. Jacob and Joseph, David and child. As someone has said: "Shall we have less sense in that life than in this?"

Conclusion

Three thoughts of Christ: sympathizing, living, powerful.

1. What is He to us?

   a. He longs to be a sympathizing Friend and a living reality, so as to be fully and always a powerful Lord.

   b. He is "able" to save—

      (1) From trial (Heb. 2:18).
      (2) From death (Heb. 5:7).
      (3) From sin (Heb. 7:28).

2. Is He all in all?

   a. Not that there will be no storm, but that we shall be kept safe in it—like village surrounded by mountains which both attract storms and protect from them.

   "God hath not promised sun without rain,
   Joy without sorrow, peace without pain;
   But God hath promised strength for the day,
   Rest for the labor, light for the way."
   (Annie Johnson Flint)

   b. Storm destroys, but accompanying rain makes fertile —so we are made fruitful by testing, and go forth to tell others. "Wherefore comfort one another with these words" (1 Thess. 4:18).

33

CHRIST AND JOHN THE BAPTIST
(Luke 7:18-35)

THE stories of those who came in touch with Jesus Christ are wonderful revelations of human nature. It was fore-told of Him that by Him "the thoughts of many hearts may be revealed" (2:35). Here we have the impact of Christ upon His Forerunner as reported by the latter's disciples.

We are told by the Apostle Peter of those who "stumble at the Word" (1 Pet. 2:8). The Lord's ways also are often very "stumbling," and they were especially so to John the Baptist at this time. How indifferent Christ seemed to him, and His course how unlike that which John had expected!

The episode reminds us that John is not the only worker who has had doubts and fears concerning his Master. In Scripture we read of David offended by God's severity (2 Sam. 6:8); Jonah offended by God's mercy (Jon. 4:1-3); and Martha offended by Christ's delay (John 11:21).

I. *The Worker Perplexed* (vs. 18-20)

   1. The Cause of the Perplexity.

      a. John could not understand Christ's ministry—not ac-companied by full Messianic program, especially judg-ment—so wondered if another was to come. Cf. other doubters (John 7:3-5; 14:5-12). But He had come this time to save, not to judge.

      b. John himself was in desperate circumstances and had special difficulties, so he was naturally impatient of Christ's quiet methods.

2. The Cure for the Perplexity.

    a. Sent straight to Jesus for answers. Doubts should always be brought direct to Him—if hidden, they will fester; if uttered to others, "offense" may spread.

    b. Received sympathetic hearing. "God is not wounded by a reverent challenge." Cf. Psa. 42:9.

II. *The Worker Enlightened* (vs. 21-23)

1. Truth taught by sight and hearing of fact—deeds supernatural, merciful, spiritual, gently reminding inquirer of Scriptures apparently overlooked, e.g., Isa. 29:18; 35:4-8; 61:1-3.

2. Trust encouraged by commendation of one not "offended," i.e., who is not hindered by what Christ is doing and who does not ask for other proofs. Gr. root is same as for our word "scandal"—that which can be a snare, or trap, of error.

N. B. C. G. Moore has said: "I know of no hours more trying to faith than those in which Jesus multiplies evidences of His power *and does not use it* . . . There is need of much grace when the messengers come back saying: 'Yes, He has all the power, and is all that you have thought; but He said not a word about taking you out of prison . . . No explanation; faith nourished; prison doors left closed; and then the message, 'Blessed is he whosoever shall not be offended in me.' That is all!'"

3. Christ will not explain Himself, but instead He will reveal Himself, as He did to David, to Jonah, to Martha, and to John.

III. *The Worker Approved* (vs. 24-28)

1. Consideration of his service—people, having heard message (v.23), must not obtain wrong impression of serious rebuke. Neither depreciation nor eulogy, but fair appraisal.

2. Commendation of John's character by asking and answering same question three times. He was—
   a. Not a reed, which is unstable—more like cedar.
   b. Not a courtier living in luxury—desert no place for such.
   c. But a prophet, and much more—a herald of Christ, a Divine messenger, bearing unflinching testimony.

3. Correlation with the kingdom of God:
   a. John was great, but even he did not know what Calvary would mean.
   b. So smallest diamond is greater than largest flint.

IV. *The Worker Vindicated* (vs. 29-35)

1. The Result—twofold effect of John's work:
   a. People and publicans, having heard him, "justified God," i.e., bore witness that God is just and true by submitting to John's baptism.
   b. Pharisees and lawyers "rejected the counsel of God," i.e., nullified or frustrated God's counsel or purpose for them by refusing what was involved in John's message. This was because they were unwilling to submit stubborn wills and be baptized by him. This led to—

2. The Rebuke—solemn, searching, even scathing.
   a. Christ likened generation to children dissatisfied with entertainment and unwilling to play at either "wedding" or "funeral"—rejoicing or mourning.
   b. John's austerity and Christ's gentleness alike had failed to appeal; yet wisdom was still proved by the wise, i.e., it was part of wisdom to heed God's call.

Conclusion

1. Are we ever "offended in" Jesus Christ? By—
   a. Partial knowledge—like John the Baptist.
   b. Mistaken conclusions—also like John (Cf. 1 Cor. 1: 18) .

   c. Proud preconceptions, expecting God to follow human patterns rather than submitting to His leadership—like rulers.

   d. Knowledge despised, either by abuse or over-emphasis—also like rulers.

2. Are not these attitudes indicative of the so-called "scientific" method of today?

   a. The scientist examines, inquires, then draws conclusion and so is led to proof.

   b. Unaided reason, however, is poor test of spiritual realities.

   c. Verse 22 may be applied spiritually.

3. What was the difference between John's offense and that of the rulers?

   a. His was born of sincere doubt, theirs of insincere controversy.

   b. First is preferable to second, but both to be avoided, remembering our Lord's words to Thomas in John 20:29.

4. How shall we avoid being "offended in" our Master?

   a. By being teachable—cf. message to John, an appeal to facts.

   b. By being willing by faith to accept Him as He is, after we have learned all we can about Him.

Then will come the blessing, for Christ will be realized in the fulness of grace, not as a stumbling-block, but as a stepping-stone (Cf. Psa. 118:22; Luke 20:17). When doubt arises it must be met by the assertion that He reigns, He knows all, and He makes no mistakes. Then are we content to be baffled by His doings and determined to trust Him whatever He does.

34

TWO SINNERS
(Luke 7:36-50)

THERE are many differences between secular history and sacred history. The former records the progress of civilization—discoveries of science, revolutions in government, fluctuations in commerce, and the lives of those who control nations and empires. Sacred history, on the other hand, while it records the movement of both group and individual, deals mainly with their relation to God and to truth, with the working of heart and conscience, mind and emotion, and with the revelation of human character.

The passage now before us, peculiar to Luke, contains one of the most remarkable revelations of heart in all Scripture, and shows Jesus Christ in relation to two widely dissimilar persons —a Pharisee and woman. It is as though a magnet were seen attracting to itself a handful of steel pens and at the same time failing to make any effect whatever on some scraps of iron ore nearby.

We are accustomed to speak of "the woman a sinner" (v.37) when we tell this story; but we must not forget that Simon the Pharisee was a sinner also. So let us note, first—

I. *Simon the Sinner*

He was—

1. Respectable.

This man of position invited Jesus to his house, probably because of—

a. Curiosity—strange deeds done by Jesus.

b. Vanity—Jesus popular.

c. Ambition—thinking to patronize Jesus.

2. Self-righteous.

Simon made a wrong estimate of—

  a. Jesus—"this man, if he were a prophet" (v.39).

    (1) Could not read Christ's nature and therefore undervalued it.

    (2) Thought accessibility of Christ due to ignorance instead of to compassion.

    (3) Mistook His way of rescuing from sin for failure to keep sin at distance.

  b. Himself—"spake within himself" (v.39)

    (1) Did not know own heart which was hard. One saved from sin by love is softened by love, but one kept from sin by pride is hardened by pride.

    (2) In spite of pride, omitted ordinary expressions of politeness (vs. 44-46).

    (3) Rejected Christ's salvation, for that comes only through mercy.

  c. The woman—"what manner of woman . . . for she is a sinner" (v. 39).

    (1) Saw her only as repulsive sinner to be despised.

    (2) Did not see that new life had entered into her heart.

3. Condemned.

  a. By his answer to Jesus—"I suppose" (v.43) —no convictions.

  b. By the argument of Jesus in parable (vs. 41,42,47);

    (1) Both Pharisee and woman were sinners.

    (2) One way for both—forgiveness.

    (3) Two degrees of love—little and much.

  c. By his attitude to Jesus—selfish, indifferent, neglectful.

N.B. How many are like Simon! Respectable, well-to-do, cultivated, even orthodox. Too refined to be vicious—of too good taste to be wholly worldly—but, nevertheless, lost sinners.

II. *The Woman the Sinner*

In sharp contrast with Simon—

1. Repentant, she was saved.
   Gift of ointment, action, and tears showed old life over and new life begun. Narrative clearly implies previous acquaintance with Christ had brought wonderful result—"Her sins . . . *are* forgiven; for she *loved* much . . . Thy faith *hath* saved thee" (vs. 47,50).

2. Saved, she was assured.
   Having repented and trusted Christ for forgiveness, she was on this occasion granted complete assurance of perfect pardon and resulting peace (vs. 47,48,50).

> "Go in peace;" the Lord hath spoken,
>   Hast thou faith? That faith avails.
> Not one word of His is broken,
>   Not one promise ever fails.
>
> Pardon He hath freely given;
>   Fear not; all is well with thee.
> Sin is gone, and bonds are riven;
>   Jesus says so; thou art free.
>
> Saved through faith! Believe it, live it,
>   Do not doubt thy soul's release.
> His the word; all honor give it,
>   Jesus saves thee—"Go in peace."
>   (Frank P. Britt)

3. Forgiven, she was grateful.
   Faith produced love, love produced service. Love does not compare, or argue, or neglect, as Simon did. Love finds ways of service and surrender—gifts, as ointment—ministry, as washing with tears and wiping with hair—all especially typical of woman's way of serving the Master, but applicable to all.

N.B. How many are like this woman? Perhaps not so respectable, or cultured, or well-to-do as Simon, but loving, devoted, grateful.

Conclusion

1. *Two Contrasts*

   a. Reality and unreality in religion. Christ's severest words directed not against gross sins of flesh avoided and condemned by respectable people, but against sins of insincerity and uncharitableness—far greater moral perils. Cold-hearted selfishness most terrible defect in human nature.

   b. Attitude of Christ toward two classes as typified here. To one He is solemn, searching and stern in condemnation; to other He is sympathetic, tender, loving, forgiving. Penitence, not Pride, leads to Pardon.

2. *Two Principles*

   a. Forgiveness precedes and causes love.

   b. The measure of forgiveness is also the measure of love.

Here, then, behind the two sinners, "great" and "small," stands the Saviour, offering love, forgiveness, assurance, peace. Is He yours?

> Gifts without love are rarely counted dear,
> Yet the Lord noticed that they wer not given
> By the proud host who knew not, though so near,
>   The dis-crown'd King of Heaven.
>
> But—can it be that e'en His own forget?
> Love's tender tokens He from them may miss?
> So busy in the Master's work, and yet
>   No welcome, and no "kiss."
>
> So full of zealous aims the life appears,
> Its current set towards the things above,
> But where is now the wonder or the "tears,"
>   Or the heart's fragrant love?
>
> Round the guest-table talk of many things
> That make for good. but not a word of Him,
> And though to lofty aims the heart still clings,
>   The eye of faith grows dim.

And from the busy work is something lost,
Music grows harsh without its deepest tone,
The Message lacks the throb, when needed most,
    Learnt in the heart alone.

O Christ, if e'er such danger me surprise,
Breathe in some whisper Thy reminding word,
Till like a breaking fount my heart replies—
    "I love Thee, love Thee, Lord."
                                (Constance Coote)

35

THE PARABLE OF THE SOILS
(Luke 8:4-15)

A parable is a teaching device in which a principle is concealed and a truth revealed. It gives the hearer first sight and then insight. This particular parable of our Lord is first told (vs. 4-8), and then taught (vs. 9-15) in answer to His disciples' question. It is usually known as "The Parable of the Sower," but since Christ laid emphasis on the soils, rather than on either sower or seed, let us do the same. However, let us first consider briefly—

I. *The Sower*

Primarily the Lord Jesus Himself, though He does not say so, either here or in the accounts in Matthew (13:1-23) and Mark (4:1-20); then His Apostles; and now any who speak in His Name and give forth the Word of life—mother, teacher, friend, preacher, writer, etc.

II. *The Seed*

The Word of God, as Christ definitely states (v.11), and not, as in the parable of Matthew 13:38, the children of the kingdom. It—

1. Has life—life-force.
2. Gives life—propagating power.
3. Feeds life—sustaining strength.

It is widely scattered—almost universally nowadays—yet not as productive as it ought to be. Why? Because not all the soil is "good ground." And so we come to—

III. *The Soils*

There is—

1. Wayside soil—hardness.

   a. As seed on hard-trodden path across field, so Word of God on heart hardened by evil influences—thoughts and desires unchecked and unforbidden. Truth heard, but only on surface and for short time, e.g., Pharaoh. Felix.

   b. Word then stolen as by birds, for it has no shelter—exposed instead of buried within heart. Fowls with quick eyes for food typify Satan's messengers with their thieves' training. They are—
      (1) Punctual—"immediately" (Mark 4:15).
      (2) Powerful—"catcheth away" (Matt. 13:19).
      (3) Practical— "lest they should believe" (v.12).

There is also—

2. Rocky soil—shallowness

   a. Thin layer of suitable soil on rock beneath—rapid growth, but also rapid withering.

   b. Shallow heart, superficial, emotional—easily interested and impressed, but with no depth of conviction—feeling, not faith. Cf. rich young ruler (18:18-24—see Study No. 70, p. 274; second son of Matt. 21:30, "I go, sir: and went not."
   Illus.: Tears during sermon, but next morning—?

Then there is—

3. Thorny soil—joyous reception.

   a. Wild, uncultivated, bad bit of ground—some outward growth, but no strong root—choked with thorns.

   b. Preoccupied heart already full of cares, pleasures, desire for other things. Cf. "deceitfulness of riches," no solid support but choked, with deceitfulness of poverty, heaven emphasized at expense of earth and duty. "No fruit to perfection" from either: e.g., Achan, Gehazi, Judas, Demas.

But there is also—

4. Good soil—fruitfulness.

    a. Ground cleared, ploughed, softened, watered.

    b. Honest heart—recognizing, receiving, returning, re-producing. *Illus.:* Child asked what he would request: "I'd ask for a new heart."

Conclusion

1. Let us note that—

    a. Here are three failures and but one success, yet one Sower and one type of seed for all.

    b. All four may be part of one case.

    c. All three failures may be changed—soil softened, deepened, cleared, cleansed.

2. Let us consider the different preposition used in each case:

    a. *"By* the wayside" (vs. 5,12).

    b. *"On* the rock" (vs. 6,13).

    c. *"Among* thorns" (vs. 7,14).

    d. *"Into* the good ground" (Gr. of vs. 8,15; see Matt. 13:8,23).

3. Let us therefore heed not only—

    a. *What* we hear—Gospel message, inspirational challenge, etc., but also—

    b. *How* we hear—simply, sincerely, sympathetically, surrendering lip and life, personality and possessions.

The Word of God must be received and retained in order that it may reveal. Are we doing this?

36

THE RAISING OF JAIRUS' DAUGHTER
(Luke 8:41,42,49-56)

CHRIST, having delivered several parables, crossed the Lake of Galilee at eventide and fell asleep in the boat. Then came the storm and His Divine control of it, His miracle in Gadara, and His return to Capernaum. According to Matthew (chap. 9), his own call came just at this time, after which he gave a feast in honor of the Master. While Christ was speaking to those who had gathered. He was approached by a certain ruler, Jairus by name.

Jairus came from what had been a house of joy and had become a house of illness and sorrow. But he had come to One who was ready for what seemed like unexpected calls and sudden alternatives, and who could take the leading part in utterly dissimilar scenes. The home life here depicted shows Christ as no mere healer but as the One who "went about doing good," even in the house of death. Let us consider—

I. *The Distressed Parent* (vs. 41-48)

  1. The Alarming Illness (v.42).

     a. Only daughter probably only child—at appealing age between childhood and maidenhood.

     b. Father was influential, honored man—sorrow keeps company with rich as well as poor.

  2. The Earnest Entreaty (v.41).

     a. Attitude of worship—urgent petition.

     b. Expression of confidence—"my little daughter . . . lay Thy hands . . . she shall live" (Mark 5:23)—no one else—cf. own doctor, mother, priest.

c. Cf. Jairus' position—of class against Jesus, and probably proud. Yet sorrow drove him to Master and pride was lost. Sorrow and need, great levellers, make short work of prejudice.

3. The Tested Faith (vs. 43-48).

a. Delay tested—did not find father wanting—as though he could be patient knowing Christ was Lord of time. Unselfishness shown as well, for sick woman needed Christ too.

b. Delay strengthened—gave him new evidence of Christ's power—heard "Thy *faith* hath made thee whole," and did he not have strong faith? Did he, hearing mention of "twelve years" of woman's sickness, think, "Why, that's my little daughter's *age!*"? Blessing often withheld for time, to give greater one.

II. *The Sleeping Child* (vs. 49-53)

1. The Servant's Message (v.49).
   a. More sorrow for Jairus—may well have queried delay then, if not before.
   b. But greater opportunity for Jesus—"disappointments His appointments."

2. The Lord's Assurance (v.50).
   a. Fear forbidden meant comfort and sympathy.
   b. Faith enjoined was counsel for time when all seemed hopeless.

3. The Crowd's Behavior (vs. 52, 53).
   a. Multitude thronging—curiosity.
   b. Mourners sorrowing—genuine or not, probably some of each—in excess of expression, as always in East, and sometimes elsewhere also—"minstrels . . . making a noise" (Matt. 9:23).

III. *The Glorious Lord* (vs. 51,52,54)
1. His Perfect Knowledge (v.52).
   a. World's opinion—death, gloom.
   b. Christ's certainty—sleep, graciousness.

2. His Complete Control (vs. 51,54).
   a. Dismissal of crowd—so evidently they had neither faith nor sympathy (v.53).
   b. Choice of those who had faith—inner circle of disciples, parents. Did not allow child to be center of curious gaze, but desired calmness and tolerated no doubt of His ability.

3. His Almighty Power (v.54)
   a. Touch of love—first regard was for child, and word used was equivalent to "My little pet lamb."
   b. Speech of authority—with voice dead hear was given command dead obey.

IV. *The Happy Home* (vs. 55,56)
1. *The Restored Child* (v.55).
   We may imagine her first prostrate in death, then erect in life given her by Christ:
   a. Fever of suffering, which had become paleness of death changed to rosy flush of health.
   b. Eyes filled with agony, which had become glassy in death, gazed in awe into Jesus' own.
   c. Smile in spite of suffering, which had hovered about lips in death, now widening towards parents.
   d. Lips tortured in illness, which had stilled in death, now filled with glad speech.

2. The Astounded Parents (v.56).
   a. Sorrow dispelled—joy restored.
   b. So always if Jesus is in home.

3. The Considerate Lord (v.55).

    a. Kindly impulse for child's physical need of strength.

    b. Thought for opportunity of lesser service by parents.

    c. Proof of reality and completeness of miracle—not only true conquest of death, but healing from illness as well.

4. The Natural Result (v.56).

    a. Galilee excited. Opposition growing, therefore silence enjoined.

    b. But see Him there—in grand composure, in joy at human joy.

Conclusion

Death of child or young person especially sad, as only parents know—seems premature to our limited vision. Yet even then Christ can bless. In this story is His threefold message for bereaved or troubled home:

1. *"Fear not: believe only!"*

    a. "Only," but also much—great faith needed.

    b. Yet implies confidence in a Person rather than mere acceptance of a truth.

    c. So if Jesus Christ real, He is to be trusted.

2. *"Not dead, but sleepeth!"*

    a. Contrasts temporal death and spiritual death—Jews knew only former, therefore wailed at its coming.

    b. But Jesus knew latter was *the* death, so thought primarily of that—it was substance of which other was shadow.

    c. Therefore He spoke these words—no wonder Jews laughed.

   d. So now, bereaved Christians should not grieve **as** those without hope.

   e. But in the "second death" there is no comfort.

3. *"Maid, arise!"*

   a. Christ intended her not only to arise from death to earthly life, but also to arise to higher spiritual life than before.

   b. So we may know our Christian loved ones have indeed arisen to immeasurably higher existence and will share in Christ's Return.

   c. Also, we have certainty of reunion which is to last forever.

Let us, therefore,—

1. Have faith instead of fear.
2. Count death but sleep for the body.
3. Know that the soul has "come up higher."

37

A WOMAN HEALED
(Luke 8:43-48)

O<small>NE</small> of the most interesting and helpful books for a young medical student to possess would be the diary of an able, experienced physician. Similarly, one of the most valuable volumes in the library of a Christian worker is one entitled "A Pastor's Sketches." Both contain stories of people and give an insight into ways of dealing with them, body or soul.

The Gospels, particularly this one written by "Dr. Luke," form the "diary" of the Great Physician, the "Shepherd and Bishop" of souls. In them we see how He deals with the most difficult cases. We note His thorough diagnoses, His marvellous skill, and the wonderful cures which are the result of His ministry.

Consider this incident as the history of a soul in relation to Christ as both Physician and Pastor:

I. *The Sad Need*

  A. *The woman's illness caused—*

    1. Helplessness.

     Her malady was—

     a. Severe—chronic haemorrhages, in modern parlance.

     b. Persistent—of twelve years' duration—cf. whole life-span of Jairus' little daughter.

    2. Hopelessness.

     She had—

     a. Tried many doctors.

     b. Spent all her living on them, yet—

     c. Was no better, but rather worse (cf. Mark 5:26).

B. *Sin is just like such a disease*:

1. The sinner is helpless against—

   a. Restlessness of thought.
   b. Forebodings about the future.
   c. Pangs of conscience.
   d. Slavery of habit.

2. The sinner is hopeless because—

   a. All panaceas are ineffectual, in spite of—

      (1) Amount of money spent.
      (2) Religious ceremonials observed.
      (3) External reformation experienced.

   b. The longer these efforts are made, the worse the condition. Cf. this age—more hopeful than any other on everything save religion.

II. *The Simple Opportunity*

It was—

1. Given.

   a. On way to home of Jairus, seemingly casual interception.
   b. Providence and grace harmonize.
   c. So now, how often person strays into church or Gospel hall, or takes up book. Cf. story of Zacchaeus (19:1-10 see Study No. 72, p. 281). Encounter appears to be mere chance, but not really. This one was also—

2. Grasped.

   a. Any "chance" seized at extremity of need.
   b. Probably struggled through crowd—cf. Mark 5:27.
   c. So now, opportunity must be not only given but grasped, not only seen but seized, or of no avail.

III. *The Splendid Work*

1. Contact.

   a. She but touched border or hem of Christ's garment (v.44; cf. Matt. 9:20,21).

  b. Power of touch, in spite of her ignorance and despondency.

  c. Faith was in Him evidently, not in truths spoken or deeds done.

 2. Health.

  a. Thorough—not like so many so-called "faith healings" today.

  b. Immediate—not even word necessary.

IV. *The Searching Test*

 1. The Enquiry of Christ.

  a. Recognition of "virtue," or special power of healing, gone out from Him.

  b. Response to mere touch of hers—or ours.

 2. The Error of the Disciples.

  a. No distinction between "touch" of woman and "press" of multitude.

  b. One real and resolute, the other curious and casual.

  c. So today—two attitudes to, e.g., the Lord's Supper:

   (1) Crowds throng.

   (2) Faith touches.

 3. The Education of the Woman.

  a. She had drawn forth privately His power to heal; so now He draws forth publicly her confession.

  b. Declaration doubtless to elicit from her avowal that she thought more of Healer than of health, and was not merely self-absorbed—also for benefit of others.

  c. Some today do not serve Christ fully when out of sight of fellows.

  d. Some do, but lose blessing because of failure to confess Him.

V. *The Special Blessing*

1. Assurance.

    a. "Daughter"—because woman did not know Jesus she first feared Him, but His opening word was reassuring.

    b. "Be of good comfort"—double assurance to her soul.

    c. "Thy faith hath made thee whole"—not "thy finger." So today we do not need physical touch, only exercise of faith, however small, in Christ.
    Illus.: Woman known for beautiful Christian life once told by caller: "I am so glad to see you; you are the woman of the strong faith!" "No, sir," she replied, "I am the woman of the weak faith in the strong Saviour!"

2. Anticipation.

    "Go in peace"—what a great gift is peace—precious, increasing, permanent, eternal!

Conclusion

    Is this life yours?

    1. First touch, then testimony.
    2. First faith, then faithfulness.
    3. First power, then peace.
    4. First comfort, then consecration.
    5. First healing, then holiness.

> The folks kept croodin' roun' aboot,
>   And jostlin' ane anither;
> For Jesus cured, beyond a doot,
>   First ane and then the ither.
>
> To ask wha touch'd Him sounded queer,
>   And Peter thocht it funny;
> Sae up he spak, "What needs ye speir
>   When jostled by sae mony?"

Yet ane there was wha ken'd fu' weel
    The touch the Savior meant,
For she alane was made to feel
    The virtue that He spent.

"Wha touch'd me?" yet again He speir'd,
    As 'f might be to forbid it,
When oot she cried, though unca fear'd,
    "Twas me, guid Lord, that did it."

But list we what the Saviour said
    As in aboot she stole,
"Gae hame in peace, be not afraid,
    Thy faith hath made thee whole."

(From A Sermon in the Scottish
Dialect by J. M'Combie Murray)

38

ENOUGH AND TO SPARE
(Luke 9:10-17)

THIS important episode in the life of Christ contains the only miracle recorded in all four Gospels. It was a turning-point in His ministry. It marked the end of the year in Galilee, the preparatory stage, and introduced His main work. This miracle is also connected with the disciples' report of their first preaching tour. This was a crowning hour, and yet to Jesus it must have been a sad and bitter hour because, in spite of the miracle, many went away and only the few remained.

I. *The Story*
  1. *A Busy Time* (vs. 10,11)
     a. Both Master and disciples needed rest for they had wrought and taught much.
     b. They were under heavy pressure and greatly in demand.
     c. Amid gathering crowds Christ was calm—this still time for sowing, not reaping.
     d. He had a deep compassion for crowds.
     N.B. The rest of today is often a new opportunity for service.

  2. *A Pressing Need* (vs. 12,13)
     a. Place was uninhabited, hence no source of food—hunger and want.
     b. Time was late—fatigue and weakness.
     c. Demand was great—200 pence equal to about $24.

d. Supply was scanty—if reckoned without Christ.

N.B. The secret of today for the task of today is that service is not measured by human ability but by Divine enabling.

3. *A Full Supply* (vs. 14-17)

a. Orderly arrangement—involved not only faith on part of disciples to seat crowds, but also faith on part of crowds to sit down when bidden.

b. Devout testimony to Father by blessing of food.

c. Generous bestowal on multitudes.

d. Entire satisfaction, not merely partial—significance of twelve basketfuls remaining may have been that each disciple have his rightful share.

N.B. The task of today is great; the means of today are ample; the need of today is faithfulness.

II. *The Sign*

1. Christ's Motive—compassion—on suffering multitudes, and also on disciples' faith. He is ever concerned with both spiritual and physical needs.

2. Christ's Manner—calmness—no uncertainty, but rather assumption of full authority and sufficiency.

3. Christ's Method—co-operation—could have performed this miracle without assistance from disciples, but through them He chose to work on that occasion, and through believers He chooses to work today.

III. *The Symbol*

The whole episode typifies the work of Christ (cf. account in John 6, with discourse following)

1. *The Perishing World*—The Multitude.

a. Weakness—then, through lack of physical food; now, through sin and loss of presence of God.

b. Weariness—then, it was evening and crowds had journeyed far; now, it is nearly 2000 years later and world is jaded from wandering.

c. Want—then, of evening meal, for when hungry nothing but food satisfies; now, "Thou hast made us for Thyself, and our hearts are restless till they rest in Thee" (Augustine).

2. *The Powerless Church*—The Disciples

a. Insufficiency—then, of food to supply crowds; now, of spiritual resources for starving world.

b. Inability—then, to buy food. Was it money or opportunity that was lacking? Perhaps both. Now, in presence of heathenism, pagan civilization, indifference, worldliness, sin—no spiritual food to offer—shameful condition unwarranted by available provision of grace. Then followed:

(1) The Request—"Send the multitude away." All that could be done in human power was to "send away" (v.12). But where? It is the same today; but again, where? (Cf. John 6:68, after discourse on the Bread of Life)

(2) The Reminder—"Give ye." There must be sacrifice, complete and continuous, on the part of believers.

(3) The Rejoinder—"We have no more but . . ." a little —"five loaves and two fishes"—"small fishes," adds John (6:9), and tells us they were a lad's lunch. Yet—"little is much if God is in it."

3. *The Perfect Saviour*—The Master

a. The Command—"Make them sit down." There must be absolute obedience. Instruments must be fully yielded.

b. The Secret—"He took." Disciples were in presence of Power Incarnate; so His followers today.

c. The Blessing—"He blessed." Work ineffectual without benediction of Father; so ours today.

d. The Supply—"They did eat, and were all filled."
Enough and to spare; still blessedly true today.

His Compassion, Capability, Care—beyond our need, our
deserving, our comprehension.

Conclusion

Christianity does not supply inherent ability; but it does
demand maintained dependence—the secret of salvation first,
then of holiness, and also of power. The worth of Christian
work is in exact proportion to the devotion of God's people.
Christ must be all in all or not at all; if He is not Lord of all
He is not Lord at all.

> "I take—He understands;
> I have faith—He is faithful;
> I trust—He is trustworthy."

39

A FULLY YIELDED LIFE
(Luke 9:12-17)

THERE must be some special reason for the prominence of this miracle, the only one found in all four Gospels. It occurred at a time of crisis in our Lord's ministry and stirred the people to such a depth of feeling that they tried to make Him a King. But the miracle was a symbol of our Lord's higher spiritual work, for He had not come to be King in the current Jewish sense, but to offer Himself as the Bread of Life for the world.

This miracle may also be taken symbolically in another way, as a parable for workers, since in it are many points of vital interest for all who are called upon to serve Christ. We may see in it what the Lord still desires to do, and also some of the greatest principles of Christian service.

I. *The Deep Need* (v.12)

1. People had journeyed far into desert and were weary and weak through lack of food.

2. Disciples, helpless, requested Jesus to send them away for food and lodging.

3. So today, as we contemplate awful needs of world, we realize task of filling them almost beyond imagination.

4. Nothing sadder than state of human nature through sin, and nothing more striking than absolute impossibility of providing anything to meet need, except through Christ.

II. *The High Privilege* (John 6:5)

1. John tells us Christ's response was question addressed to Philip: "Whence shall we buy bread, that these may eat?"—thus taking counsel with disciples and associating them with Himself.

2. This is what He is always desirous of doing—of making us co-workers with Himself (Cf. Gen. 6:13; 10:17; Psa. 25:14; Amos 3:7; John 15:15; 2 Cor. 6:1).

3. This joy, privilege, honor, inspiration of all work for Christ—association with Him and fellowship with His purposes.

4. He might and could have worked without us, but instead has been pleased to permit us to carry His bread to world.

III. *The Great Task* (vs. 13-15)

1. When disciples confessed insufficiency of food supply and obvious inability to obtain more, Christ uttered startling command: "Give ye them to eat"—to all appearances utterly impossible task, and yet He also said of people: "They need not depart" (Matt. 14:16).

2. Strong confidence is clear, and means Christians have what world needs—because Christ Himself is behind every word He says (cf. John 6:6).

3. So today, in spite of depressing presence of world's dark heathenism, pagan civilization, and spiritual indifference, and Church's scanty means and lack of power and wisdom, Christ knows His own grace and sufficiency.

IV. *The Simple Secret* (v.16)

1. Christ utilized five loaves and two fishes as foundation of supply. Could have done without them, but used them nevertheless.

2. This suggests one of greatest principles of God's working —His use of means. Miracle in both Testaments usually wrought through already existing agencies—natural

means employed to full extent, and then supernatural power added. This miracle no new creation, but simply use of available supply as channel of Divine power.

3. So today, Christ uses natural characteristics and resources of His disciples—takes us as we are and utilizes what we have for His glory. Thus, one thing only disciples had to do—bring what they possessed to Master. He blessed these and made them sufficient for people's need. Otherwise, "loaves unblessed are loaves unmultiplied."

V. *The Wonderful Result* (v.17)

1. Through blessing of Christ on ordinary food, five thousand men, "beside women and children" (Matt. 14:21), were "filled."

2. Cf. Moses' rod—ordinary shepherd's crook of his daily calling—transformed by power of God (Exod. 4:2,3).

3. So today, our ordinary life, though weak, and our natural capacities, though few, can be employed by God to produce remarkable results. Size never determines power. *Illus.*: Zinzendorf, while at school, founded "Guild of the Grain of Mustard Seed"—result today, Moravian Church.

Conclusion

1. It is marvelous what Christ can do with fully yielded life—almost infinite possibilities in smallest and humblest. Cf. merchant in office, workman in factory, mother in home, soldier on service. Blessings often found under most unfavorable conditions.
Illus.: In St. Nicholas' Church tower in Amsterdam is keyboard struck by wooden gloves. Only clatter and clanging heard there, yet exquisite music of bells floats over city, and men at work pause to listen.

2. Be it ours, therefore, to surrender everything to Christ, trusting Him with everything, obeying Him in everything. Then He will send us forth, blessed and blessing, to fill and satisfy hungry souls.

Only one talent small,
Scarce worthy to be named,
Truly He hath no need of this.
Oh! art thou not ashamed?
He gave that talent first,
Then use it in His strength,
Thereby, thou know'st not, He may work
A miracle at length.

Many the starving souls,
Now waiting to be fed,
Needing, though knowing not their need
Of Christ the Living Bread.
If thou hast known this love,
To others make it known,
Receiving blessings, others bless;
No seed abides alone.

And when thine eyes shall see
The holy, ransomed throng,
In heavenly fields, by living streams,
By Jesus led along.
Unspeakable thy joy
And glorious thy reward,
If by thy barley loaves one soul
Has been brought home to God.

40

CONFESSING CHRIST
(Luke 9:18-26)

T<small>HIS</small> passage sums up for us what we ought to "say" about Jesus Christ (vs. 18,20), or, in other words, the believer's opinion of the Son of God.

I. *His Character—as Saviour* (vs. 18-20)

1. According to popular opinion (v.19).
2. According to apostolic opinion (v.20).

II. *His Cross—as Sufferer* (vs. 21,22)

1. His Deity to be hidden at that time (v.21).
2. His Passion revealed to disciples (v.22).

III. *His Call—as Leader* (vs. 23-25)

1. Self to be denied—"repudiated, disowned," as in 22:57; Matt. 10:33; 2 Tim. 2:12—not denial *to* self, but repudiation and denial *of* self.

2. Cross to be taken up daily—not mere suffering or trial, but death of self with Christ, as in Gal. 2:20; 5:24,25; Rom. 6:11; and certainly not any personal tendency, such as temper or despondency. These are not crosses, but sins.

3. Christ to be followed—which is impossible without two steps preceding. As He lived His earthly life He denied self, and as He went towards Calvary He bore His Cross.

4. Life to be lost—in order to be saved. Divine paradox—true "saving" of life will include all the rest.

IV. *His Claim—as Lord* (v.26)
  1. Glory:
     a. His own.
     b. His Father's.
     c. The holy angels'.

  2. Shame:
     a. Of Him.
     b. Of His words.
     c. Of the believer.

Conclusion

"What think ye of Christ?" Character, Cross, Call and Claim. On this one question hang issues of eternity. May we all acclaim Him Saviour, Sufferer in our stead, Leader, Lord!

41

THE TRANSFIGURATION
(Luke 9:28-36)

THIS remarkable incident in the life of Christ occurs midway between His Incarnation and His Ascension—the one representing the institution of our hope and the other its anticipation. The teaching recorded in the sixth chapter of John's Gospel had turned Christ's popularity and had increased the opposition in Galilee, so that the character of His ministry underwent a change at this point. He abandoned the performance of miracles and devoted Himself to the Twelve Apostles. Together they took longer journeys—to Tyre and Sidon, to Caesarea-Philippi.

The unique experience of the Transfiguration has thus great meaning at this stage in Christ's earthly life.

I. *The Transfigured Lord*
  A. *The Time*
    1. "About an eight days after"—Why does each Gospel (Matthew and Mark, "after six days") record a time element? "These sayings" (v.28) most important (see above), and include—
      a. Peter's confession (v.20).
      b. Christ's revelation (v.22) for the first time of His death.
    2. These two apparently irreconcilable, so probably disciples spent six days in gloom and wonder.

  B. *The Purpose*
    1. To disciples—to show glory and give encouragement. Deity and death not irreconcilable after all—no contradiction, but consistency—means to great end.

2. To Jesus—who, though sorrowful because of rejection in Galilee behind and in Jerusalem ahead, solicits no human sympathy. Divine approval—cf. His baptism (3: 22), and one other time of crisis (John 12:28). Foretaste of glory.

C. *The Character*

1. While praying, countenance and raiment showed plainly indwelling Divinity—glory from within—body steeped in splendor natural to Himself.

2. Thus, glorification of humanity by Divinity.

II. *The Attendant Saints*

A. *The Persons*

1. Moses and Elijah, lawgiver and prophet—not patriarchs—spiritual heroes rather than secular.

2. Moses representing Law and Elijah Prophets, both remarkable as to death:

   a. Moses' death was mysterious.

   b. Elijah's death was miraculous.

3. Clearly there in person, because Christ conversed with them before disciples awoke from sleep.

B. *The Conversation*

1. Subject was "His decease"—literally, His exodus, departing—His death, resurrection and ascension, route He would take out of this life and back to heaven. Would be end of Law and fulfilment of Prophets.

2. "Which He should accomplish"—literally, perform, execute, as something appointed and prescribed by God the Father.

3. "At Jerusalem"—center of Jewish life and religion.

C. *The Meaning*

1. To Jesus.

   a. Homage of Lawgiver and Prophet conferring on His death—interested in it and prepared for it as culmination of Old Testament. "Moses would have talked of the Lord's coming exodus as Redemption, and Elijah as Restoration, each according to the character of his own earthly mission, and the Saviour's exodus accomplished both. For He redeemed us from sin and Satan, and restored us to holiness and to God" (H. J. Horn).

b. Encouragement of Christ's human soul to go on because of sight of two who had passed on to glory—one by natural death but Divine burial, and the other by translation—symbols of two classes of believers at second coming of Christ (Cf. John 11:25, 26).

2. To disciples.
   a. Cross understood by inhabitants of heaven if not by those of earth.
   b. Glimpse by anticipation of what Kingdom of God really meant—spiritual, not temporal.

III. *The Astonished Disciples*
   A. *The Men*
   Why three only—"Peter, John and James"?
   1. Perhaps because benefit to all through fittest.
   2. If others also, perhaps dazzled with grandeur and Judas incited to worldly ambition.
   3. Perhaps these three only saved situation by keeping it secret (v.36; Mark 9:9,10) —until 1 Peter 1:15-18 was written.
   4. Cf. unfitness of other nine as shown by lack of power over demon in boy at foot of mountain (v.40).
   5. Thus, God's revelation only to fitted ones whose devotion is real though faith frail.

   B. *The Impression*
   1. "It is good for us to be here"—passage often quoted, yet original cannot bear out meaning usually given.

2. Not that worship and fellowship are not to be private, or that adoration of God is to be undertaken for honor, for it is written: ". . . not knowing what he said" (v.33).

3. Rather, since word translated "good" is not precious, or valuable, but excellent, fortuitous, best, Peter here showed he found only advantage in Christ's ministry, i.e., no idea of Cross.

4. So statement means: "It is opportune, of service to us, that we are here"—thought of crisis—Kingdom has come, so place of sojourn needed.

5. How like Peter, well-meaning but blundering!

IV. *The Divine Testimony*

   A. *The Cloud*

   Why?

     1. God's will thus shown when Peter suggested remaining in mount.

     2. Probably his words hastened departure, and now cloud hid figures.

   B. *The Voice*

     1. Peter had lowered Christ to level of Moses and Elijah —disciples as Jews probably glad Jesus of Nazareth connected with Old Testament heroes.

     2. So now hour is come for departure of Law and Prophets.

     3. Also, reminder comes—"Hear Him"—especially as to Cross (Cf. Isa. 42:1-7; Heb. 1-14).

V. *The Practical Outcome*

   A. *The Fear and its Removal*

     1. Awed, disciples fell on their faces (Matt. 17:6).

     2. But "Jesus came and touched them" and spoke reassuringly (Matt. 17:7), leading them back to their own life from His.

B. *The Sight and the Lesson*

   1. "Jesus only" (Matt. 17:18) —Law and Prophets gone.

   2. Chosen three never forgot experience—cf. John 1:14; 2 Peter 1:21.

Conclusion

  1. *God's Motive*

    a. To make real a truth already received.

    b. Cf. idea of Messiah in John 1—nothing really new here.

    c. Cf. statement of Peter at Caesarea-Philippi (Matt. 16:16) —needed to translate creed into life.

    d. Intellectual grasp not enough—not new views but new vitality needed.

    e. So today, we may be orthodox, yea evangelical, and yet there may be lack in heart and life.

  2. *God's Method*

    a. Face to face with Christ, soul will leave all else, even Moses and Elijah.

    b. All leading to Him—books, friends, experiences, etc.

    c. Times of communion may be times of transfiguration.

    d. Emphasis on Death—Atonement the Center!

    e. Emphasis on Glory—Resurrection the Consequence!

So, *Jesus Only*—

    a. Salvation for sinner.

    b. Subject for preacher.

    c. Solution for student.

    d. Sanctification for believer.

    e. Solace for sorrowing.

    f. Satisfaction for all—forever!

"Jesus only! In the shadow
 Of the cloud so chill and dim,
We are clinging, loving, trusting,
He with us and we with Him.
All unseen, yet ever nigh,
Jesus only all our cry.

Jesus only! In the glory
 When the shadows all have flown,
Seeing Him in all His beauty,
Satisfied with Him alone.
Then, among the ransomed throng,
Jesus only all our song."

42

THREE SPIRITUAL DIAGNOSES
(Luke 9:46-56)

HERE we may say that the writer of the Gospel, Luke the Beloved Physician, shows us Jesus Christ as the Great Physician of Souls, the Heavenly Diagnostician. The spiritual diseases diagnosed are:

I. *Pride* (vs. 46-48)
1. Reasoning as to Messianic hopes, and recent distinction accorded to Peter, James, and John lead other disciples to dispute.
2. Jesus uses child as object lesson. Law enjoined care of feeblest.
3. Indicates three steps:
   a. Receive child in His Name.
   b. Receive Him.
   c. Receive His Father.
4. So self-seeking is contrasted with self-abnegation—all members of one body.
5. Love always stoops—true greatness in serving lowest and least. Service, not lordship, constitutes greatness in Kingdom.
6. Our Lord having taken upon Himself "the form of a servant," His true disciples become great only as they follow His example.

II. *Prejudice* (vs. 49,50)
1. Confession in v.49 suggested by Christ's use of word "name" in v.48.

2. Fear and jealousy of other methods, and love of complete uniformity, curse of past. Cf. Num. 11:27-29.

3. Life should be dynamic, not static.

4. Broad and narrow views of life—narrowness shows disciples were beginners in faith (see Matt. 8:26; 18:1-6).

5. Christ's reply should be compared with His words in 11:23—both true in different circumstances:

   a. Cf. brethren in other bodies.

   b. Cf. those in own ranks who differ within truth as it is in Christ.

III. *Persecution* (vs. 51-56)

1. Here, at v.51, begins new section of Gospel—Galilee to Jerusalem for final conflict. Again He "must needs pass through Samaria" (John 4:4).

2. Samaritans (Cf. Acts 8:14; 2 Kings 1:3)—spirit so different as to be alien. Should have made "ready" for Jesus, but even so He declares His disciples also must be of different "manner of spirit," because He came to save, not to destroy (v.56).

Conclusion

1. Pride leads through prejudice to persecution.

2. Humility leads through tolerance to understanding.

> The Lord Christ wanted a tongue one day
>   To speak a message of cheer
> To a heart that was weary and worn and sad,
>   And weighed with a mighty fear.
> He asked me for mine, but 'twas busy quite
> With my own affairs from morn till night.
>
> The Lord Christ wanted a hand one day
>   To do a loving deed;
> He wanted two feet, on an errand for Him
>   To run with gladsome speed.
> But I had need of my own that day;
> To His gentle beseeching I answered "Nay!"

So all that day I used my tongue,
  My hands, and my feet as I chose;
I said some hasty, bitter words
  That hurt one heart. God knows
I busied my hands with worthless play,
And my wilful feet went a crooked way.

And the dear Lord Christ, was His work undone
  For lack of a willing heart?
Only through men does He speak to men?
  Dumb must He be apart?
I do not know, but I wish today
I had let the Lord Christ have His way.

43

THREE TEMPERAMENTS
(Luke 9:57-62)

IN THESE six verses we have thumbnail sketches of three very different men who came into contact with Christ. All were aspirants to permanent, close discipleship, and the reception their protestations received from the Master revealed His marvelous insight into human temperament, based as it was on principles eternally applicable. This supernatural knowledge of His was a fulfilment of one of the prophecies concerning Him uttered by Simeon at His circumcision—"that the thoughts of many hearts may be revealed" (2:35). There is a striking difference in His treatment of these three types. First, there is—

I. *The Impulsive* (vs. 57,58)
   A. *The Man*
      1. What he was:
         a. A scribe (Matt. 8:19).
         b. A disciple (Matt. 8:21).

      2. What he said:
         a. "Master"—which was good name for Christ.
         b. "I will follow"—recognized claim of Christ.
         c. "Whithersoever"—would throw in lot with Christ.

      3. How he seemed:
         a. Charming, warm, hearty, magnanimous.
         b. Enthusiastic, confident.
         c. Everything coming easily—learning, popularity, etc.

B. *The Master*

1. Did not show disapproval, but saw beneath surface and did not disguise anything. Knew man's impulse had been too quick, so tested him, asking him to—
   a. Consider His homelessness.
   b. Remember how He was ostracized.

2. In man's enthusiasm, saw—
   a. Egotism.
   b. Self-deceit.
   c. Instability.
   d. Blind confidence in own strength.

3. Result of test was silence. Did he follow Christ? Doubtful.

C. *The Message*

1. Excited feelings vs. enlightened heart.
   a. Prospect of glory and advancement.
   b. Superficial devotion.
   c. Fascinated but not convinced.

2. Impulse vs. will.
   a. Everything seems easy? Yes, but also—
   b. Sin, discouragement, recoil, broken word—all easy.

3. Counting the cost.
   a. This needed before resolution or self-sacrifice.
   b. Includes separation and hardship.

4. Any place for impulsive?
   a. Yes—cf. Peter before and after Pentecost.
   b. Keynote for balance—steadfastness, as in 1 Pet. 5:9; 2 Pet. 3:17—impulsive nature speaking from experience.

5. But this man needed to consider—he was too speedy! Then there was—

II. *The Cautious* (vs. 59,60)
Familiar and even trite to say no two natures alike—but this one exact opposite of foregoing—impulse vs. caution. One

might be said to be ready, but unwilling; the other, willing, but unready. Christ used different methods, checking one nature and stimulating the other.

A. *The Call*

Only one recorded in all three encounters.

1. What? Words often in Gospels—"Follow Me"—meant two things only:
   a. Trust.
   b. Obey.
   or, Believe My Word, and do what I say!
2. How? Implication always—
   a. Immediately.
   b. Fully.
   c. Continually.
   i.e., Christian life summed up in word "follow."

B. *The Response*

1. *The Meaning.*

   a. Not literal one—in Orient, funeral was held same day and family did not emerge until it was over.
   b. Seems unfeeling, but—*Illus.*: George Adam Smith and Kelman once offered Scottish education to young son of Bedouin chief, and at once he replied: "Suffer me first to bury my father!" But father close by!
   c. Means "home ties first"—cool, dilatory, pleading to stay home till death of father frees son from filial duty.

2. The Tendency.

   a. Wary and reflective even to excess.
   b. Not despising or scoffing at claims of Christ, but putting other things first.
   c. Procrastinating—making best of both worlds, material and spiritual, meanwhile.

    d. Intending to use Gospel later, but not now.
    e. Needing more than laudable purpose.

C. *The Solution*

Christ evidently saw power of devotion in this life, and His answer was intended to correct and stimulate:

1. To recognize relative value in conflicting duties—let spiritually dead do work which needs no spiritual life. Cf. regulation regarding priest (Lev. 21:11) — so for us, as "priests unto God" (Rev. 1:6).
2. To give precedence to primary duty—only spiritually alive can save from spiritual death.
3. To enter upon true consecration—but he was too slow!

III. *The Vacillating* (vs. 61,62)

When Elijah called Elisha to succeed him, Elisha answered, "Let me, I pray thee, kiss my father and my mother, and then I will follow thee" (1 Kings 19:20). This request was granted, but now that similar one is made of our Lord, it is refused. Explanation would seem to be that Elisha was sincere and obedient in his response to call to service. Not so this vacillating one, apparently.

A. *His Decision*—"I will"

1. Good in itself—"trust and obey"—Christ to have disposal of life.
2. Sincere in intention—meant it at time—apparent determination, but real irresolution.
3. Offered self at first, but temporized.

B. *His Desire*—"but"

1. Apparently natural, like Elisha's—but—
2. Really weak—perhaps—
    a. Afraid of losing friends, or
    b. At least of causing their displeasure, or
    c. Irresolute—needed to examine facts and come to definite decision, or

      d. Too tender-hearted—home ties too strong.

   3. What is our "but"?

C. *His Danger*—"no man"

   1. Eastern salutations and leave-takings long, involved —man liable to forget call and not return.

   2. Feelings change when one looks back—some natures need complete severance with past.

   3. Plough needs undivided attention, eyes front to make straight furrow.

   4. Needed concentration—but he was too soft!

Conclusion

Too speedy, too slow, too soft. Which are you? But, by the grace of God—

1. The Impulsive becomes steadfast—

   a. On human side, by—

     (1) Deliberation.

     (2) Dedication.

   b. On Divine side, by—

     (1) Reception.

     (2) Transformation.

Till "these are they which follow the Lamb *whithersoever* He goeth" (Rev. 14:4) .

2. The Cautious becomes consecrated, because of—

   a. The danger of delay—can he be sure his good desires will continue?

   b. The unworthiness of indecision—can he bear to be a time-server, putting the Lord Jesus Christ last?

   c. The necessity for decision—can he doubt that to postpone is to reject, in view of uncertain future?

"Now is the accepted time," the day not only of "salvation," but of consecration.

3. The Vacillating becomes whole-hearted, because while—
   a. The warm-hearted may be too speedy,
   b. The cold-hearted will be too slow, and
   c. The half-hearted will be too soft,
   d. The whole-hearted is straight, staunch, and sincere. First, conversion—then, consecration—then, concentration. And so we admire and rejoice in—

4. Christ's infinite wisdom in dealing with diverse cases of human aspiration, for "He knew what was in man."
   a. Our warning—let nothing keep us from Him.
   b. Our comfort—none is beyond His skill.
   c. Our duty—to live close to Him, now and ever.

44

THE SENDING OF THE SEVENTY
(Luke 10:1-24)

T HE GALILEE ministry is now closed, and the long, slow journey to Jerusalem begun. Time is short and many are being given their first and last opportunity to receive Christ. Rejected largely by the Jews, He sends the Seventy to Samaria also, so this missionary journey of theirs typifies foreign missions in general and includes all mankind. It also has a bearing on the evangelization to be carried on after Christ had gone, and so there is here a useful study of Christian workers, their work and their characteristics.

I. *The Preparation* (vs. 1-4)

A. *Appointed by the Lord* (v.1)

1. The laborers.

   a. "Other seventy also"—suggests distinction from Twelve—temporary appointment, to prepare way for His coming to Jerusalem.

   b. Number thought to be reminiscent of elders in Israel (Exod. 24:1; Num. 11:16).

2. The appointment—"the Lord appointed"—foundation of all true Christian work.

3. The mode—"two and two"—why not one by one, so that more places might be reached?

   a. "Two are better than one" (Eccles. 4:9-12). Thirty-five tasks well done preferable to seventy poor ones.

   b. Sympathetic incitement and encouragement—two together more efficient than two separately.

    c. Usual Divine plan—examples:
      (1) Moses and Aaron—mutual support.
      (2) Joshua and Caleb—unity.
      (3) David and Jonathan—friendship.
      (4) Peter and John—energy and love.
      (5) Paul and Barnabas—conviction and consolation.
      (6) Luther and Melancthon—fighter and scholar.
      (7) John and Charles Wesley—organizer and soul-winner.
      (8) Moody and Sankey—preacher and singer.

4. The work—"whither He Himself would come"—fore-runners, giving opportunity to all to hear.

B. *Encouraged by the Lord* (v.2)
He tells them of—
1. Broad fields.
2. Abundant crops.
3. Ripened grain.
4. Few laborers.
The honest idler must say, "I'm doing nothing"—not, "There's nothing for me to do."

C. *Instructed by the Lord* (vs. 2-4)
1. Prayer—"pray"—put first as most important and some-times most difficult service. Says A. J. Gordon: "You can do more than pray after you have prayed, but you cannot do more than pray until you have prayed."
    a. Motive—"therefore"—contrast between "great" harvest and "few" laborers.
    b. Object—"send forth"—has force of "thrust."
    c. Recipient—"the Lord of the harvest"—so, all will be well.

2. Action—"go"—own effort often answers believer's prayer. Relation of prayer and work as started by Evan Roberts of Welsh Revival fame: "God wants a

thing done; God moves a believer to pray that it may be done; God does it in answer to that prayer."

a. Confidently—"behold, I send"—He was behind them.

b. Mildly—"lambs"—to show gentleness and inoffensiveness.

c. Realistically—"among wolves"—must expect contrast and opposition.

d. Unencumbered—"carry neither"—sacrifice even of travelling necessities to show sincerity and trust.

e. Seriously—"salute no man by the way"—Eastern greetings complicated and time-consuming—no time for empty compliments, though distinguish between true politeness (v.5) and mere etiquette. *Illus.*: This not out of date: many church members have time for sports, amusements, social life—but none for Christian work.

II. *The Plans* (vs. 5-11)

A. *Salutation* (vs. 5,6)

1. Opening word "peace" characteristic Hebrew greeting and also special feature of their message.

2. Household benediction showed breadth of Christian courtesy (Gal. 6:15; Col. 4:10).

3. Peace to descend on those fitted to receive it.

B. *Ministration* (vs. 7-9)

1. Behavior (vs. 7,8)—"such things"—Life must tell for Christ, so it is emphasized that—

a. First duty to think of Master, last to think of self; but win to self first and then to Him.

b. No false dignity here—accept what find and not find fault. *Illus.*: Some today act as though Christ sent them to detect weak spots in church, sermon, choir, etc., and then report to Him.

2. Work—"heal the sick"—Help the helpless ones—great seal to their ministry.

3. Testimony—"say"—Kingdom of God opportunity before all.

   a. Christ about to come—we, as they, forerunners.

   b. Our message—"Lift up your heads!"

   c. Our field—this passage suggests work in home, called sometimes "fireside ministry" or "front yard evangelism."

      (1) Friends first, then outside converts. Said M. D. Babcock: "Show the new life where the old one was lived. It will cost but it will count."

      (2) Best work based on friendliness—in conversation, habits, business, recreation.

      (3) Get close to people, dealing with them one by one. *Illus.*: Easier to be enthusiastic over evangelization of native in foreign land than when he comes as immigrant to our shores and gets so near we can smell garlic on his breath.

N.B. Behavior and work must lead up to testimony. In Kingdom of God supreme good is not healthy body, but saved soul.

C. *Opposition* (vs. 10,11)

   1. It will come (v.10).

   2. It must be dealt with (v.11).

      a. Testimony given—dust wiped off.

      b. Warning offered—"notwithstanding"

         (1) Responsibility of hearing.

         (2) Loss of opportunity.

III. *Prediction* (vs. 12-16)

   A. *Opponents condemned* (vs. 12-15)

      1. Day of reckoning to come—Christian workers need not be surprised if no results follow faithful witness.

2. Fearful doom for rejectors—terrible to know and yet not to do.

B. *Hearers honored* (v.16)

Hearing servant means hearing Master.
1. Privilege.
2. Responsibility.

C. *Rejectors dishonored* (v.16)

Not only—
1. Servant and Master involved, but—
2. Christ and His Father—God Almighty "despised" by those who refuse His Son.

IV. *Proofs*

Not known how long mission took, but probably very brief time.

A. *Joyful Return* (v.17)
1. To Master with work done.
2. Reporting success—"even the devils."
3. "With joy"—always so—spiritual victory most satisfying in life.

B. *Wise Warning* (vs. 18-20)
1. Christ noted work but, says Godet, "while they were expelling the subordinates their Lord was noticing the chief of the demons" (v.18). Power of enemy was real, attractive, subtle. Satan's fall from heaven suggests Paul's teaching about presence of evil in heavenly places (Eph. 6:12).
2. Christ explained success—to be expected by means of His power—and gives added assurance (v.19). He had said, "Behold, I send you forth" (v.3)—now He says, "Behold, I give you power" (v.19)—same power manifested all through His ministry now given to believer—in own personal life, and on behalf of others bound by sin. "The Lord's biddings are His enablings."

3. Christ warned against pride—all of grace, so rejoice in personal relationship with heaven rather than in work accomplished.

C. *Divine Satisfaction* (vs. 21-24)

1. Christ's Joy (v.21) —especially after Galilean ministry. One of few instances of rejoicing in earthly life of Man of Sorrows—"exulted in the Spirit" might be read here. It was a threefold joy, over—

   a. Divine gifts (v.17).

   b. Divine grace (v.20).

   c. Divine glory (vs. 21,22).

2. Christ's Witness (v.22) —that He knew God and that others would have more knowledge after obedience.

3. Christ's Encouragement (vs. 23,24) —spiritual perception given to simple-minded men while truths hidden from "many prophets and kings."

   a. Who are "the wise and prudent"?

      (1) "Wise"—those with knowledge and capacity.

      (2) "Prudent"—those with insight, knowledge in exercise. Mental power may be great and yet meet with moral failure.

   b. Who are "babes"?
      Those with child spirit which manifests itself in humility, wonder, reverence, trust.

Conclusion

1. *The Call to Service*

   a. Christ as Lord expects followers to work, especially in view of great need and scarcity of helpers, first by prayer, than by effort.

   b. Note enlarging circle of workers: the Twelve, the Seventy, the Five Hundred (1 Cor. 15:6), and at length the entire Church, the Body of Christ (1 Cor. 12:12-31).

2. *The Character of the Worker*

Carefully considering all our Lord's words in this passage, we see necessity of:

a. Simplicity.

b. Earnestness.

c. Winsomeness.

d. Faithfulness.

If our work barren of result, test by these four characteristics. Our fruit will never be better than our personal character.

3. *The Result of Labor*

As seen in this passage, they are:

a. Blessing to the soul.

b. Knowledge of the truth.

c. Fellowship with the Lord.

d. Satisfaction in the life.

Our position as laborers in the vineyard is at once difficult and delightful, arduous and glorious. It is the noblest and highest kind of living, for there is nothing more wonderful than to be, as are the angels of heaven, "ministers of His that do His pleasure." Chosen by Christ, consecrated to Christ, charged and counselled by Christ, we shall be conquerors through Christ.

45

KINDNESS AND GOOD WORKS
(Luke 10:25-37)

Our Lord's questioners approached Him with a wide variety of motives. Here is a man who is described as a "lawyer," or scribe, one versed in the Mosaic Law. Today's equivalent is the word theologian, one who had made a special study of the Word of God. But this questioner was evidently not sincerely desirous to know the truth, for by his inquiry, we are told, he "tempted" Christ (v.25).

I. *The Appeal* (vs. 25-29)

  1. *The Captious Questioner* (v.25)

    Scribe should have known answer from own work, but enjoyed asking Christ. Many today ready to discuss theology or ecclesiastical law, but not really interested in "eternal life."

  2. *The Great Question* (v.25)

    In many respects the greatest in life. Aspiration in appeal grand, if sincere.

  3. *The Adroit Counter-question* (v.26)

    It had two parts:
    a. "What—?" His knowledge of the law.
    b. "How—?" His application of the law.
    Both necessary, showing law sufficient up to then, if rightly used.

> "How readest thou?" Christ's question must concern
> Each eager, praying one, who would discern
> The real meaning of the Book of books,
> When through its pages he with patience looks.

Some read to bring themselves into repute,
While showing others how they can dispute;
And others read it with uncommon care,
But all to find some contradiction there.

Some read to prove a pre-adopted creed,
Thus understand but little what they read;
And every passage of the Book they bend
To make it suit that all-important end.

'Tis one thing, friend, to read the Bible through,
Another thing to read to learn and do;
'Tis one thing, too, to read it with delight,
And quite another thing to read aright.

4. *The Evasive Rejoinder* (v.27)

   a. Sufficient knowledge—could recite appropriate passage.

   b. Insufficient application—in realm of intellect only.

5. *The Wise Reply* (v.28)

   a. Christ transferred subject to realm of conscience—"this do."

   b. This struck home—"the shoe pinched."

6. *The Attempt at Self-justification* (v.29)

   a. Question while shielding was really accusing him—virtual admission that he had never loved his neighbor or he would have known him.

   b. Question showed him obtuse, as if duty to God ever done otherwise.

   c. Question really, "Whom am I obliged to love?" But love as obligation not worth much—anxiety to mark bounds no sign of love, e.g., "May I go there? May I do that"? Christian life free, spontaneous, all-inclusive. If Christ had told him whom to love he might have limited both love and interest.

II. *The Answer* (vs. 30-35)

   How would we have replied? Impatiently, probably—but not so Christ. He told story, not strictly parable but incident, as example of neighborliness. He drew graphic picture of—

1. *Suffering* (v.30)
   a. The unfortunate traveller—going distance of 17 miles.
   b. The cruel treatment—from thieves—highway robbery.
   c. The forlorn condition—stripped, wounded, abandoned, dying.

2. *Neglect* (vs. 31,32)
   On the part of—
   a. The priest.
      (1) Opportunity and knowledge, but indifference.
      (2) May not have been actually unfeeling, but too proud.
      (3) Yet conduct true test of position and profession.
   b. The Levite.
      (1) Opportunity and knowledge also, but curiosity preceded indifference.
      (2) Has been suggested that priest left case to Levite, and Levite thought it not one for him because ignored by priest.
      (3) Religious work does not make worker religious.
         Illus.: Sexton would rather not be "doorkeeping in the house of his God" if higher wages elsewhere.

   N.B. 1. Only too possible to have heartlessness and pitilessness in church.
        2. Causes: self-absorption instead of devotion to Christ; formalism instead of reality.

3. *Relief* (vs. 33-35)
   On the part of the "Good Samaritan," as he has been known. This made his nationality synonymous with kindness and good works in spite of other phases of its history—e.g., hospitals named for him. Group thus judged

by individual member, as often, though sometimes erroneously and unwisely. But this Samaritan showed—

a. True humaneness.

  (1) By sight—different to looks of priest and Levite.
  (2) By sympathy—"compassion"—or suffering with victim.
  (3) By service—
     (a) Unselfish because also in peril from thieves.
     (b) Thorough—thinking of everything.
     (c) Continued—even to next day.

b. True humanity.

  (1) By brushing aside nationalities and any other distinctions.
  (2) By giving first himself (cf. 2 Cor. 8:5), and then lesser but necessary gifts.

III. *The Application* (vs. 36,37)

Leading up to it, see first:

1. *Another Appeal*

Christ turned questioner, but note contrast:

  a. Lawyer asked, "Who is my neighbor?" (v.29)
     Christ asked, "Which . . . was neighbor unto him?" (v.36), or, Whose neighbor am I?
  b. Appeal not to selfishness—men's claims on me—but to love—my debts to men.
  c. Emphasis not on object of love—but on spirit of person showing love.

2. *Another Answer*

  a. Asked his opinion of three men, lawyer—
     (1) Was compelled to recognize third's true neighborliness.
     (2) Avoiding use of term "Samaritan," emphasized act by which mercy was shown and character shown by mercy.

And now came—

3. *The Practical Application*

    a. Christ clinched whole argument by very practical exhortation:

        (1) To activity—"go thou"

        (2) To action—"do likewise"

    b. Best proof of possession of eternal life would be—

        (1) Feelings of love.

        (2) Works of neighborliness (cf. Jas. 2:1-26) —where one and only qualification is need.

    c. If spirit right, no need to ask who is our neighbor.

    d. It is not defining of neighbors that gives us love, but experience of love makes all neighbors.

    e. Love finds or makes neighbors not by marks in them, but by its own spirit—true neighbor is man of compassionate heart. If you want to know who neighbor is, *be* one!

    f. Love not canal artificially drawn and only those in line included—but torrent, free, spontaneous, all-embracing.

Conclusion

    1. The world's idea of "neighbor"

    Literally, one who dwells near:

    a. Nearness of residence.

    b. Habitation of same country.

    c. Blood relationship.

    d. Friendship or acquaintance.

    2. The Christian's ideal of "neighborliness"

    a. Springs from love as law of life (cf. 1 John 4:7-21), because all men are "nigh" to him in their common—

        (1) Origin—human

        (2) Nature—sinful

        (3) Needs—suffering

        (4) Heritage—perilous

    and in—

(5) The grace which is available to all.

b. Shows itself in different forms:

    (1) In family—tender care.

    (2) In neighborhood—courtesy.

    (3) In friendship—sympathy.

    (4) In business—integrity.

    (5) In distress—mercy.

    (6) In nation—patriotic sacrifice.

    (7) In world—benevolent service.

    (8) In church—brother love.

Word "philanthropy," meaning love of man as man, essentially due in strongest, best, and widest form to Gospel of Christ. If we live in presence of God, and His love fills our souls, we shall not be able to avoid loving others. This story, therefore, shows love's duty made plain, left undone, and rightly accomplished. Where do we stand?

46

LOVE IN ACTION
(Luke 10:25-37)

T HE ENTIRE story is concerned with love. Love in the New Testament is always associated with giving, doing, serving, and is never to be regarded as mere thinking or feeling.

I. *Love Required* (vs. 25-28)

1. The question.
2. The counter-question.
3. The requirement.

II. *Love Refused* (vs. 29-32)

By—

1. Evasion.
2. Abuse.
3. Indifference.

III. *Love Revealed* (vs. 33-37)

By—

1. Feeling.
2. Helpfulness.
3. Sacrifice.
   The Good Samaritan gave:

   a. Eyes.
   b. Heart.
   c. Feet.
   d. Hands.
   e. Thought.

f. Time.
g. Beast.
h. Speech.
i. Money.

Conclusion

We are to "go, and do likewise," so note:

DUTY:

> Discussed by the Lawyer
> Defined by the Lord
> Declined by the Priest and the Levite
> Done by the Good Samaritan

—who showed himself to be

Pitying
Prompt
Practical
Persistent

47

PRACTICAL CHRISTIANITY
(Luke 10:25-37)

THESE verses have an essential bearing on what is often called practical Christianity. There is really no need of the word "practical," since Christianity is nothing if it is not that. But because there is a tendency to forget its definite bearing on human life it is perhaps necessary to use the phrase. Three things should be noted:

I. *The Standard of Practical Christianity*—The Word of God

1. The Word written.
2. The Word read.
3. The Word understood.
4. The Word practiced.

By it we should test all of our life.

II. *The Source of Practical Christianity*—The Love of God

Includes God's love to us and our love to Him. God loves each one of us—

1. Singly.
2. Earnestly.
3. Actively.
4. Thoughtfully.

Our love to Him should be similarly shown in whole-hearted devotion.

III. *The Stream of Practical Christianity*—The Love of Man

Like the Samaritan, we are to show our—

1. Interest.
2. Sympathy.
3. Helpfulness.
4. Self-sacrifice—whether of—

   a. Time.
   b. Money.
   c. Ease.
   d. Prejudice.

This is all to be for the sake of Jesus Christ our Saviour, who has done so much for us.

> "Do all the good you can
> To all the folks you can,
> In all the ways you can,
> In all the places you can,
> As long as ever you can—
> For Jesus' sake."

> "I am but one—but I am one;
> I cannot do much—but I can do something;
> What I can do I ought to do;
> What I ought to do, by God's help, I will do!"

48

JESUS WITH MARTHA AND MARY
(Luke 10:38-42)

THE SCENE was Bethany, a village near Jerusalem, as we know from other references. In this place, as it has been pointed out, the Master revealed Himself in four different ways: as the Gracious Teacher (in the present passage); as the Sympathizing Friend who is also the Lord of Life (John 11:1-44); as the Suffering Saviour (Mark 14:3-9; John 12:1-11); and as the Ascending Christ (24:49-53). In this passage there is a delightful picture of home life and of Christ resting. As someone has said: "The heart ought not to be an inn where the Lord sometimes comes, but a home where He always abides."

It is clear from the use of the word "also" in verse 39 that both sisters, Martha and Mary, were disciples of Jesus; and, from John 11:3, that their brother Lazarus was too.

I. *Martha's Concern for the Master* (vs. 38-40)

1. Martha evidently older and more prominent sister, owner of home, for she was the one who "received him into her house" (v.38).

2. Had sat at Jesus' feet on another occasion (v.39), but this time was more anxious to do Him honor by hospitality (v.40).

3. "Cumbered about much serving" of elaborate meal (v.40). Even necessity may be distraction, robbing of spirituality.

4. Complained that Mary had left her to "serve alone" (v. 40).

5. Demanded that Guest use prerogative of Master and "bid her (Mary) that she help" (v.40).

II. *The Master's Concern for Martha* (vs. 41,42)

Christ as Teacher was personal, patient, practical, and powerful. Note what He taught here:

1. Said, "Martha, Martha"—one of double calls of Scripture —this time in protest (Cf. Gen. 22:11; 46:2; Exod. 3:4; 1 Sam. 3:10; Matt. 23:27; Luke 22:31; Acts 9:4).

2. Reminded her (primary meaning) that—
   a. Too many things (dishes) troubled her, and—
   b. But one thing (some one plain, simple food) was necessary.

3. Then lifted subject into high realm of things spiritual and said Mary had chosen something better than natural food, i.e., the nourishment of His teaching.

4. Doubtless recognized two different temperaments—active and contemplative, practical and spiritual.

   Illus.: Great Murillo painting in Louvre shows kitchen in which workers move to and fro—one putting kettle on fire, another lifting pail of water, third taking plates from dresser, etc. Faces radiant, forms beautiful, and not clad in ordinary garb, they are white-winged angels. Charm of picture lies in fact that no incongruity strikes beholder. Title, "The Angels in the Kitchen"—that is spirit of our Christian faith.

"Lord of all pots and pans and things, since I've no time to be
A saint by doing lovely things, or watching late with Thee,
Or dreaming in the dawnlight, or storming heaven's gates—
Make me a saint by getting meals and washing up the plates!

Although I must have Martha's hands, I have a Mary's mind;
And when I black the boots and shoes, Thy sandals, Lord, I find—
I think of how they trod the earth, what time I scrub the floor;
Accept this meditation, Lord, I haven't time for more.

Warm all the kitchen with Thy love, and light it with Thy peace;
Forgive me all my worrying, and make all grumbling cease.
Thou who didst love to give men food, in room or by the sea,
Accept this service that I do—I do it unto Thee."

5. But this difference not main point of episode—not blame for Martha and praise for Mary, but emphasis on condition of soul. Activity not based on spirituality will distract. Contrast here is between "many things" and anxiety about them and "one thing." i.e., "that good part," and choice of it.

> "I cannot choose; I should have liked so much
> To sit at Jesus' feet—to feel the touch
> Of His kind, gentle hand upon my head,
> While drinking in the gracious words He said.
>
> And yet to serve Him! Oh, divine employ
> To minister and give the Master joy,
> To bathe in coolest springs His weary feet,
> And wait upon Him while He sits at meat.
>
> Worship or service—which? Ah, that is best
> To which He calls us, be it toil or rest—
> To labor for Him in life's busy stir,
> Or seek His feet, a silent worshipper."

III. *Mary's Concern for "That Good Part"* (v.42)

We may call this "personal religion" and note:

A. *Its Character*

1. Mary no contemplative mystic—original clearly shows she also had served for a time. When action needed, was as ready as Martha (cf. John 11:29; 12:3).

2. But Mary had grasped more clearly relative importance of earthly and heavenly things (cf. Matt. 6:33).

3. Thus, comparison of good things (earthly) with better things (heavenly) not contrast between bad and good or between not having Christ and having Him.

4. But indicative that Martha's was not wrong action; instead, it was right action in wrong spirit and at wrong time.

5. Real difference lay in motive—one duty, the other love. Being right with God comes before working for Him.

> "I will not work my soul to save,
> For that my Lord has done;
> But I will work like any slave
> For love of God's dear Son."

B. *Its Characteristics*

1. Lowliness—"at Jesus' feet"—cf. disciple and Master with hostess and Guest. "The meek will He guide in truth" (Psa. 25:9).

2. Learning—Mary "heard His word"—made Him her Teacher, His Word her food and her lamp.

3. Love—"hath chosen"—fellowship involves more than discipleship or teaching—means definite act of will and devotion, going on to meet highest purpose of God in all His dealings with mankind (cf. 1 John 1:3).

C. *Its Necessity*—"needful"

1. Because of sin, causing us guilt, weakness, blindness, inability to respond to God's claim.

2. Because we need personal relationship between soul and Christ—"Come unto *Me*"—"Abide in *Me*," etc. Brief hours of fellowship not lost but, rather, must come first.

3. Because we need improved relationship between ourselves and others—influence comes only through character. We admire activity and possessions but are more impressed by character. "I seek not yours, but you," wrote Paul to Corinthians (2 Cor. 12:14). Impact of one spirit on another needs full, ripe spiritual experience and healthy condition of soul, only possible "at Jesus' feet." Cf. Gal. 5:22, "love, joy, peace, etc." Said Evan H. Hopkins: " 'One thing is needful'—to know what that one thing is, is the

first great lesson of life. To possess that one thing is the great blessing of life. In proportion as our mind is brought into agreement with God's mind, so do we discover that the true life is after all the the simple life—the life of one aim, of one path—of one controlling passion. The aim is the glory of God. The path is the will of God. And the passion is the love of God. We find our lives so difficult because they are so complicated. We try to attain so many ends. We try to walk in more than one path at a time, and we let various motives influence us in rapid succession.' "

D. *Its Possession*

1. It is precious—"good"
   a. Leads to salvation, sanctification, satisfaction, service.
   b. Lessons learned; guidance realized; strength received.

2. It is permanent—"shall not be taken away"
   a. Continued by abiding in Christ.
   b. Maintained by becoming like Christ.

CHRIST never asks of us such heavy labour
    As leaves no time for resting at His feet;
The waiting attitude of *expectation*,
    He oft-times counts a service most complete.

He sometimes wants our ear, our rapt *attention*,
    That He some sweetest secret may impart;
'Tis always in the time of deepest stillness
    That heart finds deepest fellowship with heart.

We sometimes wonder why our Lord doth place us
    Within a sphere so narrow, so obscure
That nothing *we* call *work* can find an entrance:
    There's only room to suffer—and endure.

Well, God loves patience! Souls that dwell in stillness,
    Doing the *little things*, or *resting* quite,
May just as perfectly fulfil their mission—
    Be just as useful in the Father's sight,

As they who grapple with some giant evil,
  Clearing a path that every eye may see.
Our Saviour cares for *cheerful acquiescence*,
  As much as for a busy ministry.

And yet He does love service, where 'tis given
  By grateful hand that clothes itself in *deed;*
But work that's done beneath the *scourge of duty*,
  Be sure to such He gives but little heed.

Then seek to *please Him*, whatsoe'er *He* bids thee,
  Whether to *do*, to *suffer,* or *lie still;*
'Twill matter little by what path He led us,
  If in it all we sought to do His Will.

Conclusion

Much of our knowledge of Christ today comes from various sources: books, papers, other Christians, all "second-hand," illustrating the difference between "knowing" and "knowing about." Therefore personal contact is necessary—not only for the sake of others, nor for our own intellectual benefit, but also for our spiritual growth and as defence against error. How is this contact to be established, this "good part" to be possessed? By—

1. *An Act*

    a. Deliberate choice.
    b. Full service.

2. *An Attitude*

    a. Absolute surrender.
    b. Continual fellowship.

"Here we offer and present unto Thee, O Lord, ourselves, our souls and bodies, to be a reasonable, holy, and living sacrifice unto Thee" (Book of Common Prayer).

> "I acknowledge myself a sinner;
> I believe the Father sent the Son in love;
> I embrace Jesus as Saviour;
> I welcome the Holy Spirit as Sanctifier;
> I take His Word as my guide;
> I dedicate myself to Christ forever;
> I take His people for my company;
> I make His glory my aim."

49

VITAL LESSONS ON PRAYER
(Luke 11:1-13)

IN THE preceding chapter we may note two sides of the Christian life: doing (10:25-37), with the Good Samaritan as model, and hearing (10:38-42), as exemplified by Mary of Bethany. Here is a third and equally important side, namely, praying. This lesson on prayer was part of the training which Christ gave to His disciples during the latter months of His ministry on earth, and no lesson was more vital.

I. *The Necessity of Prayer* (vs. 1,2)
   A. *Christ's Example*—"as He was praying" Note—
      1. His habit of prayer—habitual prayerfulness.
      2. His times of prayer—cf. 3:21; 5:16; 6:12; 9:18,28.

   B. *The Disciples' Request*—"Lord, teach us to pray"
      1. Incited by His example—perhaps had prayed aloud.
      2. Conscious of need for teaching.
      3. Shows John the Baptist was man of prayer also.

   C. *Christ's Response*—"When ye pray, say . . ."
      Who more fitted as teacher than He, the God-Man, by—
      1. Knowledge—of God and of man.
      2. Experience—in His human dependence on God.

II. *The Model of Prayer* (vs. 2-4)
   Not to be followed slavishly or exclusively, nor even to be repeated often, but given as guide and suggestion. Emphasis here in Luke on form—"say" (v.2); in Matthew (6:9-13) on type—"after this manner" (v.9).

A. *The Address*—"Our Father which art in heaven"
   1. "Father"—conscious sonship—child's loving confidence, submission, and yearning for reassurance.
   2. "Our"—only in true Church of God is true brotherhood of man—sonship through Christ includes brotherhood (John 1:12).
   3. "Which art in heaven"—recognition of God's unlimited sphere as distinct from human fatherhood (cf. v.13).

B. *The Attitude*—"Hallowed be Thy Name"
   1. God first—prayer not as beggars but as worshippers—more worship needed in church: much religion selfish, many services self-centered. *Illus.*: Many hymns no more than pretty songs about self to which we ask God to listen or, someone has put it, versified histories of feelings, failings and fallings! Prayers often similar.
   2. First of three uses in prayer of word "Thy"—true worship takes one out of self and into presence of Almighty God.

C. *The Appeal*—"Thy kingdom . . . from evil"—note—
   1. Coming of Kingdom of God includes doing of His will on earth—"as . . . so . . . also."
   2. Bread to be asked for, not luxuries—sufficiency, not surfeit.
   3. Forgiveness, leading, deliverance.

D. *The Attributes*—"For Thine . . . for ever. Amen" (see Matt. 6:13b)
   1. Spirit of prayer: filial, fraternal, reverent, missionary, obedient, dependent, forgiving, cautious, adoring.
   2. Thought in prayer—"Limp prayers need backbone of thought"—true devotions not characterized by absence of contemplation.

III. *The Effectiveness of Prayer* (vs. 5-10)
    A. *Illustrated* (vs. 5-8)
        1. Emphasis not on unwillingness of friend but on earnestness of suppliant, yet—
        2. Note contrasts of these verses with verses 11-13:
            a. Selfish indolence—fatherly love.
            b. Slothful indifference—perfect, never-resting beneficence.
            c. Yielding to avoid annoyance—yearning to bless.
        N.B. If persistence conquered selfishness, what will not pity do?

    B. *Promised* (v.9)
        1. Three types of prayer:
            a. Asking—simple desire.
            b. Seeking—earnest enquiry.
            c. Knocking—repeated endeavor.
        2. One type of answer: God says *"shall"*—"be given, . . . find, . . . be opened."
        3. Two means of blessing—no true Christian life without both:
            a. "Ask and it shall be given" (v.9).
            b. "Give and it shall be given" (6:38).

    C. *Assured* (v.10)
        1. To encourage—most natural law, to "receive," "find," "have opened."
        2. To strengthen—universal—"every one."

IV. *The Reasonableness of Prayer* (vs. 11-13)
    A. *Man's Need* (vs. 11,12)
        1. Not ask unless required.
        2. Reasonable to expect answer.

    B. *Human Beneficence* (vs. 11,12,13)
        1. Father's response considerate and prompt because loving.
        2. Yet giver frail, limited, "evil."

C. *Divine Bounty* (v.13)

    1. "Much more" will "heavenly Father" give "Holy Spirit to them that ask Him."

    2. Greatest Giver gives highest gift and shows largest beneficence.

Conclusion

How to pray:

1. With a feeling of need.
2. With earnestness and even with importunity.
3. In filial confidence.
4. For the Holy Spirit's enabling.

Then is the need met, the importunity prevails, the promises assure, experience confirms, and the faithfulness of God guarantees the answer.

50

MORE PRAYER, MORE POWER
(Luke 11:1-13)

THERE are certain marine creatures called cetaceans. They are neither fish nor fowl, and they never go on shore, yet even from ocean depths they must rise at intervals to breathe so as to live. Even so, it is necessary for man to mount into a higher region if he is to obtain spiritual life and grace for living it, and this the Christian does through prayer. More prayer, more power!

> "Prayer is the Christian's vital breath,
> The Christian's native air."

Our Lord, having exemplified this principle by His practice (v.1; see also 3:21; 5:16; 6:12; 9:18,28), proceeds in chapter 11 to expound it by precept (vs. 2-4), by parable (vs. 5-8), and by promise (vs. 9-13). Illustrative of the principle of prayer, we see:

I. *The Believer as a Child* (vs. 2-4, 11-13)

1. "Father"—Old Testament saints seldom addressed God thus (cf. Isa. 63:16 with Gal. 4:7).

2. It was His Son who revealed His Fatherhood—included redemption, regeneration, adoption.

3. Only as we realize Fatherhood of God in Christ, and live in this relation to Him, is our prayer a power.

4. Not only Fatherhood, but fatherliness secret of real power of God in life of believer.

5. This is brought out very forcibly in vs. 11-13: "bread," "fish," "egg," are "good gifts," all for the asking.

II. *The Believer as a Friend* (vs. 5-8)

  1. Not only Father, but Friend, is our God.

  2. Father would naturally answer (vs. 11,12), for close relationship demands and dependence necessitates.

  3. Friend more free to refuse—so appeal must be to sympathy and more on level of equality.

  4. So we need to live as friends of God (cf. Exod. 33:11; 2 Chron. 20:7; Isa. 41:8; Jas. 2:23), not as mere acquaintances.

  5. "Friends" implies our fellowship, while "children" indicates our position, "disciples" our learning, and "servants" our work.

  6. But obedience is test of all—to be, to do, to suffer (John 15:13,14).

III. *The Believer as an Intercessor* (vs. 2-4,5,13)

  1. These prayers include others:

    a. "Lord's Prayer" begins "Our Father," is couched in plural throughout and recognizes those "indebted to us."

    b. Parable of importunate man begins, "Friend, . . . for a friend."

    c. Those that "ask Him" for the Holy Spirit do so not for themselves only, but for others as well.

  2. Love seeking help for needy around needs—

    a. Urging to prayer.

    b. Conviction that help is to be had.

    c. Perseverance in supplication.

    d. Encouragement by receiving answer.

  3. If a son, believer should ask Father on behalf of brethren. Then there will be:

    a. Perfect liberty in prayer.

    b. Certain answer to prayer.

4. If a friend, believer should prove it by friendly action—intercession with God for others. This will involve, as in parable, three friends:

   a. Hungry friend needing help.
   b. Praying friend seeking help.
   c. Mighty Friend giving help.

5. Note relative proportions of personal and intercessory prayer:

   a. So often prayer mostly for self, but should be otherwise.
   b. In praying for others is own help (cf. Job. 42:10).
   c. This like Christ who had power in prayer:
      (1) King and Priest—King to help, Priest to pray.
      (2) King because Priest—"able to save them . . . seeing He ever liveth to make intercession for them" (Heb. 7:25).
   d. So with us—first, power with God, then power with man.

Conclusion

Thus the believer, whether as—

1. Creature seeking a necessary element, or—
2. Child desiring his Father's blessing, or—
3. Friend and intercessor pleading for others as well as himself,—will receive answers to his prayers, and the Spirit of grace, truth and holiness will indwell his heart.

> "More things are wrought by prayer
> Than this world dreams of. Wherefore, let thy voice
> Rise like a fountain for me night and day.
> For what are men better than sheep or goats
> That nourish a blind life within the brain,
> If, knowing God, they lift not hands of prayer
> Both for themselves and those who call them friend?
> For so the whole round world is every way
> Bound by gold chains about the feet of God."   (Tennyson)

51

THE LORD'S PRAYER
(Luke 11:2-4)

THE ONE who uses this petition comes to the Throne of grace as:

1. A Son—"Our Father which art in heaven" (cf. John 1:12)

2. A Saint—"Hallowed be Thy Name" (cf. John 4:24)

3. A Subject—"Thy Kingdom come" (cf. 1 Tim. 1:17)

4. A Servant—"Thy will be done on earth as it is in heaven" (cf. John 12:26)

5. A Suppliant—"Give us this day our daily bread" (cf. Matt. 6:26)

6. A Sinner—"And forgive us our sins; for we also forgive every one that is indebted to us" (cf. 1 John 1:9)

7. A Soldier—"And lead us not into temptation; but deliver us from evil" (cf. 2 Tim. 2:3)

52

GREATER THAN JONAH
(Luke 11:29,30,32)

ONE OF the most solemn and impressive truths connected with Jesus Christ is that, while men may receive Him as a friend or reject Him as an Enemy, they cannot possibly ignore Him (11:23). The same sun melts ice and hardens clay, though it merely shines on both. Christ the Sun of righteousness makes some His friends and others His enemies, the difference being due to the varieties of human nature and of attitude towards Him.

In meeting all these varieties and solving all of the problems involved, Christ showed a marvellously keen perception. We are told in verse 16 that some of these "others," His enemies, "tempting Him, sought of Him a sign from heaven." In the discourse which followed, Christ made a great claim which fed their strong opposition to Him. He challenged His hearers to believe that He was greater and more important than Jonah the prophet. But first, let us consider—

I. *The Demand* (v.16)

1. What?
   a. They desired direct testimony from heaven—wanted to be miraculously convinced.
   b. This is tendency today—skepticism demands the unusual and extraordinary but as often rejects it.

2. Whence?
   a. Not publicans (common people), but scribes (learned ones) were most skeptical.
   b. Such demands usually from those who have much knowledge and experience already, not from ignorant.

II. *The Refusal* (v.29)

   1. What?

      a. To give something additional while part already received is unused.

      b. To make excuse for rejection.

   2. Why?

      a. Frequency of miraculous destroys effect—tendency harmful because excludes faith.

      b. What they had seen already was sufficient—demand was no proof of earnestness—characters still "evil" (v. 29; cf. Matt. 12:39).

III. *The Claim* (vs. 30,32)

   1. What?

     "As Jonas . . . so shall also the Son of man be" (v.30). Compare—

      a. Jonah, whose name meant "death,"—

        (1) Saved shipload—Deliverance.

        (2) Was taken from death after three days and three nights—Resurrection.

        (3) Preached to Nineveh—Repentance.

      b. Christ, "the Prince of life" (Acts 3:15) —

        (1) Was to save from sin by His death—Deliverance.

        (2) Was to rise from the dead the third day—Resurrection.

        (3) Was at that time preaching to Jews and would afterwards be preaching, through followers, to Gentiles—Repentance.

   2. What then?

     "A greater than Jonas is here" (v.32). Contrast—

      a. Jonah, imperfect man,—

        (1) Saved only ship's crew.

        (2) Spent only forty days in preaching.

        (3) Preached wrath once and was heeded.

(4) Was given sign of "burial" in and "resurrection" from great fish to add to message.

b. Christ, perfect Son of God and Son of man,—

(1) Was to save all who come to Him in faith.

(2) Was spending three years in preaching, and afterwards would preach, through followers, during entire Church age.

(3) Was preaching love repeatedly, and was finally to be rejected.

(4) Was to be rejected by world in spite of greatest sign of all—literal burial and resurrection.

Conclusion

1. *The Great Need*

   a. If sight darkened by indifference, no need of light (vs. 34-36). Cf. brothers of rich man in chapter 16.

   b. Not light—eyes; not sound—ears; not knowledge—obedience.

2. *The Great Challenge*

   a. Christianity is Christ—His character, His claims, His death, His resurrection, His influence.

   b. "What think ye of Christ?" (Matt. 22:42) "A greater than Jonas"? Yea, and "my Lord and my God"! (John 20:28)

   c. Test Him! "O taste and see that the Lord is good"! (Psa. 34:8)

53

GREATER THAN SOLOMON
(Luke 11:31; 1 Kings 10:1-13)

In THIS verse we have another of the claims of Christ. He said, simply and definitely. "Behold, a greater than Solomon is here," that is to say, Himself. It was a stupendous challenge for Jesus to declare Himself greater than this important character in Jewish history, the monarch under whom their nation had reached its zenith among world powers. Our Lord's comparison warrants a reference to and spiritual treatment of 1 Kings 10:1-13, the Old Testament account of the visit of the Queen of Sheba to King Solomon summarized in this verse of Luke. Let us, therefore, compare and contrast Solomon and our Saviour in four ways: Fame, Wisdom, Wealth, Influence; and let us keep the parallels clearly before us.

I. *King Solomon* (1 Kings 10:1-13)

  A. *The Fame of Solomon*

    1. His fame was "concerning the Name of the Lord" (v. 1) —connected in queen's mind with the God of Israel.

    2. It was true—both in acts and in wisdom (v.6).

    3. It was known in "the utmost parts of the earth" (Luke 11:31) —probably hers was desert journey of a thousand miles, indicating her great longing to see Israel's king.

    4. It was exceeded only by his wisdom and prosperity (v.7).

  B. *The Wisdom of Solomon*

    1. It consisted not of mere intellectual capabilities or accomplishments, but of wisdom of God. Cf. Proverbs 1 to 29 as part of Holy Scripture.

2. It could meet "hard questions (vs. 1,3) of life, which to heathen queen must often have seemed strange and mysterious.

C. *The Wealth of Solomon*

1. Queen saw his house, meat, servants, ministers, clothing, approach to house of his God (vs.4,5) —in a word, his "prosperity" (v.7).

2. She called forth his generosity—"all her desire, whatsoever she asked, beside . . . his royal bounty" (v.13).

3. Cf. Matt. 6:28,29—"all his glory"—though this was not to be compared with mere "lilies of the field," much less with their Creator (Cf. John 1:3).

D. *The Influence of Solomon*

1. Queen gave him great gifts (v.10).

2. She also "communed with him of all that was in her heart" (v.2), and declared that "half was not told" (v.7).

3. She felt envy for even his servants (v.8).

4. She was inspired to give God glory for him, declaring the Lord "delighted" in him (v.9).

5. She "turned and went" (v.13) duty after pleasure, responsibility after privilege.

II. *Jesus Christ* (Luke 11:31)

A. *The Fame of Christ*

1. He was approved by God the Father (cf. Matt. 17:5; Luke 9:35; Heb. 1:9).

2. He is true (1 John 5:20), both in acts and in wisdom (Luke 2:52; Acts 2:22; John 7:46).

3. He is "Saviour of all men" (1 Tim. 4:10) —Prophet (Luke 7:40; 24:19), Priest (Psa. 110:4; Heb. 6:20), and King (Luke 19:38; 1 Tim. 6:15).

4. His fame (cf. Matt. 4:24, Mark 1:28; Luke 5:15, etc.), combined with wisdom and prosperity (see B. and C.) accounts for His influence (see D.).

B. *The Wisdom of Christ*

1. In Him are enshrined "all the treasures of wisdom and knowledge" (Col. 2:3) —they are His own.

2. Jesus never found life empty or strange. He saw God's eternal purpose in everything, even in His Cross (Luke 22:24). So He alone can tell us all things (Cf. John 4:29).

C. *The Wealth of Christ*

1. He told earliest disciples to "come and see" (John 1:39) —experience best argument (cf. John 7:17).

2. All our desire, "uttered or unexpressed," to be laid before Him (cf. John 14:13,14; Psa. 68:19).

3. In Him all fulness dwells (cf. Col. 1:19; 2:9) —His riches are "unsearchable" (Eph. 3:8) —"the pleasure of the Lord shall prosper in His hand" (Isa. 53:10).

D. *The Influence of Christ*

1. He does not require great gifts from us—"Nothing in my hand I bring"—but does impel us to come to Him —"Simply to Thy Cross I cling."

2. Only asks: "My son, give Me thine heart" (Prov. 23: 26) —union and communion.

3. Our privilege not only to "stand continually before" Him and "hear" Him (cf. 1 Kings 10:8), but to dwell with Him "for His work" (1 Chron. 4:23) —"whose service is perfect freedom"—"whom to serve is to reign"—"reign in life" (Rom. 5:17).

4. In original of Luke 3:23, we read that God "delighted" in His Son.

5. Cf. Peter on Mount of Transfiguration (Luke 9:33, 37). After every revelation there remains the King's business, until at last comes one unbroken communion above.

Conclusion

Yea, verily, "a greater than Solomon" once came to earth "for us men and for our salvation." "If before the wise man who yet became a fool; if before the proverb-maker who himself became a proverb; if before the richly endowed man whose glorious abilities were lent to the utter folly of idolatry; if before the king whose kingliness became vanity, the 'Queen of the South' bowed herself: how much more should we bow before the unfading Wisdom, the unsullied Purity, and the eternal Kingship of the Lord of all?" (H. J. Horn). Let us enthrone Him on the throne of our hearts, while He waits for the glorious day when, as Solomon did before Him, He shall sit on "the throne of His father David" (Luke 1:32).

54

THE PARABLE OF THE RICH FOOL*
(Luke 12:13-21)

THERE were sharp contrasts among Christ's hearers, expressive of every attitude towards Him from passive indifference, through dawning interest, to either deep devotion or downright hostility. We have the record (Luke 11:14 to 13:9) of a continuous discourse during which there are several interruptions or interpolations. One of them (12:13) was the occasion for a parable illustrative of Christ's teaching against the sin of covetousness.

I. *The Spirit of Covetousness* (vs. 13-15)

  A. *Manifested* (v.13)

    1. Circumstances are matter for conjecture. Inquirer's cause may have been just, or it may not. Elder brother's portion was supposed to be double that of younger. Probably claim in this case was right but spirit behind it was wrong, for following reasons:

      a. Unusually blunt exhibition of worldliness, especially considering Christ's words immediately preceding. Hearer seized upon His reference to law (v.11) and pricked up his ears.

      b. His need prompted his speech, and he thought he saw chance to get benefit of law gratis and win his case.

      c. To him, therefore, Christ was only a good lawyer. No response from spiritual side of his nature—was listening to God Incarnate, and yet no stirring in his soul.

---

* Also in *Sermon Outlines*, p. 33.

d. Often so with us: we are off on stream of our own plans while we seem to be listening to Christ's message, and so His words fall off our consciousness, leaving no effect behind.

e. This man judged situation by his own wishes and cravings; how often we do likewise!

f. Many ready to call Christ Master for own advantage. *Illus.*: Beggar at minister's door promising glibly to come to church; boy at Sunday School with idea of getting good position through church influence; those who attend services for what they can get—"rice Christians," as such are known in Orient.

g. But saying "Master" or "Lord" does not make disciple.

2. Christ refuses request, disapproving, as it were, mixing religion and politics, things spiritual and things temporal, in man's mind. He is thinking of two ways of change:

a. External, leaving conditions, cases, and even men as they were before;

b. Internal, changing man himself and thus conditions and cases are changed also. Cf. holiness: love in heart makes for new life because of new character. In spiritual sphere, love and truth adjust personality to highest form.

B. *Shunned* (v.15)

1. Covetousness appears in many forms. Cf. two:

a. Clutching what is already possessed.

b. Grasping for more.

2. "Take heed, and beware"

a. It has stealthy approach.

b. It has terrible end.

C. *Condemned* (v.15)
 1. An Incontestable Fact.
  Worldly goods cannot keep soul alive. Not even abundance of them can do this, since in this case abundance is no better than mere sufficiency.
 2. A Humbling Fact.
  a. If life is primarily spiritual, not what it has but what it is counts.
  b. "How much is he worth?" is question often asked. It should apply more to character than to possessions.
  c. Man distinct from his possessions and cannot amalgamate with them. Possible to buy books and yet be illiterate. All depends on capacity and appropriation.
 3. An Inspiring Fact.
  There is hope for spiritual condition of those who recognize these distinctions.

II. *The Course of Covetousness* (vs. 16-19)
 A. *A Worldling* (v.16)
  1. Rich man of Christ's parable was doubtless considered provident, enterprising and influential citizen—sort of person who nowadays would preside at meetings and to whom hats would be doffed with great respect. Was example of "getting on in life," one "looked up to."
  2. But his story gives us insight into great problem of rich—where to invest money. He had not seen "prospectus" of Prov. 19:17: "He that hath pity upon the poor lendeth unto the Lord; and that which he hath given will He pay him again."
 B. *His Worldly Goods* (v.16)
  1. Were evidently not gained wrongly; sin came after gain.
  2. It is not sin to have, only to hoard.

C. *His Worldly-Wise Attitude* (vs. 17-19)

1. His Meditation (v.17).

   a. There was difficulty in project of storing goods.
   b. He consulted no one.
   c. What he had was not godsend, but windfall.

2. His Mistakes (vs. 18,19).

   a. He mistook Body for Soul.

      (1) Production—cultivated his land well—no objection to that, but ship should be in water, not water in ship.

      (2) Prosperity—model farmer, showing industry and diligence deserving of success, which is great test—still no objection.

      (3) Pondering—what to do with accumulated wealth—still not essentially wrong, unless accompanied by undue anxiety or selfishness.

      (4) Proposal—eating important to him. Here he errs, in thinking exclusively of body. Souls do not eat, nor live by bread alone. In such a life there is often chaff for starving mind: money, athletics, pleasure, position, business success—but no spiritual satisfaction whatever.

   b. He mistook Self for God.

      (1) Consideration — "with himself" — no other. There should be thought but not of self alone.

      (2) Center—"I"—"all my"—first person is often Devil's own pronoun which, if used exclusively, shuts out God and brother-man alike.

   c. He mistook Time for Eternity.

      (1) Anticipation—"years"—thought he could lay up time as well as goods.

      (2) Announcement—no mention of "if the Lord will."

III. *The Penalty of Covetousness* (vs. 20,21)

    A. *Classed with Fools* (v.20)
        A fool is one utterly devoid of mind—so this man's sagacity much in question.

    B. *Cut off from Life* (v.21)
        He thought of years but could not reckon on one night. "It is certain we can carry nothing out" (1 Tim. 6:7).

    C. *Poor for Eternity* (v.21)
        He left all behind—except himself, and he was worthless.

Conclusion

    1. *The Sin*

        a. Covetousness is not confined to the wealthy.

            (1) Wealth measured by position and claims.

            (2) Any man wealthy who finds he has more than enough.

            (3) Love of gain in poor man is as serious as sin of rich man here.

        b. Covetousness is self first in everything.

            (1) Pleasure—comfort, indulgence, protection—in a word, selfishness.

            (2) This is prevalent among all, rich or poor, small or great.

    2. *The Remedy*

        a. Denial of Self

            (1) The word "deny" has two meanings—refuse and ignore.

            (2) Cf. Peter's "denial" of Christ—he disowned and he repudiated. Our attitude to self should be as strong as this, and it should be shown daily.

        b. Displacement by Christ.
        This will be accomplished by—

(1) Crowning Him as Lord;

(2) Being concerned with Him, absorbed in Him, doing His will;

(3) Perpetually recognizing Him—nothing apart from Him;

(4) Having not one penny nor ten minutes, except in Him.

Thus was Christ Himself in His devotion to the Father. To assert self is to displace Christ. To displace by Christ is to deny self. So let us yield, abide, obey, that "in all things He might have the pre-eminence" (Col. 1:18).

55

SOLICITUDE *
(Luke 12:22-34)

Christ often used general circumstances in specific cases. "Therefore" (v.22), He says, trust is the antidote for a grasping spirit such as has just been under discussion (vs. 15-21). Let us take the word "solicitude" as the key to our study. A dictionary definition of a "solicitous" person is one who is "full of anxiety or concern, as for the attainment of something."

There can be—

I. *Vain Solicitude* (vs. 22-30)

We are told not to be vainly solicitous—

A. *Because of the Nature of Life* (vs. 22,23)

1. Roger Bacon said in 1611, "A man died of thought." What would he say today? When anxiety prevails, sad looks and deep furrows tell.

2. Anxiety wrong—same temper as "rich fool" in preceding verses—self-consuming care.

B. *Because of the Care of the Creator* (vs. 24,27,28)

1. Ravens an interesting illustration—not eagles or nightingales, but birds of ill omen, of prey. Complete improvidence yet sure maintenance mark these inferior members of creation.

2. Lilies speak of beauty as well as of life—"much more" includes food, raiment, all.

---

* See also Sermon Notes, p. 51.

C. *Because of the Uselessness of Anxiety* (vs. 25,26)
   1. Does not go deep enough—accomplishment greater without it.
   2. Foreboding opposite of foresight and destroys it.

D. *Because of Pagan Character of Anxiety* (vs. 29,30)
   1. Brings discredit on God, as though He were not real and true.
   2. Little difference between this attitude and atheism— "a-theism," or "no-God-ism."

II. *True Solicitude* (vs. 31-34)

We are told to "seek," or be solicitous for, the "kingdom of God."

A. *Because this Attitude Secures the Present* (v.31)
   To "consider" and then to "seek" bring "all these things."

B. *Because it Assures the Future* (v.32)
   1. Feebleness recognized.
   2. Fearfulness forbidden.
   3. Victory assured.

C. *Because it Regulates Life* (v.33)
   Principle is scatter, yet increase. "God first" strikes balance.

D. *Because it Insures Character* (v.34)
   Heart follows its treasure. Picture in Paris of physicians examining dead body reminds us that death is always due to "absence of heart"—so in spiritual realm.

Conclusion

We may find key phrase in verse 29: "Neither be of doubtful mind." Greek has sense of not being tossed about on open sea when one may be anchored safely in roomy, sheltered haven.

1. *The Sea*—Care
   Constant restlessness, dangerous instability, long separation.

2. *The Anchor*—Trust
   Peaceful, safe, homelike.

3. *The Harbor*—Fatherhood (v.30)
   A relationship—
   a. Endearing—"your Father"—a delicate child is shielded.
   b. Interested—"knoweth"—a timid child is encouraged.
   c. Individual—"ye"—an infirm child is helped.
   d. Enduring—"have need"—a tempted child is protected.

   Therefore, let us trust all to "Our Father who art in Heaven," and rest in Him.

56

A MIRACLE OF HEALING
(Luke 13:10-13)

T HE WORLD is full of mysteries, among them the forces that lie in both Nature and the mind of man. Many natural processes in our everyday experience are insoluble enigmas. One of the greatest is the problem of suffering—bodily pain and mental anguish. Why do so many suffer during all, or a large part of, their lifetime? Yet suffering is but an aspect of a larger problem, that of sin, for sin is the original source of all evil; and in dealing with sin one is dealing with sorrow and suffering as well. Herein lies the glory of Christianity. It points toward that day described in Revelation when there shall be "no more death, neither sorrow, nor crying, neither shall there be any more pain" (21:4); and of "that great city, the holy Jerusalem," it is written that "there shall in no wise enter into it any thing that defileth." What is more natural, therefore, than that in the Gospels as in the present portion, we see Christ dealing not only with suffering, but with sin?

I. *Suffering* (vs. 10,21)

  A. *The Sad Object*

    1. "A woman"—one who so often suffers—"eighteen years" —whatever her age, great portion of her life.

    2. "A spirit of infirmity"—literally, "a spirit which had caused infirmity," indicating supernatural power behind physical trouble, not that she had been born with malformation or deformity (cf. v.16).

      a. Evidently possession by Satan had effect of curvature of spine—may have worked on nervous system.

  b. Not quite thus now—yet sin does affect nervous system and result often baffles medical skill.

  c. This type of suffering hardest to bear—strength gone and foundation sapped.

3. "Was bowed together"—bent double.

  a. Erectness of human form unique characteristic—no other animals completely so. Man only made in image of God, with onward and upward look to hope of life beyond.

  b. Greek word for man means "upward-looking"; conversely, downward sign is symbol of earthliness.

  c. Many bodies bent on account of disease, yet upright souls often found in such; while sin always lowers soul, even in body admired for grace and strength, beauty of proportion and features.

  d. Sorrow also bends—but better to submit in trust and not be crushed, for he whose soul is bent sees neither sky nor face of his Father.

  e. Care bends—heavy burdens make prematurely old.

B. *The Noble Soul*

  1. "Could in no wise lift up herself"—"in no wise unbend"—indicates she tried—not willing to give up—not weak spirit, but patient and brave.

   a. Many such today—noble, heroic, often unknown.

   b. Sorrowing, suffering, they refuse to look on gloomy side, but turn eyes away to light.

   c. Did this woman know sin was secret of suffering and do her best to remedy it?

  2. "In one of the synagogues on the sabbath . . ." —notwithstanding her terrible infirmity, she was in place of worship at appointed time.

   a. Surely excuse for her to be absent from God's house! No, most infirm are often most regular.

   b. What she would have missed that day had she been absent! Blessing always in path of duty.

   c. Someone has said that *"Morbus sabbaticus"* or "Sunday sickness" attacks at certain hours on the Sabbath, but recovery is rapid! Symptoms vary, but patient can always sleep well night before and can always eat hearty Sunday dinner or supper shortly after acute attack! Generally called "indisposition" —yes, indisposed towards church!

   d. Not so this woman—testified to God in and through suffering. There is indeed ministry of submission as well as of speech.

II. *Sympathy* (v.12)

A. *The Ready Look*

"Jesus saw her"

1. Immediately drawn to poor woman's need.
2. More remarkable because women's part of synagogue separate from that of men.
3. People known by what attracts them.
   a. Some eyes sharp for defects, things off square or out of proper place.
   b. Other eyes keen observers of beauty, of Nature— cf. artist's for color, doctor's or dective's for character.
4. But Christ quick to see suffering, so woman's presence at once noticed. Chords of sympathy vibrate—one of signs of fitness to work with and for others.

B. *The Loving Call*

"He called her to Him"—His call was—

1. Audible—tone must have been capable of being heard at distance.
2. Personal—for her alone.
3. Definite—meant something.

    4. Cheering—gave her hope.
This Saviour still sees and calls.

III. *Service* (vs. 12,13)

Sympathy quickly vanishes if not expressed by service.

  A. *The Assuring Word*

    "Woman, thou art loosed from thine infirmity."

    1. His voice would reassure her—though could have performed miracle without if necessary.

    2. Word used in Greek indicates immediateness and permanence of ensuing action.

    3. "Loosed"—manifestation of special relationship of her infirmity to powers of evil (cf. v.16).

  B. *The Healing Touch*

    "He laid His hands on her"

    1. His word of sympathy was followed by His touch of power—confirmation and cheer in pressure of hand.

    2. Impartation of power. Christ seems never to have touched one actually and presently possessed of evil spirit, but this woman had been influenced eighteen years before and only physical results remained. Pity for miserable condition and prompting of kindly heart overcame Divine antagonism to Devil.

This our Saviour now—One who can effect immediate, permanent cure for spiritual ills of long standing.

IV. *Satisfaction* (v.13)

  A. *The Loving Saviour*

    "Immediately she was made straight"

    1. We may imagine His intense joy to see woman healed. Overcoming not only suffering, but sin, was foretaste of future.

    2. Then, amid blame and praise, hate and joy, He showed indignation against critics (see following Study).

B. *The Worshipping Woman*

"And glorified God"

1. Immediately knew she had been made straight and given strength, vigor, ease, power, joy.

2. Gave praise where due—by lip and then, we hope, by life.

This Saviour still loves and waits.

Conclusion

1. *An Invitation*

   a. Christ still sees—

   > "Thy kind but searching glance can scan
   > The very wounds that shame would hide."

   b. Christ still able, ready, willing—

   > "Thy touch has still its ancient power,
   > No word from Thee can fruitless fall."

   c. Christ still hears—

   > "Hear in this solemn evening hour
   > And in Thy mercy heal us all."

   d. Christ still calls—

   > "Once more 'tis eventide, and we,
   > Oppressed with various ills, draw near."

   e. Christ still gives—

   (1) For sin's guilt, pardon—

   (2) For sin's bondage, power—

   (3) For sin's defilement, purity.

2. *An Inspiration*

   a. There is hope for the worst. Christian workers may lift up their hearts as they consider this poor woman —eighteen years baffled, despondent, despairing. "Let not your heart be troubled" (John 14:1).

b. There is pledge of final victory. Fiat goes forth—question of time only. "We see Jesus," and past victories are pledge of future: sin destroyed, sorrow dispersed, care dispelled, in presence and by power of same Lord Jesus. Then shall we rejoice in His rejoicing and triumph in His triumph: "Then the ransomed of the Lord shall return, and come to Zion with songs and everlasting joy upon their heads; they shall obtain joy and gladness, and sorrow and sighing shall flee away" (Isa. 35:10).

57

CHRIST AND THE SABBATH
(Luke 13:14-17)

During this last journey of Christ, when growing opposition must have given the disciples a sense of deepening gloom, the healing of a woman on the Sabbath day provided the Pharisees with a case against Him and spurred them on to bolder attack. Their opposition was not only because of the miracle of healing, but also and chiefly because of Christ's teaching on the subject of the Sabbath.

I. *The Indignant Protest* (v.14)

A. *Unwarranted Anger*

1. Blindness and coldness of formalism—to ask for miracle, yet to object when one is performed.
2. It passed by splendid power, gentle generosity, loving instinct, practical relief from pauperism.
3. Indignation instead of reflection—"Little pots soon boil."

B. *Unfair Appeal*

1. Afraid to attack Jesus direct, so blamed people.
2. But had anyone, even woman, come to synagogue for purpose of healing? More likely for worship, and also to hear Christ's teaching (cf. v. 10).

C. *Unrighteous Attitude*

1. Really against miracle regardless of day or circumstances, but chose to emphasize propriety.

2. Ruler of synagogue was ecclesiastical martinet so callous that he would rather hundred people suffered than one rule be broken.

3. Need for more humaneness and less pedantry.

II. *The Triumphant Vindication* (vs. 15-17)

A. *Because of Usual Custom* (v.15)

1. Title given "Thou hypocrite" (R.V., "Ye hypocrites"), indicated Christ's knowledge that they were not really concerned for Sabbath law, also His righteous severity.

2. Reminder of what they would readily do for mere animal on Sabbath.

B. *Because of Greater Need* (v.16)

1. Contrast—
   a. "This woman"—"his ox or his ass"
   b. "Whom Satan hath bound"—"from the stall"
   c. "These eighteen years"—"on the Sabbath"
   d. "Had a spirit of infirmity" (v.11)—"to watering," viz., mere physical thirst.

2. Recognize relationship—"daughter of Abraham"— and repulsiveness is forgotten. Christ sees below scars. *Illus.*: Driver of vehicle told overworked doctor how often he changed horses and how necessary was expense of new ones. Said doctor: "But if *I* work myself to death, another *doctor* will cost nothing!"

C. *Because of Popular Testimony* (v.17)

1. "Adversaries" (plural) ashamed, but still plotting,

2. Christ rejected because He threatened their power with people—not merely because of Sabbath law.

III. *The Sabbath Principle*
1. Note history—from Genesis 2:3 onwards, before entrance of sin, suggesting it was fundamental, permanent, and universal—one day of rest in seven originally connected with rest in creation.

2. Confirmed later in connection with Jews (Exod. 20:8-11)—only one of Ten Commandments beginning with admonition to "remember" what God had already appointed.

3. Two great premises laid down by our Lord:
   a. Sabbath made for man;
   b. He was Lord of Sabbath.

4. Here and elsewhere He upholds it, and explains more fully relationship between public worship of God and deeds of love to men—separating accidental from essential.

5. Yet differences on Sabbath subject of controversy all through ages.

6. Necessary to get back to principle that humanity is above mere enactment—Sabbath is to keep up man even more than man is to keep up Sabbath.

7. Appropriate that "the Lord's Day" should be continuance and development of Jewish Sabbath—commemorates God's rest in redemption set forth by Christ's resurrection, and anticipates God's great, eternal Sabbath-keeping. Cf. Heb. 4:9-11.

8. Consider it in true light:
   a. Gift even more than command—privilege of permitted service as well as needed rest.

   b. Freedom, not restriction—respite from ordinary life. Children should be taught this from earliest years.

   c. Rest, not dissipation—recuperation between periods of labor. "A change is as good as a rest."

d. Benediction, not ban—prevents bigotry of formalism and may be made one of choicest blessings of life.

e. Inspiration, not just institution—must not be lost in mere tradition.

f. Symbol, not consummation—promise of future (Cf. Heb. 4:1-11).

Conclusion

1. True believer has no difficulty, no bondage, but rejoicing in Lord's Day—all that is gracious and glorious connected with it.

2. Profits from resting one day in seven.

3. Cherishes blessed memories of past with old friends, in old scenes.

4. Finds it character-moulding influence on family, such as quiet of Sunday evening.

5. Looks forward to great future by means of it.

   Rest—worship—service—praise God for recurring opportunity for all these!

58

SALVATION AND SERVICE
(Luke 14:1-35)

In THIS chapter we may distinguish several feasts: One, probably dinner, actually took place in the home of a Pharisee, and to it our Lord was invited (vs. 1,7,12,15). It is remarkable how many lessons arose out of this invitation. Three other feasts found places in His discourse while at meat: a wedding feast (vs. 8-11); a "dinner or supper" (vs. 12-15); and a "great supper" (vs. 16-24). With the first of these He taught humility, and with the second unselfishness, while in connection with the third the Gospel of salvation, or Conversion, is uppermost in His teaching.

Incidentally, three other important suppers are found in the New Testament: "the Lord's Supper," or Communion (1 Cor. 11:20-34); "the marriage supper of the Lamb," or Consummation (Rev. 19:7-9); and "the supper of the great God," or Condemnation (Rev. 19:17,18). The figure of a supper is appropriate since eating is not only natural and necessary, but it possesses great potentialities for pleasure or the reverse, according to the participants and the circumstances.

Our chapter, then, has four broad headings in relation to four different types of people. The first two types were rebuked by our Lord, and the last two were given solemn warnings:

I. *Rebuking the Hypocritical* (vs. 1-6)

1. Pharisees at meal determined on open, active hostility.
2. Watched Christ in hope of catching Him, especially on Sabbath.

3. Man with dropsy presented to Christ:
   a. Call for His healing power, and—
   b. Cause for challenge of enemies by Him as to lawfulness of Sabbath healing.
4. Their silence was significant—man was healed and let go, also in silence apparently—and then Christ put forth argument, based on their own Sabbath experience, which they could not answer.

II. *Rebuking the Proud* (vs. 7-14)

Then Christ turned from hosts to—

1. Guests (vs. 7-11).

   a. The occasion—efforts to secure best places prompted our Lord to give definite, suitable message on danger of pride.
   b. The principle—also urged by Him at other times (cf. 18:14; Matt. 23:12)—"exalted . . . abased." Even from guests' own selfish standpoint modesty shown to be worth while, but Christ urges absolutely real humility as well.

Then He turns back to the—

2. Host (vs. 12-14).

   a. The principle—duty of unselfishness: not that rich are never to be invited, but that poor should not be overlooked. Welcoming of friends means personal enjoyment which easily becomes selfishness. New Testament very strong on duty of hospitality, evidently outstanding feature of early Church life (cf. Rom. 12:13; 1 Tim. 3:2; Titus 1:8; 1 Pet. 4:9).
   b. The promise—Christ points to future recompense at "resurrection of just." N.B. Implies another resurrection, that of unjust (cf. 20:35; John 5:28,29).

III. *Warning the Indifferent* (vs. 15-24)

A. *The Platitude of the Pious Pharisee* (v.15).

Perhaps state of mind of guest expressed undue com-

placency in view of Christ's mention of future. As D.
M. McIntyre puts it: "One of those present tried to
turn the sharp edge of His words by giving utterance
to a pious platitude . . . as much as to say, 'Oh, yes, we
shall all be very happy when we get to heaven.' Jesus
turned to him with a parable which had for its motive
the question, Are you sure that you shall be there?"
Then follows—

B. *The Parable of the Great Supper* (vs. 16-24).
   Why "great"? Because of—
   1. Great Preparation.
      a. This parable to be carefully distinguished from
         that in Matt. 22:1-14.
      b. "Certain man" represents God Himself, and
         "great supper" is Gospel.
      c. Point apt to be overlooked: interval between first
         invitation and second, or between invitation and
         reminder ("bade . . . sent . . . to say," vs. 16, 17).

         (1) First invitation may be said to be indicated in
             Gen. 3:15.
         (2) Then followed wonderful preparation of God
             all through Old Testament, from time of Adam
             to appearance of Christ—4000 years.
         (3) Hints to antediluvian patriarchs—believed by
             Abraham, foretold by Moses, expressed in Le-
             vitical law, hailed by David, announced by Pro-
             phets, even in outside Gentile world.
         (4) Ample time given for people to hold them-
             selves free to accept but, quite unconcerned,
             they even showed ingratitude.
         (5) Then Jesus Christ appeared and led life of
             ministry till He died on the Cross saying, "It
             it finished!"

   Such was preparation and completion of process.
   Is it not grand, showing God's infinite love and

concern for men? Salvation not hastily but carefully arranged.

2. Great Provision.

    a. Victory won—promise fulfilled—atonement offered —Jesus ascended—Holy Spirit given. So now, full and perfect, "a great supper."

    b. Host—God of heaven and earth; guests—enemies; provision—pardon, eternal life, guidance, deliverance—all pertaining to life and godliness—beyond need and remaining to eternity as testimony to God's love.

Then comes—

3. Kind Reminder.

    a. Guests notified "all things are now ready." What things? Things of God, provision for salvation— Old Testament looks forward to that which is to be done; New Testament looks backward to that which is done.

    b. Guests bidden to "come." God might have dealt with us as rebels and said, Submit! But He speaks as father and says, Come! Action needed is merely to take, receive Him and His Gospel, offered and provided by Christ. What could be fuller, or freer? Surely all will accept. But no, there is—

4. Evasive Response.

"They all with one consent began to make excuse." Note—

    a. Absurdity of excuses:

        (1) Piece of ground—but bargain closed, so no real hurry to see purchase again.

        (2) Oxen bought—also bargain closed, so no real hurry to prove them once more.

(3) Wife married—also "bargain" closed—but perhaps had wedding feast of own.

D. M. McIntyre says: "A bad excuse is worse than none, and all these excuses were bad. A landowner does not generally add to his estate without first surveying the ground he is to purchase. A farmer is not in the habit of buying oxen which he has not proved. A young wife would willingly accompany her husband to a festival. These are excuses, not reasons; there is no *reason* for refusing the gifts of the Son of God." Another writer says: "In the excuse of each, there was of course a lie; there nearly always is in an excuse. You can always give a reason without telling a lie, but it is very hard to make an excuse without telling a lie. A reason exists, in the memory; but you have to manufacture an excuse, and it is not worth the material out of which you make it . . . Men make their excuses just the same today, and they make them in a plausible way and in a most polite manner."

b. Dishonesty of excuses.
   (1) Did these men think host was deceived by what they said?

   (2) Men today speak and act as though God is deceived, but instead they are self-deceived—"Be not deceived; God is not mocked" (Gal. 6:7).

   (3) These excuses typical of others—circumstances matter not— no valid reasons. But if honest this would be seen, and if fellow-man offered such excuses he would reap scorn and doubt.

c. Madness of excuses.
   D. M. McIntyre: "To turn away from Christ and His salvation is altogether irrational. It is stark, downright folly."

(1) These men missed all—nothing else to come—supper, not mid-day meal—no "midnight snack" in next world! No other way to God—no other name to plead.

(2) These men each made wrong choice:

(a) First placed property before God.

(b) Second devoted himself to business instead of serving God.

(c) Third idolized wife instead of worshipping God.

N.B. All mentioned lawful pursuits—land-owning, ploughing, marrying. "More killed by meat than by poison," by abuse of lawful than use of unlawful. What more honorable than commerce, agriculture, and marriage? But—

(3) These men had false values:

(a) Instead of buying land or oxen, first two were bought by them; instead of influencing wife to accompany him, third was influenced by her or because of her to stay away.

(b) Not wrong to have secular life, but wrong to let secular life have us. First interests not material but spiritual. "Seek ye first the kingdom of God" (Matt. 6:33).

(c) Christian may be in world, but world must not be in him. *Illus.*: Ship may be in water, but not water in ship.

5. Final Result.

Shown by Christ in verses 21-24.

a. Host not to be set aside and preparations made to go for nothing—others, poor, maimed, halt and blind brought in until house filled.

b. God will not allow His marvellous preparation to be lost. Christ already rejected in various places, so it became necessary to speak frankly of consequences.

c. Story seems to suggest distinction between Jews and Gentiles: Chosen People having rejected Christ as Messiah, He is offered to hitherto unprivileged Gentiles as universal Saviour.

d. Host angry at refusal—invitations of God, like those of royalty, have force of command.

IV. *Warning the Shallow* (vs. 25-35)

Severity of Christ in these verses is strikingly different from invitation in preceding parable (cf. vs. 16,17), and His own attitude to outcasts in following chapter (15:1,2). This is keynote passage on true discipleship as opposed to thoughtless or hasty profession. Christ's words were addressed to "great multitudes" (v.25), and were of most searching nature as He laid down the conditions of discipleship:

1. The Cross to be borne (vs. 25-27)

   a. Attitude of willingness to follow, even unto death.

   b. Love of Christ first, with all other loves only in and through Christ.

2. The Cost to be counted (vs. 28-32)
   Illustrated by two metaphors:

   a. Building — risk was of non-completion — therefore, count money!

   b. Battle—risk was of defeat—therefore, consider forces! Whether building or battling, failure to face consequences causes spiritual disaster.

3. The Possessions to be renounced (v.33)
   Application of foregoing—true disciple must be ready to "forsake all."

4. The Influence to be exerted (vs. 34,35)
   Third metaphor of passage, salt, suggests quality of discipleship—risk was of insipidity—therefore beware!

Conclusion

Two categorical negatives are found in this chapter:

1. *As to Salvation*—"None of those men which were bidden shall taste of My supper" (v. 24)

   a. Men of property and business, what profit if you lose your own souls?

   b. Young men, as you marry, take heed of spiritual values!

   Are you making excuses to God? If so, they are as old as Adam. Or are you really stating reasons? If so, be sure they will stand in the light of eternity for, remember, excuse or reason, the statements in the parable were accepted.

2. *As to Service*—"He cannot be My disciple"—three times over (vs. 26,27,33) —if there is no—

   a. Surrender to Christ (v.26). Christ first in the heart means we are to take care that no interest or love is put before Him;

   b. Suffering for Christ (v.27). Christ first in the life means bearing our cross and following Him, being ready to be, or do, or suffer whatever may be God's will for us.

   c. Substance for Christ (v.33). Christ first in the possessions means that not only all we are, but all that we have is to be His.

Well may the chapter close with the familiar yet solemn words: "He that hath ears to hear, let him hear."

59

LOST: SHEEP, SILVER, SON!
(Luke 15:1-32)

THIS IS perhaps the best-known chapter in the New Testament. It contains three oft-told stories—of the Lost Sheep, the Lost Silver, and the Lost Son. These were called forth by the contrast presented in the first two verses of the chapter between the inquiring "publicans and sinners" and the murmuring "Pharisees and scribes." The former group were strongly attracted to Christ, and He, though separate from them, felt closest to them. He saw through them but did not loathe them, as did the Pharisees. This latter group regarded the Master as hopeless, so puzzled were they by His preference for outcasts; although obviously it is not easy to devote one's life to evangelism or philanthropy and yet keep up with what is called "good society." The Pharisees, as H. J. Horn points out, "were offended that He should come to bring a common salvation, by a common faith, to the common people. But the very genius of the Gospel lies in this, that those who have must give to those who have not. The shielded must help the exposed, the found must go after the lost, the free must loose the slave, the strong support the fainting. And in the glorious process, caste gapes and dies, exclusiveness is trampled under foot by the hurrying steps of charity, 'Society' is merged into society, and grace lifts all from their petty distinctions into the eternal and unutterable distinction of the sons of God."

I. M. Haldeman calls this "The Threefold Parable" and says it is "the one parable which illustrates God's Way, God's Grace, and God's Joy in saving the sinner, whether he be a wanderer, a lost value, or a squanderer." Why, indeed, the repetition of teaching by the use of three similar stories? It has been suggested that they indicate the place in evangelism of each Person of the Holy Trinity. Fanciful? Perhaps, and yet we shall see that the Son, the Holy Spirit, and the Father, respectively, may be shadowed in the three stories. D. M. McIntyre says: "In this chapter there is only one parable (v.3). It represents the action of the Good Shepherd, who is Himself the Son; the diligence of the Church, filled and possessed by the Holy Spirit; and the love of the Father. There is the lost sheep, one of a hundred; the lost piece of money, one of ten; there are only two sons, and both of them are lost—one in the far country, the other in the Father's house. The elder brother may represent the Pharisees, self-righteous and unloving."

The reply of Christ being not in one general form, but in three special ones, let us think of three Pharisees as perhaps having "murmured" in turn. To each He may be said to have responded with an apologia for His work.

The first Pharisee simply asked, Why? And Christ answered in effect:

I. *Love* (vs. 3-7)

Because of compassion of heart—standpoint of Shepherd, or the Son.

A. *The Parable*

1. Loss of one in hundred (v.4), or 1 per cent, not serious, not cause of search.
2. Helplessness and misery of animate object promoted search. Cf. "which was lost" (v.6).
3. Love shown in—
   a. Perseverance—search "until he find it" (v.4).
   b. Care—"on his shoulders" (v.5)—"home" (v.6).
   c. Joy—"rejoice . . . have found" (v.6).

B. *The Point*

1. Compassion for man's misery prompted God to redeem (cf. John 3:16).

      a. Search was spontaneous and persistent.

      b. Finding brought tenderness.

      c. Return caused joy.

  2. This compassion natural—"what man of you" (v.4)—and God not inferior to man.

  3. This love individual and therefore tender:

      a. Not like sentiment of employer—fill up ranks.

      b. Not satisfied except with finding and nearness.

  4. This love unwearying—cf. our own weariness in "well doing," even in seeking lost.

So our first Pharisee is silenced. But another says, True, but the object of the search is not worth the trouble. And so Christ pointed in effect to—

II. *Loss* (vs. 8-10)

Because of value of human soul—standpoint of coin's owner, or the Holy Spirit.

A. *The Parable*

  1. Loss of one in ten (v.8), or 10 per cent, quite serious—probably from row on headdress. Some Eastern women had many rows sewn together and hanging over brows, with largest coins in center and tapering at each side to smallest; but even one piece lost would destroy effect.

  2. Search was persevering — by lighting candle, sweeping house, and seeking diligently—"till she find it" (v.8).

  3. Joy over finding especially personal—"I had lost"—as compared with "was lost" (vs. 6,32). Could suggest Holy Spirit's special striving with lost soul. Cf. *soul* of man with Holy *Spirit* of God, or the Holy Spirit through the Church, as often typified in Scriptrue by a woman (see Eph. 5:23-27; Rev. 19:7-9; 21:2, 9), seeking to save sinner.

B. *The Point*

1. Man is valuable to God—mind, will, heart, conscience, viz., whole personality—as coin to woman. Only God's love knows true worth of human soul.

2. Man is lost—

   a. To God. God suffers loss in sinner who departs. Pharisees could not grasp this.

   b. To world. Cf. coin isolated, not fulfilling purpose.

   c. To self. True natural falls into disuse.

3. Man is imperishable—

   a. Coin may have been defaced, but still bore "image and superscription." Man damaged by sin, but still "made in the image of God."

   b. Coin was still ornament, and so may regenerated man "adorn the doctrine of God our Saviour" (Tit. 2:10).

So our second Pharisee is silenced. But the third says, Granted the love of God, and the loss to God, but the new status of the sinner will not last; such a man is incorrigible, he will revert to type. And then Christ pointed in effect to—

III. *Longsuffering* (vs. 11-32)

Because there is hope for worst—standpoint of father, or God the Father.

A. *The Parable*

Loss of one in two (v.11), or 50 per cent, most serious of all. Central figure is father (God), or even elder brother (Pharisee), not prodigal (sinner)—he only shows father in sharp relief.

   1. The Son.
      a. Restrained by home, attracted by world. Beginning of all sin is incapacity to find fullest enjoyment in God's presence, love, and ways.
      b. Wants liberty and means of enjoying it.
      c. Soon finds liberty limited by self and by outer circumstances, and become license.
      d. Then realizes, repents, and returns.

   2. The Father.
      a. Grants request, but never forgets.
      b. Never loses hope—watches continually—recognizes quickly.
      c. No hesitation—no standing on dignity—no rebuke.
      d. Pardon, restoration, joy, because of love.
      e. Same love shown to elder brother by thought, word, deed, and manner.

B. *The Point*
   1. God's longsuffering—in history and individually, "not willing that any should perish" (2 Pet. 3:9).
   2. God's interest—not insensible, but ever thinking and feeling.
   3. God's love—deep, wide, lasting, personal.
   4. God's welcome—all forgiven, forgotten, restored, and rejoicing.

Thus did Christ answer His critics, and thus did He hearten and cheer with great hope those whom the world of His day despised and set at nought. His love, His loss, and His longsuffering should be the threefold reason why His followers ought to take up the same position; and in each of the three parables are four parallel thoughts: (a) losing, (b) seeking, (c) finding, (d) rejoicing. H. J. Horn reminds us that "he that 'receiveth sinners, and eateth with them,' in the practice of the Gospel, finds the sinner brought to Christ and holiness, and himself blest."

Conclusion

1. **Our goal today:**

   Compassion — Consideration — Continuance — three essentials for all Christian work.

2. Our power today:

   Only as we realize and manifest Spirit of Christ will our work tell for God.

3. Our secret today:

   Love with Christ—abide in Him—see life and mankind from His standpoint—be in fellowship with His purpose.

60

THE PARABLE OF THE LOST SHEEP *
(Luke 15:1-7)

In the parallel passage in Matthew 18, this story is prefaced by the beautiful, well-known words: "The Son of man is come to save that which was lost" (v.11). From its application to a sheep (vs. 12,13), we can see what it means when it refers to a man or woman. The sinner is lost to himself, to others, to all that is good and useful, but above everything else he is lost to God.

In Luke's version we see:

I. *The Attractiveness of Christ* (v.1)

    1. The fact—characteristic of Gospels.

    2. The reason—blend of tenderness (14:21), and sternness (14:25f.).

    3. The truth—separated yet close—sinners seen by Him and yet loved. Cf. sympathy based on sinlessness (Heb. 4:15).

    Illus.: Benevolent doctor takes pity on drunkard, etc.

II. *The Attack on Christ* (v.2)

    1. Testimony—the Gospel in a grumble —"This man receiveth sinners!"

    2. Truth—He did! He does!

    3. Today—what is Christianity's attitude to sin and to sinner?

III. *The Answer of Christ* (vs. 3-7)

    1. Appeal—"What man of you . . . ?"

    2. Illustration—Both Old Testament and Gospels full of similar instances:

* See also I in Study No. 59, p. 241.

a. Losing—helplessness, foolishness, want, misery. Cf. **Isa.** 53:6—artists' theme throughout ages: loss of ship, waif, sheep and lambs. Many lost are also indifferent, thoughtless, reckless.

b. Seeking—the Good Shepherd did "go" for 33 years "until"—.

"None of the ransomed ever knew
How deep were the waters crossed.
Nor how dark was the night that the Lord went through
'Ere He found His sheep that was lost."

c. Finding—"layeth it on his shoulders"—"home"—cf. "much more" (Rom. 5:9,10).

d. Rejoicing—own sheep, but wanted others to join in— as Pharisees should have done with Christ over "publicans and sinners." Then Christ adds testimony of One who knows heaven as well as earth, that "likewise joy shall be in heaven over one soul that repenteth."

Conclusion

1. *The Reason*

Loving compassion—spontaneous search—yearning tenderness—joyful satisfaction.

2. *The Rebuke*

Heaven more interested in one repentant sinner than in 99 that "need no repentance"—or think so.

3. *The Reminder*

Compassion—Considerateness—Contact—Continuance.

4. *The Rejoicing*

Joy on earth too—there is nothing to compare with it. Is it often ours?

61

THE PARABLE OF THE LOST SILVER*
(Luke 15:8-10)

T HERE have been many sermons preached on the Lost Sheep, more on the Lost Son, but few on the Lost Silver. It is the shortest of the three parables in this chapter, and apt to be overlooked. Yet it is important, for though it may be said to be similar to the first of the three it is also different.

Presenting aspects of the Divine attitude to man, the first parable shows His Love and the third His Longsuffering. This second parable portrays His Loss.

I. *The Loss*
   1. To the woman.
      a. What? One coin out of ten—valuable object—large proportion.
      b. Why? Probably belonged in her headdress—awkward gap.
      c. How? In dust—in wrong place.

   2. To God.
      a. What? Mankind—valuable to Maker—whole personality.
      b. Why? Man lost—
         (1) To God—who would have used him.
         (2) To world—for he is isolated by sin.
         (3) To self—dust of earth no fit place for coin or man.
      c. How?
         (1) Like coin's image, God's likeness, in which man was made, not wholly defaced—imperishable.

---

*See also II in Study No. 59, p. 242.

(2) Like coin, unable to restore self—must wait to be found.

(3) But, unlike coin, though he does not now realize own worth, can be made to, during—

II. *The Search*

1. By light—"light a candle"—illumination of God's Word (cf. Psa. 119:105).
2. By sweeping—"sweep the house"—conviction of Spirit (cf. John 3:8; Acts 2:2).
3. By earnestness—"diligently" (cf. Prov. 22:29).
4. By persistence—"till she find it" (cf. v.4).

III. *The Result*

1. Discovery—"hath found it" (cf. 5,32).
2. Joy—"Rejoice . . . I have found . . . which I had lost" (cf. v.6, "was lost"—suggests striving of Spirit with soul contrasted with mere going astray).

Conclusion

1. *The significance of the individual*—"one." Christ often dealt with one person alone. No mention of other nine coins—personality important, socialism or communism to the contrary.

2. *The moral value of the individual*—"sinner." Question is not intellectual but moral—note interest of heaven.

3. *The permanent usefulness of the individual*—"that re- penteth." Above all else, a turn-about-face in the life.

4. *The heavenly satisfaction over the individual*—"joy . . of angels of God." They know and are deeply interested. No "foreign coins" among redeemed! Gravity of loss often indicates value. God's loss was so great because of sin that He gave the highest price to "seek and to save." Have you been "lost and found"? Then are you trying to reach other valuable souls till you "find" them for God?

62

THE PARABLE OF THE LOST SON*
(Luke 15:11-32)

THIS MAY be called "The Parable of the Loving Father"**instead of "The Parable of the Prodigal Son." It has also been referred to as "The Pearl of Parables."

In Scripture, the words "I have sinned" are said by eight different men. Four times they are said without reality:—by Pharaoh, Balaam, Saul, Judas. Four times they are said in sincerity:—by Job, Achan, David, the Prodigal Son. In this last instance we are told in detail the steps to and from the utterance of the phrase. We are given the history of a sin, with the experience of the sinner made very clear.

I. *Downward*

  A. *Seven Steps*

    1. Restraint.

      a. Life bright with every opportunity, but son of home under law, rules of household. Liberty is regulated freedom, not abuse of law, which is license.

      b. So man and God—freedom within bounds (Gen. 3:2,3) —but sin makes conscious of them.

    2. Restlessness.

      a. Son not satisfied, chafed, hemmed in—wanted to get away from father and home—could not find enjoyment.

---

* See also III in Study No. 59, p. 249.
** Also in Sermon Outlines, p. 10, under this title.

b. So man, in natural state incapable of finding fullest satisfaction in God, is restless.

3. Request.
   a. Emphasis on word "me." Wanted possessions, not presence, of father. Unlawful because not yet due, but son was determined on freedom.
   b. So man wants to be let alone, to be "free."

4. Responsibility.
   a. Granted—now own master, free to do as he liked.
   b. So sinful nature—self will, independence of God. "Portion"—endowments of life. God always respects man's individuality and independence, even though expressed through self-assertion and self-will. This condition has been described as "lord of himself, that heritage of woe."

5. Recklessness.
   a. Off at once—waste, riotous living—no thought of responsibilities—freedom only consideration—has his "fling."
   b. So sin always wastes—living for self is waste.

6. Retribution.
   a. "Harmony with environment" a principle of moral law. Tendency of sin or of virtue to gather corresponding surroundings.
   b. So fortune goes, famine comes. Life within and circumstances without often agree. Famine around matched by emptiness within.

7. Reproach.
   a. Menial task for Jew to be swineherd, especially when employed by "citizen" of another country. No friend near—everyone left when money gone.

b. So isolation of sinner—homelessness; degradation of sinner—emptiness.

B. *Sin*

1. Germ of Sin—self-will—own way.

2. Growth of Sin—gradual, not precipitate—distance from God.

3. Goal of Sin—complete degradation and disaster—entire separation from God.

II. *Upward*

A. *Seven Steps*

1. Reflection.

a. "Came to himself"—so before he was "beside himself" (moral madness). "Said"—or thought (talking to himself)—and first thought was of his father and servants of household.

b. First step up is always to think, and this brings realization of own plight and claims of others.

2. Recollection.

a. Past comes before him—conditions abandoned so carelessly. Servants better off than himself now.

b. Second step is letting memory work—great power to lead men back to right path.

3. Realization.

a. "I perish"—no blame to any but self.

b. Third step is to stop blaming others and become conscious that loss is through own sin.

4. Resolution.

a. "I will arise"—"I will go"—"I will say."

b. Conversion is "turning around" and starting off in opposite direction, right one.

5. Repentance.

a. Means entire change of mind. Forsaking of sin necessary to prove reality of determination.

  b. Horace Bushnell, telling of young man who, through reading of book on Christianity, found Christ, states belief that conversion came when he had determined to read book and follow its light; and so decision of prodigal was turning-point in his history—way home incidental. Essential thing: under purpose of will he arose and went towards his father.

6. Restoration.

  a. Beautiful picture—while son "yet a great way off," father "saw," "had compassion," "ran." No rebuke —"not 'forgiven' but 'loved' " as far as expression was concerned.

  b. Reconciliation included robe, ring, shoes—all showing sonship and service—imputed righteousness.

7. Rejoicing.

  a. "They began to be merry"—and we are not told when they left off! Love requited brings enduring joy: of repentance, of recovery, and of restoration.

  b. So joy in heaven and in the heart of God over "one sinner that repenteth," for not only joy of angels but joy "in the presence of the angels."

B. *God.*

1. Grace of God—longing and watching love—quick reconciliation—full welcome—entire restoration.

2. Greatness of God—reconciliation possible because of—
  a. God's character;
  b. Christ's atonement.

3. Glory to God—new life to prodigal, but better still if he had never wandered. Life of elder brother more exemplary—"ever with me" and "all that I have is thine"—so in this story there is no premium on sin. But elder brother should have emulated father in

attitude to returning prodigal, instead of, as it has been said, becoming in turn a "prodigal"—hard, cold, unforgiving.

Conclusion

The characteristics of the prodigal's return were:

1. Consciousness of loss (vs. 14-16).
2. Conviction of truth (v.17).
3. Confidence of love (v.18).
4. Courage of faith (v.18).
5. Confession of sin (vs. 18,19,21).
6. Contrition of heart (v.19).
7. Conversion of will (v.20).
8. Conduct of life (v.19).

Where are we? Going down, or going up? If down, why farther? God says, "Return!" Will you not say, "Behold, I come"?

63

BRIEF OUTLINES OF THE PARABLE OF THE LOST SON
(Luke 15:11-24)

A. *A Life Drama in Five Acts*
   1. The Old Home—a Father's love available (v.11).
   2. The Far Country—a Father's care despised (vs. 12,13).
   3. The Swine Food—a Father's help needed (vs. 14-17).
   4. The Return Journey—a Father's forgiveness sought (vs. 18-20).
   5. The Joyful Welcome—a Father's home regained (vs. 20-24).

B. *Steps Down and Steps Up*

Desire	Rejoicing
Demand	Restoration
Division	Reception
Departure	Return
Danger	Repentance
Destitution	Resolution
Desertion	Remembrance
Degradation	Reflection
Dying	

C.

The SON was:	The WAY was:	The FATHER was:
Selfish	Wicked	Fair
Sinning	Wasteful	Faithful
Sorrowful	Woeful	Forgiving

D. I perish
   I will arise
   I will go
   I will say
   I have sinned
   I am no more worthy

E. I want to do as I please — BUT
   "Christ pleased not Himself" — AND
   He said: "I do always those things that please HIM" —SO
   "Teach me to do the thing that pleaseth THEE."

F. "All that I have is thine" (Luke 15:31).
   "Abraham gave ALL that he had unto Isaac" (Gen. 25:5).
   "Shall HE not with HIM freely give us ALL things?" (Rom. 8:32)
   "His divine power hath given unto us ALL things" (2 Pet. 1:3).
   "ALL things are yours" (1 Cor. 3:21).

64

THE PARABLE OF THE UNJUST STEWARD
(Luke 16:1-13)

THIS chapter and the one preceding, Luke 15 and 16, form one complete section of the Gospel illustrative of the conflict between Christ and the Pharisees. The present parable and the following one (vs. 19-31) are definitely linked with the preceding threefold vindication of Himself receiving sinners (see "also," 16:1). This parable illustrates a right use of life, leading to blessedness.

I. *For Whom Was It?*

1. For disciples (v.1), in application to them of Christ's own attitude to sinners.

2. Parable difficult of interpretation, but apart from particular details leading idea is clear: From—

   a. A life of injustice (v.1), and—
   b. An act of shrewdness (vs. 2-8), is brought out—
   c. A message of faithfulness (vs. 9-13).

II. *What Was It?*

Our Lord's counsel to do righteously what steward did unrighteously:

1. By being prudent and practical (v.8) —mental plane.
2. By making friends of poor (v.9) —spiritual plane.
3. By being faithful (v.10) —moral plane.

Conclusion

Our Lord here teaches a threefold lesson:
1. Of Wisdom ("wisely").
2. Of Love ("friends")
3. Of Faithfulness ("least . . . much")
Be first trustful and then trustworthy!

(N.B. See fine treatment in Latham's *Pastor Pastorum*)
Thus the disciples are taught to do the very thing that their Master did in receiving and eating with sinners.

65

PARABLE OF THE RICH MAN
AND LAZARUS
(Luke 16:19-31)

IN CHAPTER 15:1,2, the Pharisees murmur; in 15:3-32, Christ justifies Himself; in 16:1-13, He applies the principle under discussion to His disciples; in 16:14-18, the Pharisees, overhearing, deride Him, and our Lord rebukes them as an "abomination in the sight of God." Then follows the second parable in this chapter, intended to be a searching application of all the preceding section to the callous Pharisees in their indifference to the poor and outcast. Let us be careful, therefore, that we apprehend Christ's primary object—not to teach the details of the future life, but to drive home the awful danger of making a wrong use of this life, thus leading to eternal misery. This is done in a series of striking contrasts, punctuated by two parallels:

I. *Present Conditions* (vs. 19-22)

   A. *Wealth*

      1. Rich man ("Dives," from Latin word for "rich" in Vulgate) not depicted as having obtained wealth unrighteously, or as being cheat or miser. Perhaps not especially selfish, since poor man was laid daily at his gate for what was probably pharasaic almsgiving, not refuse.

      2. But Dives, being surrounded by comforts and luxuries, enjoyed them to full and was indifferent to real needs of those around. There is nothing that so "pet-

rifies the feelings," to use phrase of Robert Burns, as selfishness in face of real need. For this there are two penalties:

a. Hardness of heart here. Well-known fact that emotions become hardened: love, benevolence, sympathy, can be checked by stifling of feelings and restraint of compassion toward those in distress. *Illus.*: John Wesley asked help in building church, and man replied: "I have disposition but not means." Later, when man had received large legacy and Wesley asked him again, he said: "I have means but not disposition."

b. Condemnation of works hereafter—momentous issues hang upon thread.

B. *Poverty*

1. Contrast very impressive—only gate divided. Beggar, his name, Lazarus, only one used in any of parables, and meaning "God is my help," was both sick and hungry.

2. Contrasts today between homes of rich and slums. But still true that Christ never denounced riches as such (cf. 1 Tim. 6:9,10). Recognized general fact and right of private ownership, but also taught unmistakably principle of stewardship. As Christians, we are stewards, not owners responsible to God for what we do with His gifts put in our charge (cf. sixfold command to rich in 1 Tim. 6:17-19).

3. One essential element in stewardship is personal interest in those to whom we give.

> "Not what we give, but what we share,
> For the gift without the giver is bare." (Lowell)

4. Christianity preaches not saintliness of poverty, but special peril of wickedness in wealth. Cf. "deceitful-

ness of riches" (Matt. 13:22), but there can be "deceitfulness of poverty" too, such as fancied inability to give or share.

> "The least flower with a brimming cup may stand.
> And share its dewdrop with another near."

5. John Wesley gave three rules for use of money:
   a. "Get all you can." There is duty of proper acquisition, justified by Scripture and human experience.
   b. "Save all you can." Vital safeguard against waste and wrong use of means.
   c. "Give all you can." Safeguard against selfishness, and also against getting and saving in wrong way.

6. A.T. Pierson listed seven ways of giving:
   a. Careless—giving something to everything and everybody.
   b. Impulsive—giving without proper consideration and inquiry.
   c. Lazy—giving by means of bazaars, church suppers, etc.
   d. Self-denying—saving cost of luxuries by using only what is actually necessary.
   e. Systematic—one-tenth, one-fifth, or some other proportion.
   f. Equal—giving God as much as we spend on ourselves.
   g. Heroic—limiting our expenses to a certain small sum and giving remainder to God.

Now comes the first parallel:
Death

1. Common heritage of rich and poor.
2. Only contrast here was probably in type of funeral. Rich man "was buried," possibly with ceremony, but since nothing said about Lazarus perhaps his body had only hasty attention.

II. *Future Conditions* (vs. 23-26)

Again contrast was complete, sudden, startling:

A. *Misery*

1. "Hades" rather than "Hell"—retribution, separation, torment.

2. Aggravation by contemplation of blessed.

B. *Blessedness*

1. "Abraham's bosom"—Hebrew concept of ease and comfort.

2. Recognition of others.

Now comes the second parallel:

Permanence

1. Of justice—"good things . . . evil things"—"lifetime . . . now."

2. Of separation—for each was "great gulf fixed."

Here our Lord might have ended His parable, but Pharisees, willing to justify themselves, could then have called it a fancy sketch, claiming Abraham, their "father," would have warned them if true. So Christ goes on to show there is no excuse, for there is—

III. *The Relation of Past and Present to Future* (vs. 27-31)

A. *Penalty Dreaded*

1. Dives' own experience leads to apprehension for brothers.

2. In his prayer for help, "send Lazarus" different from "a certain beggar"!

B. *Miracles Demanded*

1. Refused because possession of Scriptures, "Moses and the prophets," was sufficient.

2. Futile because no miracle can compel belief against will.

C. *Opportunities Cited*
   1. Lost ones not regained.
   2. Existing ones sufficient.
   3. No others effectual, even appearance from dead—they would not "be persuaded," much less "repent."

Conclusion
   1. Salvation comes through opportunities but *by* faith. Therefore choices, not chances, determine whether life shall lead to eternal blessedness or eternal misery.
   2. Have we used our many opportunities and (a) exerted a saving faith in the Lord Jesus Christ; (b) become faithful stewards of God's blessings?

66

CHARACTER
(Luke 16:19-31)

With this parable of the Rich Man and Lazarus Christ teaches the reversal of human judgments. Man fawns on the rich, but God loathes such a standard of values. The essence of things is not in their appearance, for "the things which are seen are temporal; but the things which are not seen are eternal" (2 Cor. 4:18). Meanwhile, present circumstances are designed by God as training for His saints.

I. *Character is the Basis for this Reversal of Judgment.*

   1. Moral element or principle was real test in parable.

   2. "Remember . . . thou . . . good things, . . . Lazarus ("God is my help") evil things."

   3. Not circumstances, but character before God.

II. *Character is Being Formed Now and Continually.*

   1. Rich man not monster—only indifferent to others and neglectful of opportunities.

   2. Negative, not positive—but destiny affected.

   3. Such characteristics as sullenness or thoughtlessness help to fix destiny.

III. *Character Ever Tends to Permanence of Condition.*

   1. Close relation between present and future—life connotes future continuance as product.

   2. Character not easily altered, so Lazarus not sent back to rich man's brothers.

   3. By our life here we determine our own eternity hereafter.

IV. *Character Based on Living Relationship with God.*

   1. Rich man self-centered, self-contained, isolated.

   2. Practical atheism means rule of head, not of heart.

   3. Practical Christianity means rule of heart—love **God**, love brother.

V. *Character has Everything Needful for Formation.*

   1. Not more light, but faithfulness to light we have.

   2. Light not deficient, but heart often averse (cf. 2 Pet. 1:3).

   3. If we follow self-devised plan instead of God's, we suffer, but see John 13:17.

   4. Character cannot grow in atmosphere of anxiety—all forces go in other direction. Someone has said: "Character requires a still air." *Illus.*: Gardener answers inquiry about stake beside rose tree: "It is not there to keep top steady, but to keep roots still, or tree will not grow."

> "Take time to be holy,
> The world rushes on;
> Spend much time in secret,
> With Jesus alone;
> By looking to Jesus,
> Like Him thou shalt be;
> Thy friends in thy conduct
> His likeness shall see."

Conclusion

   1. Faithfulness in the use of what we have will bring satisfaction with Christ, with His Holy Spirit, and with life.

   2. If what the conscience sees the will acts upon, we are led on to higher things.

   3. Character thus formed stands the test here and hereafter.

   4. If we are faithful to what we know, we shall receive more knowledge and more power. "If any man willeth to do His will, he shall know of the doctrine" (John 7:17 R.V.). "Then shall we know, if we follow on to know the Lord (Hos. 6:3).

67

"THOUGH ONE ROSE FROM THE DEAD"
(Luke 16:31)

THERE is a remarkable stress laid on the fact that our Lord showed Himself after His resurrection only to His disciples (cf. Acts 10:41). Why? Surely the best way to convince, confuse and confound His enemies would have been to appear before their very eyes in resurrection form. No, for "neither will they be persuaded though one rose from the dead." The resurrection was a manifestation not realized except by those who recognized—

I. *Our Lord's Purpose*

   1. Not to compel, which is in fact to repel, but—
   2. To impel—to "persuade"—
      a. Giving reasons—consider
      b. Making impressions—remember
      c. Eliciting decisions—resolve
   3. To preach repentance—change of mind leading to change of heart—not regret, but revolution.
   4. To overcome Satan's dissuasions, of which there are so many.

II. *Our Lord's Method*

   1. Making adequate provision—"Moses and the prophets," revelation of God to prepare us.
   2. Urging faithful use. In craving talents and opportunities he has not, man often neglects those he has—e.g., business, books, ministry.

III. *Our Lord's Warning*

Hopelessness for future if God's provision neglected. But suppose one did rise from the dead!

1. Could he give better credentials? How to prove he was from God—by what testimony? Cemeteries contain wicked dead as well as good.

   a. By words? Can be deceptive.

   b. By works? Even wicked spirits have power.

2. Could he preach more vital truths?

   a. If from God, either same or different. If same, what advantage?

   b. If different, how shall he be accepted?

3. Could he come more convincingly?

   a. Supernatural appearance is likely to cause panic, not conviction.

   b. Mediaeval church did believe in ghosts and superstitions. Was it any more religious? Are such people so today?

   c. Persons have come from grave: e.g., Witch of Endor, Daughter of Jairus, Son of Widow of Nain, Lazarus of Bethany. Have large numbers believed in Christ because of these? *Illus.*: Chink of light will arouse waking man, but full light often makes no impression on one sleeping heavily.

Conclusion

Now, besides Moses and the Prophets, we do have Christ who "rose from the dead," but it is still "one by one" they come who believe on Him. "Now is the day of salvation"—"Today if we will hear His voice."

68

THE HEALING OF THE TEN LEPERS
(Luke 17:11-19)

THIS IS another incident of the long, slow journey to Jerusalem, and at this point Luke's narrative commences a new cycle (see 9:51 and 13:22). The route was notable as the scene of former labors, but no particulars of place are available, the interest being in the story itself. Like other miracles, it is a record of the past with lessons for the future—"symbolic history."

I. *The Great Need* (vs. 11,12)
1. In unknown village, afflicted company providentially met the Lord as He journeyed to His death with His face "steadfastly set" (Mark 10:32).
2. Group consisted evidently of nine Jews and one Samaritan. Notwithstanding hostile relations of two peoples, these representatives had been united by common disease. "Adversity makes strange bedfellows."
3. "Stood afar off" because of leprosy—loathsome, destructive, infectious, often incurable, almost always fatal (cf. Lev. 13:46), and therefore type of sin.

II. *The Earnest Cry* (v.13)
1. In dire need lepers "lifted up their voices"—because of being "afar off."
2. Cry of their hearts is significant:
   a. "Jesus, Master"—suggesting faith in Christ and recognition of His authority: "Jesus"—Saviour from sin; "Master"—superintendent, authoritative one. Believed

He could and would heal—when this, no doubt of issue.

    b. "Have mercy on us"—suggesting consciousness of sin and need of pardon.

III. *The Prompt Response* (v.14)

    1. Quick observation—woes experienced by suffering humanity recognized by compassionate Deity.

    2. Definite direction:

        a. To honor law and recognize authorities.

        b. To give adversaries another proof.

        c. To test faith already expressed—reversing usual order. Here trust without sight—faith in word followed by obedience to will always sure way of blessing. Note variety of Christ's methods—may well characterize our evangelism too.

IV. *The Immediate Outcome* (v.14)

    1. Believed—although "afar off"

    2. Obeyed—still "afar off"

    3. Experienced—Christ's power felt at distance.

    4. Imagine glow of health returning to poor leprous bodies!

    5. Then followed restoration to society and readmission to temple.

V. *The Grateful Acknowledgment* (vs. 15,16)

By one of ten:

    1. Experience—"saw that he was healed."

    2. Expression—

        a. "Turned back"—after first instinctive start to obey.

        b. "With a loud voice glorified God"—cf. probable faint voice of leprosy.

        c. "Fell down . . . at His feet" to praise—cf. "afar off" (v. 12) to pray.

d. "And he was a Samaritan"—evidently unexpected reaction. But Lowell speaks of "the deep religion of a thankful heart."

Illus.: Serene old lady, asked her secret, told of "pleasure book" in which she set down things like beautiful sunset, comforting text, kind word. Trifles? Yes, but thanking God for such keeps mind sweet and heart content.

VI. *The Sad Disappointment*

1. Christ's wonder expressed, though He knew both how many and where they had gone (cf. 8:45), to impress lesson of gratitude. Should precede even obedience, for presumably nine had started for Jerusalem or nearest priest. But Samaritan returned first.

2. Christ's pain at ingratitude of nine—possible explanations are:

a. Underestimating their blessing.
b. Forgetting their Benefactor.
c. Considering acknowledgment unnecessary.

All are selfish—but cf. our own prayers without acknowledgment of past answers—safety, guidance, help, healing, etc. We may be startled if we consider.

> "There is no God," the foolish saith,
> But none—"There is no sorrow,"
> And nature oft the cry of faith
> In bitter need will borrow.
> Eyes which the preacher could not school
> By wayside graves are raised,
> And hearts say, "God be pitiful!"
> Which n'er said, "God be praised!"

3. Christ's selflessness marked—"give glory to God." Lost sight of self in desire for Father's glory (cf. John 17:4).

VII. *The Full Reward*

Expressed gratitude acknowledged by—

1. Higher position attained — symbolized by command "Arise."

2. Larger blessing given—
   a. Physical soundness confirmed.
   b. Moral health included.
3. Nobler life assured.

Illus.: Old lady told inquirer she felt better because she had moved to healthier place—had left Grumble Alley for Thankful Street—and change agreed with her!

Conclusion

1. *Sin is still troubling.*
   Whether we realize it or not—like speck in apple spreading decay, or like start of leprosy.
2. *Christ is still passing.*
   Opportunity for help and salvation still open.
3. *Grace is still working.*
   Only Christ can help and save.

> "The healing of His seamless dress
> Is by our beds of pain."

4. *Ingratitude is still surprising.*
   a. Its Forms—many:
      (1) Thinking of gifts, not Giver.
      (2) Taking benefits as matter of course—e.g., health until sickness, safety until accident.
      (3) Ignoring many mercies in single sorrow—cf. "all" in Gen. 42:36 with Rom. 8:28.
      (4) Forgetting answers to prayer and failing to follow specific prayers with equally specific praise.

   b. Its Causes—also many. Now, as in case of the nine lepers:
      (1) Callousness—underestimating benefit.
      (2) Pride—considering thanks unnecessary because only getting due.
      (3) Selfishness—making sure of blessing first.
      (4) Thoughtlessness—not reflecting.
      (5) Cowardice—fearing Christ's foes.

(6) Calculation—wondering if response will involve discipleship.

(7) Weakness—willing if others are, but not otherwise.

(8) Procrastination—putting off till later, and sometimes till too late.

(9) Worldliness—forgetting Christ in other interests.

5. *Gratitude is still glorifying.*
   a. We note what came to Samaritan leper through his acknowledgment of Christ's mercy:
   (1) Larger blessing—complete healing.
   (2) Higher position—"afar off" to "feet of Jesus" to "arise."
   (3) Nobler life:
       (a) Consecration follows when God's love is sensed.
       (b) Duty changes aspect when thankfulness expressed.
       (c) Sorrow loses gloom when accepted thankfully as discipline.
       (d) Life is glorified when praise is keynote—cf. Rom. 12:1.

   b. We note what caused St. Paul to express thanks to God:
   (1) Redemption (2 Cor. 9:15)
   (2) Deliverance (Rom. 7:25)
   (3) Service (1 Tim. 1:12)
   (4) Victory (1 Cor. 15:57; 2 Cor. 2:14)
   (5) Kindness (2 Cor. 3:16; Phil. 1:3)
   (6) Obedience (Rom. 6:17)
   (7) Fellowship (2 Tim. 1:3)

If we are grateful for what grace gives gratis, let us—
Trust and take.
Think and thank.
Prize and praise.
Consider and confess.

69

TWO PARABLES ON PRAYER
(Luke 18:1-14)

Following the healing of the Ten Lepers, the opponents of our Lord questioned Him about the Kingdom of God (17:20). His reply to them was enigmatic, but He went on to inform His disciples as to His Second Coming which should usher in the Kingdom (17:22-37). Then come lessons on their right attitude meanwhile, in view of the great future, particularly in their prayer relationship with God. If chapter 11 was a general treatise on prayer, this one gives some special messages. It is in two parts, verses 1-8 and 9-14, and between these there is a close connection.

I. *Perseverance* (vs. 1-8)

    A. *The Principle Enforced* (v.1)

        1. Positively—"men ought always to pray."

        2. Negatively—"not to faint" ("never lose heart"—Weymouth). H. J. Horn says: "It is only the *always* that will prevent the fainting."

    B. *The Principle Illustrated* (vs. 2-6)

        1. The judge—"feared not God, neither regarded man" —thus characterized so as to suggest attention not to be expected—regardless of plea or duty, thought habitually only of own ease.

        2. The woman—"a widow"—therefore greatest possible claim on justice—continued pressing until heard.

        3. The reward—"I will avenge her." At last he relents. but only "lest . . . she weary me"—"unjust" indeed.

C. *The Principle Applied* (vs. 6-8)

1. The first question. Is not God altogether different from this unrighteous judge—concerned for needs of "His own elect" even though He waits with longsuffering for them? D. M. McIntyre says: "It is a daring comparison to liken God to this unjust judge. But the point of the parable is, even he is moved by importunate prayer to do that which is so pathetically pleaded for . . . Into the reasons for delay the Lord does not enter . . . But what He wishes us to understand is the power of persistent and believing prayer—prayer that will not accept a refusal, prayer that will not be denied."

2. The second question. In view of great future already referred to (17:22-37), will such faith as this, enduring long waiting, be in existence at time of Christ's Second Coming? Does not and cannot mean no faith in Him at all. Answer already given by anticipation in 17:26. Plummer says: "The majority, not only of mankind, but of Christians, will be absorbed in worldly pursuits, and only a few will endure to the end."

II. *Pride and Penitence* (vs. 9-14)

A. *Pride* (vs. 9-12)

1. Separating. Pharisee stood out among devout Temple worshippers, but did not really pray—struck attitude and posed conspicuously.

2. Despising. Said "God"—not even reverent address; "thank," but merely conventional—no sense of sin, so no glow of love or gratitude—arrogant and uncharitable. Measured himself with worst in sight, which is easy—not surprising to find him superior in some ways to publican. Also easy to feel glad one does not sin in one way while one is sinning in another and perhaps worse way. Spirit of Pharisee not

yet dead—many apt to think themselves better than others, while in sight of God they are worse than nothing.

3. Boasting. Used "I" five times—did more than law required: fasting twice in week instead of once in year; gave tithes of all instead of simply tithes of field and stall. Not only knew this but determined God should know it from him, and also others. Motive wrong, standard false, conduct superficial. Spurgeon said of man he knew: "I always believed he was perfect till he told me so."

B. *Penitence* (vs. 13,14)

1. Self-distrusting. In marked contrast, both in attitude and feeling.

2. Confessing. Words striking evidence of consciousness of God's righteousness and own sinfulness.

3. Receiving. "Mercy" for which he prayed. Not surprising Christ says he was "justified rather than the other"—humble distrust of self vs. arrogant exaltation.

Conclusion

1. *Prayer should be importunate.*

   a. In spite of delay, reasons for which may include:

      (1) Raising faith to highest possibility.

      (2) Perfecting character: elevating, enriching, testing, eliminating hindrances.

      (3) Growth in grace slow—no fruit unless first blossom—no top storey first. Cf. child wanting full knowledge at once; so we, shamed by fall, want full grace at once. But character not like ready-made suit of clothes—rather, process of formation. If need is humility, first humiliation, failure; if need is spirituality, something opposite felt first and overcome; if need is to be like Christ, there

is cup to be drunk and baptism to be baptized with.

b. Results of delay should include:

(1) Trust

(2) Patience

(3) Strength

(4) Courage

(5) Joy

2. *Prayer should be sincere.*

a. God demands reality.

b. But there are hindrances, such as: self-conceit, spite, grudges, prickings of conscience, idols in heart, inconsistency of life, lack of real sense of need.

3. *Note blend and balance in this.*

a. God is our Father—be persevering; our Father is God —be sincere.

b. Confidence of children, yet reverence of subjects.

c. Familiarity, and yet holiness.

And thus coming, yielding, praying, trusting, we may know the power of prayer and the meaning of "Ask what ye will." Our desires being yielded up to Christ, we shall be influenced by the Holy Spirit to pray for what *He* desires, and His Word will reveal what that is. So "rest in the Lord and wait patiently for Him, and He shall give thee the desires of thine heart"; "ask, and"—in God's time and way—"ye shall receive, that your joy may be full."

70

CHILDLIKE OR CHILDISH?
(Luke 18:15-30)

In ALL of these incidents we may trace the urgency of those who may have feared it was the last time that Jesus would pass their way. In the present passage, we see children brought for blessing, a young man coming for discussion, and the lessons from both encounters taught to the disciples.

I. *Childlikeness* (vs. 15-17)

   A. *Children Brought* (v.15)

      1. "Even their infants" (Moffatt's translation) is possible rendering of Greek, indicating parents' appraisal and approval of Jesus.

      2. Note parents' desire—babes' need—Christ's sufficiency.

   B. *Children Welcomed* (v.16)

      1. Disciples provoked by intrusive familiarity—impatient that such should be brought.

      2. But little children belong with loving Lord and merit His tender permission to come. To such belongs kingdom of God, not only to those of childlike natures (see following verse for this); and not to beautiful, strong children only—if any partiality, for plain, weak ones. Children Christ's until they reject Him, so not wise to tell them they are "children of wrath" and need conversion in adult sense. Cf. regeneration—often takes form of spiritual awakening rather than radical change of character, which is conversion.

I wonder if ever the children
  Who were blessed by the Master of old,
Forgot He had made them His treasures,
  The dear little lambs of His fold.
I wonder if, angry and willful,
  They wandered afar and astray,
The children whose feet had been guided
  So safe and so soon in the way.

One would think that the mothers at evening,
  Soft smoothing the silk-tangled hair,
And low leaning down to the murmur
  Of sweet, childish voices in prayer
Oft bade the small pleaders to listen,
  If haply again they might hear
The words of the gentle Redeemer,
  Borne swift to the reverent ear.

And my heart cannot cherish the fancy
  That ever those children went wrong,
And were lost from the peace and the shelter,
  Shut out from the feast and the song;
To the day of gray hairs they remembered,
  I think, how the hands that were riven
Were laid on their heads when Christ uttered,
  "Of such is the kingdom of heaven."

He has said it to you, little darling,
  Who spell it in God's Word today;
You, too, may be sorry for sinning,
  You also believe and obey:
And 'twill grieve the dear Saviour in heaven
  If one little child shall go wrong—
Be lost from the fold and the shelter,
  Shut out from the feast and the song.

                        (Margaret E. Sangster)

C. *Childlikeness Commended* (v. 17)

  1. The heavenly kingdom—"receive the kingdom of God" —welcoming God's rule and authority into heart and life.

  2. The lowly door—"enter"—by trust and humility. **Child** starts with what adults have already lost, innocence.

II. *Worldly-mindedness* (vs. 18-23)

  A. *Eternal Life Sought* (vs. 18-21)

    1. Question blended good and evil.

a. True earnestness and self-dissatisfaction — consciousness of unattained bliss and real longing for it— readiness to take pains—confidence in Christ's guidance. But—

b. Notion that eternal life is won by good deeds, and error as to ability to do these—superficial estimate of goodness and overconfidence in own power.

2. The Lord's reply.

a. Polite compliment shows low estimate of word "good."

b. Deepening and widening of conception of good awakens consciousness of imperfection in self. God only good and all good from Him.

c. Christ then meets young man on own ground of law, and refers him to usual duties.

3. The young man's rejoinder.

a. Shade of disappointment and impatience in protestation.

b. Thought he would be ordered to do something brilliant and unusual, but instead, ordinary obligations. Cf. Naaman (2 Kings 5:13).

B. *Eternal Life Offered* (v.22)

1. Test applied—soul lacking.

2. Test too great—why? Not riches alone.

3. Test disclosed there was trouble over riches—but that was not main trouble.

4. Test involved revelation of life—crux was "Follow" —follow Jesus, an outcast?

C. *Eternal Life Jeopardized* (v.23)

1. "Went away"—how? "Sorrowful" (cf. Matt. 19:22); "grieved" (Mark 10:22). We may imagine him also indignant, unsettled, dejected.

2. "Went away"—where? Into the world, to former companions, finally to grave and judgment. Good in-

tentions do not count—mere conviction of sin does not atone.

> "The wave is mighty but the spray is weak,
> And often thus our great and high resolves,
> In their forming as an ocean wave,
> Break in the spray of nothing."

III. *Complete Surrender* (vs. 24-30)
  A. *Surrender Possible* (vs. 24-27)
    1. Way difficult—especially for rich.
    2. Possibility divine—even if impossibility for unaided humankind. Andrew Murray calls this learning two lessons: "There is many a man who has learned the lesson, *It is impossible with men,* and then he gives up in helpless despair, and lives a wretched Christian life, without joy or strength or victory. And why? Because he does not humble himself to learn that other lesson: *With God all things are possible."*

  B. *Surrender Made* (v.28)
    1. Disciples left all—not much, but all to them. God's store includes "mites" (cf. 21:1-4).
    2. Disciples followed Christ—broke with world, which is real test (cf. v.22).

  C. *Surrender Rewarded* (vs. 29,30)
    1. Earthly increase promised.
    2. Heavenly blessings assured.
    Almost naive self-congratulation of verse 28 not rebuked —rather made appeal to faithfulness.

Conclusion

The connection between these two incidents—the coming of the children and the conversation with the young man— is the emphasis on qualification for discipleship. This was fulfilled in the first but not in the second. The key is in verse 17, the word "receive" (cf. Psa. 116:12,13). Let us contrast characteristics of childlikeness with those of childishness:

1. *Childlikeness*

    a. Love. Child cherished for months before spark of returned love kindled—believer's affection long enlisted by God (cf. 1 John 4:19).

    b. Confidence. Child, sensing dependence on and safety in care of parents, confides in them—believer trusts in Christ.

    c. Humility. Child's intelligence awakening to need of knowledge, he is willing to learn—believer eager to be taught in spiritual things.

    d. Obedience. Child, learning to do as told, is ready to obey—believer must also, sometimes by difficult lessons.

Thus childlikeness includes love, dependence, humility. obedience.

2. *Childishness*

Rich young man was example of—

    a. Selfishness—no thought of others or of God.

    b. Independence—wayward desire to go own way.

    c. Self-sufficiency—made own plans and looked out for self.

    d. Disobedience—went away because owned no authority.

Thus childishness means individual has no love for benefactor; having no sense of dependence, feels no impulse to trust; is unwilling to learn; and is not ready to obey. This attitude is not manly and he who displays it can never enter kingdom of God. Instead, humility is necessity for entrance, a power in continuing, and a secret in growing. Is our attitude, therefore, expressed in the words of Psalm 131:1,2: "Lord, my heart is not haughty, nor mine eyes lofty: neither do I exercise myself in great matters, or in things too high for me. Surely I have behaved and quieted myself, as a child"?

71

A BLIND MAN SEES
(Luke 18:35-43)

Bishop Temple used to say that the difference between the "treasure hid in a field" and the "pearl of great price" in Matthew 13:44-46 represents a difference between men in relation to the Kingdom of God. The "treasure" had to be dug for, the "pearl" was in plain sight; so men come to God in different ways. Some are unexpectedly met by Christ, some consciously seek Him even as He is seeking them. Thus, all conversions are represented by these two men in and near Jericho—the blind man outside and Zaccheus on a street of the town (see next Study). Now note how the healing of the blind man is parabolic of the sinner who seeks the Saviour and the Saviour who receives the sinner.

I. *The Sinner* (vs. 35-39)

A. *Sad Condition.*

1. Blind—eyes out of relationship to light though made for each other—so God and soul.

2. Helpless—begging because unable to work for living.

B. *Sudden Hope*

1. Circumstances: crowd, noise, inquiry, answer, opportunity.

2. Many such as he, seizing opportunity for selves, so why not he?

C. *Sincere Prayer*

1. Personal—own words, well-aimed, real. "Son of David" showed belief in Christ, whereas careless bystanders called Him merely "Jesus of Nazareth" (v.37).

2. True way to blessing—realize need and express it.

D. *Splendid Earnestness*

1. Hindrances deepened determination to use his only chance.

2. Earnestness often tested by Satan's hindrances.

N.B. Three conditions of meeting Jesus: need felt, reality shown, surrender made. Have we met them?

II. *The Saviour* (vs. 40-43)

A. *Special Interest*

1. Circumstances: taking last journey with face set—yet stood still upon hearing that cry.

2. God's attitude still—ruling world and yet listening for man's cry.

B. *Stirring Invitation*

1. Told people to bring blind man—thereby teaching humanity; spoke to man individually—thereby awakening hope.

2. Christ uses every means.

C. *Strong Encouragement*

1. Question: "What?" Test: "wilt."

2. Cf. Zebedee's sons in corresponding chapters of Matthew and Mark (Matt. 20:21; Mark 10:36).

D. *Saving Grace*

1. Sight immediate and perfect.
2. Satisfaction—assurance—peace.

N.B. Three consequences of meeting Jesus: immediate salvation, instant obedience, instinctive praise. Are these ours?

Conclusion

1. *Jesus is still passing by.*

   What is He to you—"Jesus of Nazareth," or "Jesus, Son of David"?

2. *Jesus is still able to bless.*
   Are you spiritually blind?

3. *Jesus will soon have passed by.*

   Do you realize that for you it may be now or never? "Not yet" may be "too late"—therefore, come now!

> "I heard the voice of Jesus say,
>   'I am this dark world's Light,
> Look unto Me, thy morn shall rise
> And all thy day be bright.'
> I came to Jesus and I found
> In Him my Star, my Sun,
> And in that Light of life I'll walk
> Till travelling days are done."

72

JESUS AND ZACCHEUS
(Luke 19:1-10)

CHRIST is now within seventeen miles of Jerusalem, and this is the story of the last recorded conversion except one (that of the thief on the cross, 23:40-43) during Christ's lifetime. It is a fine instance of His adaptability to individual cases. In these days of "conservation," "reclamation," "efficiency," we may learn a valuable lesson in rescuing a lost soul:— morally lost, for Zaccheus was sinful; intellectually lost, for he did not know who Jesus was; and socially lost, for he was of the despised class of publicans. But Zaccheus was also—

I. *Seeking Jesus* (vs. 1-4)
   A. *A Despised Calling*
      1. Zaccheus was what was sometimes known as "middleman," one with ordinary tax-gatherers under him, in Jericho, chief custom house of Romans—not salaried, but lived by "farming" taxes, with many chances for graft and fleecing.
      2. Office much hated by people—feelings natural.
      3. So evidently Zaccheus had acquired wealth by wrong methods.

   B. *An Earnest Desire*
      1. Though "chief among the publicans" and "rich," he for some reason wanted "to see Jesus who He was."
      2. More than curious—evidently inclined to be penitent and drawn to Christ.
      3. Now was opportunity of lifetime—"There is a tide in the affairs of men which, taken at the flood, leads on to fortune."

C. *A Strenuous Effort*
1. Personal deficiency in height led to "sycamore tree"—not American tree of that name, but Egyptian fig with low branches.
2. Disregard for appearances proves earnestness.
3. Someone has said: "Who dares to call the sycamore barren? One tree, at least, was laden with good fruit."

II. *Receiving Jesus* (vs. 5-7)
A. *Jesus Calling*
1. Use of name in Christ's call suggests Zaccheus was well known to others beside Himself.
2. At any rate, call was personal and ignored usual indifference of tax-gatherers to religion.
3. Only instance of Christ's inviting Himself—knew He would be welcome, for He never forces Himself on unwilling.
4. Words "make haste," "today," and "must" suggest pressing necessity because only opportunity for Zaccheus—peremptory but blessed.

B. *Zaccheus Responding*
1. Promptly—"made haste."
2. Heartily—"received Him."
3. Gladly—"joyfully."

C. *Opponents Complaining*
1. Ground of Pharisaic complaint same as in 15:2.
2. Reason for penitential consolation.
3. Justification of Divine condescension.

III. *Confessing Jesus* (vs. 8-10)
A. *Open Profession*
1. Response to complaint fearless statement proving genuineness.
2. Public avowal—to people as well as to Christ.

3. Words usually interpreted as future purpose, influenced by Christ and proving repentance, but verbs "give" and "restore" in present tense and, together with words "stood" and "behold," may indicate Zaccheus not of character described by enemies. This would mean he already had become penitent before Christ came, and was showing it now. Much to be said for this view.

B. *Assured Salvation*

1. But whatever view is correct, the Lord assured Zaccheus of full salvation:

   a. Present—"this day"

   b. Personal—"he also"

   c. Domestic—"this house"

2. Christ stood with him against murmurers—word "also" implies "as well as you," though they regarded man as outcast.

3. Perhaps significant use of "he is," not "he has become," strengthening view in A.3. above.

4. "Son of Abraham"—spiritually true descendant of "father of the faithful" (3:8; 13:16; Rom. 4:16; Gal. 3:7-9).

C. *Realized Redemption*

1. Repentance had been elicited.

   "For what is true repentance but in thought,
   Not even in inmost thought, to think again
   The sins that made the past so pleasant to us?"

2. Then Christ stated definitely this was just the case for Him to deal with—"for"—since He had come for very purpose of saving lost.

3. So He went on His way to Jerusalem, leaving behind in Jericho—

a. A rejoicing soul.

b. A happy home.

c. A bright prospect.

d. A clear witness to Himself.

Conclusion

Compare two rich men (see 18:18-25), both earnestly seeking. The young ruler would not part with his wealth, but Zaccheus was willing to do so and thus could indeed "inherit eternal life" (18:18).

1. This Seeker had position, means, desire, zeal.
2. The Saviour spoke personally, urgently, definitely, graciously.
3. The Saved had joy, courage, consecration, assurance.

Jesus is still passing through our city, our village, our district. It is for us to receive Him, to rejoice in Him, and to reproduce Him in our lives and in our homes.

73

LIFE'S SYCAMORES
(Luke 19:4)

I<small>T WOULD</small> seem probable that the conversion of Zaccheus and the parable that followed it were both events of the
day we now call Palm Sunday (see vs. 1,11,28). Christ's entry
into Jerusalem is the more remarkable when compared with
all His preceding earthly life, during which He kept in retreat,
checked curiosity, and enjoined silence as to His mighty works.
On this day, however, He not only was sought out, but publicly
offered Himself, permitting acknowledgment and even praise.
Why? Because the event marked the last public presentation
of Christ as Messiah to the Jews in Jerusalem, and may be compared with the opening of His ministry as recorded in John
2:13-25. He was thus the center of observation not only on
the part of an individual like Zaccheus, but also for masses of
people such as those described as "all the city" (Matt. 21:10),
and for particular groups such as the Greeks mentioned in John
12:20-22. So ought it to be now, for there are many saying,
"We would see Jesus." But how can men see Him? By climb-
ing the sycamore trees He has placed along the path that they
travel from the here and now to the hereafter.

I. *Some "Sycamores" of the Christian*
  1. *Holy Scripture.*
      a. Its inner sanctuary opens only to worshipper.
      b. Christ the great Subject of search and research:
          (1) In Old Testament He is desired, foretold, pictured.
          (2) In New Testament, He is shown to be Prophet,
          Priest, and King.

2. *Private Prayer*
   a. Lifts us to heaven—invited.
   b. Brings heaven to us—anointed.
3. *Public Worship*
   a. God's house—"to see . . . as I have seen Thee in the sanctuary" (Psa. 63:2).
   b. God's ordinances—"in breaking of bread, and in prayers" (Acts 2:42).
4. *Personal Trust*
   a. Unbelief and distrust close eyes (cf. 24:16).
   b. Trust-sight—believing is seeing, in Christian life.

5. *Humble Confession*
   a. Men say, "Confession is good for the soul" (cf. Rom. 10:9-11). Silence is not "golden" here.
   b. Tell others and in telling be blessed.
6. *Complete Obedience*
   a. Imitation of Christ (cf. 9:23).
   b. Faithfulness to Christ (cf. John 7:17).
7. *Devoted Service*
   a. Work a necessity (cf. 2 Thess. 3:10).
   b. Work a blessing (cf. Gal. 6:4).

These aids are near us, available, reliable, but there are difficulties in the way of non-Christians. Spiritually, they are like Zaccheus, short of stature, and, also like him, burdened by sin and obliged to face the sneers of others. So, then, we who have named the Name of Christ ought to be—

II. *"Sycamores" for the World*
  1. *Individually.*

   Two necessary features in a tree to be climbed:
   a. It must be accessible. So we must be available to those who need our message and our help.
   b. It must be strong. So we must be able to bear the burdens of others.

2. *Corporately.*

    a. Others must see Christ in our church (cf. 1 Cor. 14:25).

    b. We must show them that we are one (cf. John 17:21) with other "branches of Christ's Church."

Conclusion

To climb God's sycamore trees—to be God's sycamore trees —is:

1. A Responsibility.
2. A Privilege.
3. A Joy.

If we climb—if we encourage others to climb—we shall each see Jesus and hear His tender voice say: "Today I must abide at thy house . . . This day is. salvation come to this house."

74

SOUGHT AND SAVED
(Luke 19:10)

T HE SUPREME message of the story of Zaccheus lies in this verse. It consists of a single, simple sentence. Says Joseph Parker: "The whole Gospel is in these words, and yet there is not a word amongst them of two syllables . . . You cannot revise them into anything grander. If you touch it, you spoil it . . . This is infinity brought down to a scale fitted to our poor vision."

I. *The Lost*

　1. *In Sin*

　　a. How? To God, self, holiness, heaven.

　　b. Not only estranged, but guilty; not only disobedient, but cursed; not only polluted, but condemned; not only imperilled, but lost.

　2. *In the Crowd*

　　a. Zaccheus was evidently penitent, misjudged, lonely, full of doubt and fear.

　　b. Is it possible for man in business or public service to assert and maintain Christian life? Yes, for no department of life is outside application of moral principles:

　　　(1) Absolute and eternal distinction between right and wrong—wrong in morals cannot be right in business.

　　　(2) Absolute impossibility of separation between life on Sunday and life on weekdays. Christianity is not sphere of life, but atmosphere; not section of life, but influence that pervades whole field of it.

(3) Absolute necessity of truth at any cost—constant and complete righteousness in all dealings.

(4) Absolute observance of Golden Rule in business means law of love in life—essential feature of true brotherhood.

c. Some quotations: "The Ten Commandments will not budge" (James Russell Lowell); "(Theodore) Roosevelt did not discover the Ten Commandments, but the trouble came from his wanting to apply them to a lot of men who felt that they were outside those issues" (The Minneapolis Journal); "If Christ is not Lord of all, He is not Lord at all" (Hudson Taylor); "Whatsoever ye do, do all in the name of the Lord Jesus" (Col. 3:17).

II. *The Deliverer*

1. *The Son of Man Came.*

   a. Title suggests human sympathy.

   b. Word "came" suggests origin elsewhere, so Son of God as well.

2. *Why Did He Come?*

   To combine infinite love and infinite truth.

   a. Easy to glorify justice only—punishment, severity.

   b. Easy to glorify mercy only—pardon, causing contempt of law.

   c. But how bring two together? How restore without demoralizing? How can a pure God receive sinners?

   d. In Christ, in whom "mercy and truth are met together; righteousness and peace have kissed each other" (Psa. 85:10). Truth and righteousness say: "The soul that sinneth, it shall die" (Ezek. 18:4); mercy and peace say: "Seek the Lord, and ye shall live" (Amos 5:6). God thus both just and justifier (Rom. 3:26).

III. *The Work*
  1. *Seeking*
      a. Anticipating need—cf. Jesus and Zaccheus.
      b. Characterizing Christianity—"the Father seeketh" (John 4:23).

  2. *Saving*
      a. Deliverance from guilt and power of sin.
      b. Restoration to fellowship with God—love and sympathy creates bond which increases with knowledge.

Conclusion

Here is the old yet ever new Gospel. We who have been sought, saved and satisfied must seek others and show them that Christ wants to save them too.

75

THE PARABLE OF THE POUNDS
(Luke 19:11-27)

CHRIST's teaching may be said to fall under five broad headings: the Kingdom of God, the personal life of believers, His own Cross, His Second Coming, and the coming of the Holy Spirit. The parables of His last week on earth were all on the fourth of these subjects, His Coming, and they were invariably marked by solemn warnings to His disciples in the light of a great future. This parable of the pounds was clearly addressed to a mixed audience (v.11), whose hopes were high concerning the Messianic Kingdom, but who had no idea of the Cross. The parable was intended to correct these false conceptions and to teach that Christ's supreme requirement of His followers is faithfulness. It should be carefully compared and contrasted with the parable of the talents in Matthew 25:14-30 (see Conclusion).

I. *The Lord Testing* (vs. 12-15)

   A. *The Journey*

      1. Why? Our Lord evidently used current incident as basis for His story. Jericho, where He was speaking, was site of palace of Archelaus, son of Herod the Great.

      2. Whither? At about this time, Herod died and Archelaus journeyed to Rome to obtain kingdom from Emperor Augustus.

      3. What then? We must not press details, but we see from parables of unjust steward and unjust judge that even cruel, unworthy men were used by Christ in contrast to teach spiritual lessons. The "nobleman," of

course, is a type of Christ Himself, going into "far country" of heaven (cf. Acts 1:10,11).

B. *The Servants*

1. Possession—interesting description, "servants of his," implying our Lord's claim on our lives.

2. Commission—with equal gifts, amount being something like fifteen dollars, and told to "occupy" it, or trade with it, keep it busy. This suggests gift of Gospel, which is same to all professing Christians, to be known, and intended for use in behalf of selves and of others (cf. 1 Pet. 4:10).

3. Position—one of personal responsibility, full liberty, ample opportunity, future accountability.

C. *The Citizens*

1. Then. Those over whom the "nobleman" was to reign —the Jews, who were very hostile to Archelaus and who did exactly what is mentioned in verse 14.

2. Later. They would have same attitude towards "the King of the Jews" (cf. Mark 15:12,13).

3. Now. Jews still hostile to Jesus Christ, their Messiah.

D. *The Return*

1. Certain—Christ is sure to return, for New Testament full of teaching about His Coming.

2. Definite—
   a. He will demand from His followers account of stewardship essential for master to know use of his money and type of business engaged in.
   b. He will also deal with His enemies (cf. Rev. 19:5).

II. *The Lord Rewarding* (vs. 16-19)

A. *The First Servant*

1. Spoke humbly—"thy pound," not "I"—no reference to himself.

2. Had done best possible with what he had—faithfulness.

3. Given ten cities for ten pounds—greater opportunity, from trader to ruler—and also words of commendation.

4. Great principle of Christian living—faithfulness in ordinary life brings about infinitely great results by grace of God:

   a. According to power and opportunity (16:10).

   b. In work (12:42).

   c. Persisted in to end (Rev. 2:10).

   Illus.: General Howard of Civil War fame was told by General Sherman on eve of victory review in Washington that the general whom he had superseded would march at head of his Army of the Tennessee. When he protested, General Sherman said: "You are a Christian—your rival makes no such profession." Said Howard: "That alters everything for me—I will concur." "All right," replied Sherman, "and *you* will ride at my side at head of combined armies." And there Howard rode, in spite of his protests, at front of all.

B. *The Second Servant*

   1. Also spoke humbly—"thy pound."

   2. But evidently not so thorough or zealous—less in earnest.

   3. Given same proportion of cities—but no commendation. Might have been equally faithful, but had somehow failed.

   4. Like Christian worker who does "second-best." Cf. distinction in Rom. 16:12 between "labour" and "laboured much"; also in Neh. 3:5 between "the Tekoites" and "their nobles."

5. Rewards in parable symbolize rewards of grace taught in New Testament. While salvation is wholly of grace, yet our use of God's gifts in daily conduct and service will be tested before judgment seat of Christ (cf. 1 Cor. 3:13-15).

III. *The Lord Punishing* (vs. 20-27)

A. *The Third Servant*

1. Brought pound, carefully kept, and handed it back —inactivity during master's absence.

2. Justified himself—distrust of master's character.

3. But master dealt with him according to own statement, because even on that ground money should have been put into bank for interest as well as for safe-keeping.

4. To Christians, this is message concerning perversion of character, none-use of opportunity, neglect of what we possess without glaring or open sin. Someone has said answer to question, "What must I do to be lost?" is, "Nothing."

5. Striking that pound was taken from this servant and given to one who already had ten—indicates another great law of Kingdom of God, that faithfulness is guarantee of increased power, while unfaithfulness assures loss of what was once possessed (see Greek negative in v.26).

6. People pray, "Lord, give us faith." How can that prayer be answered? Will God send small portion to be used until finished, when more must be asked for? No; when our Lord's disciples said, "Lord, increase our faith," He answered, "If ye had faith, ye might . . ." (17:5,6). In other words, "Use the faith that you have and then you will have capacity to exercise more."

7. Difference between three servants in parable was due to faithfulness or lack of it, and this also applies to

our employment of Divine grace.   Possible to receive—
   a. Both commendation and great opportunity, or—
   b. Proportionate opportunity with no commendation, or—
   c. Condemnation because grace cannot lie dormant in soul.
   8. God's gifts intended for service, not for selfishness, and still less for shrinking. Our Master is not "an austere man" (v.21), but He certainly is "Jesus Christ the righteous" (1 John 2:1).

B. *The Enemies*
   1. Their hostility futile and fatal. Cf. what befell Jews in destruction of Jerusalem by Titus, forty years after this parable was uttered.

   2. Also note what is still happening to Jewish people today; but—

   3. All Christ's enemies will be dealt with in future (cf. Rev. 19:11-21).

   4. Death and destruction are always end of those at enmity with God (cf. Rom. 8:6,7).

Conclusion

Two principles of life will be taken into account at our Lord's Return:

1. *Ability*—illustrated by Parable of the Talents (Matt. 25:14-30), the truth of nature, gifts obviously unequal (1 Pet. 4:11). Man who had two and gained two more has exactly same commendation and proportionate reward as one who had five and gained five more. Faithfulness in capacity and position, according to possession of natural gifts, is what God requires.

2. *Fidelity*—illustrated by Parable of the Pounds, the truth of grace, a gift equally divided (1 Pet. 4:10). Men, starting level, produced varying results because of varying faithfulness. Cf. Eph. 4:7. Believer to be—

a. Faithful—ambassador (Prov. 13:17); witness (Prov. 14:5); servant (Matt. 24:45); steward (1 Cor. 4:2); minister (Col. 1:7).

b. Full of faith—one who trusts God's faithfulness will be faithful himself. New Testament emphatic on great truth of faithfulness of God: in connection with forgiveness (1 John 1:9); temptation (1 Cor. 10:13); protection (2 Thess. 3:3); sanctification (1 Thess. 5:23,24); and His Word is faithful (1 Tim. 4:9; Tit. 1:9).

Let us therefore judge Him faithful who has promised (Heb. 11:11), and He will count us faithful to be put into His ministry (1 Tim. 1:12); and then others will judge us to be faithful to the Lord (Acts 16:15).

76

JESUS WEEPS OVER JERUSALEM
(Luke 19:41-44)

I T IS often noted that Christ is not recorded to have smiled. But the fact that there is no such record does not imply that He never did. Could He have failed to smile lovingly at the little daughter of Jairus as He raised her from the dead, or into the innocent eyes of the children brought for His blessing? But these were not the only occasions for joy in His life. The fact is that He had a constant joy—in doing God's will (cf. Psa. 40:8). We are told He "rejoiced in spirit" (10:21) at human faith, and that He, "for the joy that was set before Him endured the cross" (Heb. 12:2). John writes that Christ spoke of "My joy" (John 15:11). It is scarcely likely that such high and holy feelings could have been experienced or expressed without a smile on that beautiful Face.

Yet, of necessity, the dark side of life was prominent in Christ's earthly experience, because of the nature of the work He came to do. So we read of His tears: "Jesus wept" (John 11:35) in the presence of death, and prayed "with strong crying and tears" (Heb. 5:7); and He is called "Man of sorrows" (Isa. 53:3). But no occasion for weeping was more remarkable than this one, on His last journey. Jericho and Bethany are behind, and He comes now to "the descent of the mount of Olives." Having received the acclaim of the crowds, He obtains His first view of the city where He is to meet His death. Amid the general rejoicing of the Passover season, His thoughts are far away. Let us dwell reverently on these tears of our Lord and try to realize their deep meaning.

I. *The Causes*

1. *Great Privileges Abused*

   a. Cf. Jerusalem in past. From David onward it was center of nation and of religion.

   b. Beautiful for situation—joy of whole earth.

   c. But now temple changed—no glory—feasts, but no reality.

   d. Sin, indifference, unreality, wilfulness supreme. *Cadno*

   e. Outward privileges—honor, renown—could not save.

2. *Great Possibilities Rejected*

   a. Days of opportunity—Christ had preached and worked there several times. *Boy Church*

   b. Days of brute force, of greatest and strongest—He humble, meek, quiet.

   c. Days of vice and hypocrisy—He rebuking sin.

   d. Days of worldly aspiration—He disappointment to Messianic hopes.

3. *Great Punishments Incurred*

   a. Ruin foreseen—Christ knew certainty of punishment.

   b. Knowing past, present, future of Jerusalem, He wept over it. *Ps 56. 8* *USA fall—our feeling*

II. *The Characteristics*

1. *Love*—because of Preciousness of Souls

   a. It is said love is blind—but Divine love farseeing.

   b. Christ's keen spiritual perception saw what dull human eyes could not see—potentialities of people.

2. *Pity*—because of Peril of Souls

   a. Their doom sealed when given up by Christ.

   b. How human and tender He was! How much He suffered!

   Illus.: Child said to mother: "Poor Mrs. Brown has lost her husband, and says she would like me to go in every day, because I comfort her so. But mother,

I don't *comfort* her—when she cries, I just put my cheek by hers and cry too!" If it is so with us **poor** human beings, how much more comforting to know that He, "in every pang that rends the heart," has His full share!

3. *Sorrow*—because of Persistence of His Soul
   a. Disappointed love and unsatisfied yearning blended.
   b. Longing to save and yet consciousness of rejection.
   c. Rebellious man can defeat wisdom, power, and purpose of God.

Conclusion Realization

Four things overlooked:

1. "Thy peace" (v.42) —reconciliation with God, harmony with self.
2. "Thy day" (v.42) —opportunity brief.
3. "Thine eyes" (v.42) —"There is life for a look at the Crucified One."
4. "Thy visitation" (v.44) —God's desire and endeavor to save.

Let us sit at Christ's feet until we learn the secret of His tears and, beholding the sins and sorrows of city and countryside, weep over them too. But let us not forget that the place of tears was the place of ascension and commission, in order that the Gospel might be preached not only "in Jerusalem," but "unto the uttermost part of the earth."

77

THE SEVEN DAYS
OF THE NEW TESTAMENT
(Luke 19:42)

Every careful student of God's Book of Nature can tell of beauties and wonders unnoticed by casual observers. The more careful his study, the closer his observation, the greater beauty and the more wonders does he see. The leaf, the moss, the petal, the eye—all reveal perfect adaptation to their objects and functions. It is the same with God's other Book—the Book of Revelation. The ordinary reader may think of it as uninteresting and even unintelligible, but the Christian student finds it full not only of blessing and power, but of wonder and beauty. And the closer and more minute the scrutiny, the more beauties will reward it—beauties of which the student had heretofore no conception.

Among these may be classed the many references in Scripture to the word "day." This word is used in different ways, two examples of which are: the seven days of Genesis, or of Creation; the seven days of the week, or of Providence. Let us now consider the seven days of the New Testament, or of Redemption, and we shall use a key word to characterize each.

I. *The Day of Jesus*
   1. Our Lord speaks in John 8:56 of "My day." This is on His human side and refers to period in which He lived on earth and wrought His work of redemption.
   2. It is a day now past, but at time He said these words He was in preparation for its full purpose and provision on Cross.

Key word: Reconciliation.

II. *The Day of Man*

    1. Marginal rendering (Greek) of 1 Corinthians 4:3 has phrase "man's day." Natural man now—

        a. Choked by worldliness (cf. Mark 4:19; Tit. 1:10).

        b. Darkened by ignorance (cf. Rom. 1:21; 1 John 2:11).

        c. Bound by Satan (cf. 13:16; Acts 26:18).

    2. Man acting as he likes—going his own way, independently of God, in—

        a. Separation from God.

        b. Enmity towards God.

        c. Rejection of God.

  Key word: Rebellion.

III. *The Day of Salvation*

    1. Paul speaks of this in 2 Cor. 6:2, quoting Isa. 49:8, and explaining that present dispensation is both "acceptable time" and "day of salvation."

    2. Note parallel—also in John 9:4 and 11:9, where we have—

        a. Day for working—i.e., ministering to others.

        b. Day for walking—i.e., manifesting our own salvation, which is, according to John 5:24:

            (1) Personal—"He that heareth My Word, and believeth on Him that sent me . . ."

            (2) Eternal—"hath everlasting life, . . ."

            (3) Complete—"and shall not come into condemnation; . . ."

            (4) Immediate—"but is passed from death unto life."

  Key word: Regeneration.

IV. *The Day of Christ*

    1. Paul speaks of this in Philippians 1:6. Christ, at His Second Coming, will be glorified—for His people, to His people, and with His people (2 Thess. 1:10). On that day there will be—

      a. Redemption (Eph. 4:30).

      b. Reckoning (1 Cor. 3:13).

      c. Revelation (Phil. 1:10).

      d. Rejoicing (Phil. 2:16).

  2. Antichrist will be on earth—Church gone—believers accepted, but not all acceptable (1 Cor. 3:15).

Key word: Reward.

V. *The Day of the Lord*

  1. According to Scripture, it is to be—

      a. Sudden (1 Thess. 5:2).

      b. Preceded by apostasy (2 Thess. 2:3).

      c. Cataclysmic (2 Pet. 3:10).

      d. Great and notable (Acts 2:20).

      e. Very terrible (Joel 2:11).

  2. Antichrist will be overcome—Christ's people with Him to end of Millennium. He and they gathered for—

      a. Victory (Rev. 17:14).

      b. Vengeance (Rev. 19:20).

Key word: Rule.

VI. *The Day of Judgment*

  1. This refers to judgment of Great White Throne. It is to be judgment according to—

      a. God's righteousness (Rom. 2:5).

      b. Men's secrets (Rom. 2:16).

      c. Men's works (Rev. 20:11-15).

  2. John tells us how to have no fear of it (1 John 4:17).

Key word: Reckoning.

VII. *The Day of God*

  1. When old heavens and earth shall be destroyed, and new ones take their place (2 Pet. 3:12,13).

  2. When God shall be all in all (1 Cor. 15:28).

  3. When God's Kingdom shall come (11:2; Matt. 6:10).

4. In meantime, He will keep believer's "deposit" (2 **Tim.** 1:12, Gr.).

Key word: Righteousness.

Conclusion

These seven "Days of Redemption" may be said to fall under two main headings, Present and Future:

1. *Present*

Within the words of our text—"This thy day"—are:

a. Reconciliation.

b. Rebellion.

c. Regeneration.

2. *Future.*

Within the words spoken by Isaiah (61:2), and significantly omitted by our Lord in His quotation of passage as applying to present (4:17-19) —"The day of vengeance of our God"—are:

a. Reward.

b. Rule.

c. Reckoning.

d. Righteousness.

Let us indeed know, in this *our* day, the things which belong unto our peace!

78

THE AUTHORITY OF CHRIST
(Luke 20:1—21:38)

I T WAS impossible for the leaders of Israel to ignore the remarkable effects of the teaching of Jesus Christ on their own city of Jerusalem, and so we find them coming with a demand that He should vindicate His position and justify His deeds. It was natural that they should require proof of a teacher's authority, though their insistence in this case was unquestionably due also to their intense animosity.

I. *Authority Required* (20:1-8)

1. Two questions by leaders (vs. 1,2):
   a. "By what authority . . . ?"
   b. "Who . . . gave . . . this authority?"
2. One question by Christ in return (vs. 3,4): "The baptism of John . . . from heaven, or of men?"
3. Two horns of dilemma for leaders (vs. 5,6):
   a. John ought to have been believed as from God and accepted, which they had not done, or—
   b. John ought to have been rejected as not from God, which they had done but would not declare, for fear of people, and lest they be convicted of wrong attitude to Baptist.
4. Two rejoinders (vs. 7,8):
   a. Leaders replied they did not know about origin of John's baptism.
   b. This naturally gave our Lord opportunity of declining to tell them origin of His authority.

II. *Authority Revealed* (20:9-16a)

Then Christ turned away, and what He would not say under leaders' unwarranted cross-examination He proclaimed to people through parable, though leaders were present and heard. While these were indifferent, uncomprehending, or downright malicious, Christ's own followers were sincere and able to understand precisely who, what and whence He was. Thus tables were turned on leaders. In following parable, God was represented by owner of vineyard, and story was summary of Jewish history, past and present:

1. *The Repudiated Servants* (vs. 9-12)
   a. Owner's arrangements—vineyard planted and let out to husbandmen before departure.
   b. Servants errand—three, one after another, sent at proper time to collect expected fruit.
   c. Husbandmen's crime — cruelties: beating, shameful treatment, wounding—rejection of both servants and master.

2. *The Rejected Son* (vs. 13-15)
   a. Owner's crowning effort—felt employees would surely reverence master's son and heir, even if not servants.
   b. Husbandmen's wicked plot—recognition of son led to conspiracy.
   c. Son's cruel murder—final rejection of owner in death of son.

3. *The Resultant Penalty* (v.16a)
   a. Owner's return certain.
   b. Husbandmen's destruction swift.
   c. Vineyard's assignment to others logical.

III. *Authority Resisted* (20:16b-19)

1. People's response to condemnation shows understanding and application of story. Says D. M. McIntyre: "The

parable of the vineyard laborers is one of the many proofs in the Synoptic Gospels that Jesus was the Son of God in the full significance of the term. He is the Heir, contrasted with all the prophets and psalmists who are servants: He is the Father's 'beloved Son' (v.12)."

2. Christ's solemn look and quick question, linking Psalm 118:22 and Daniel 2:34,35 to present situation, imply that this was exactly what was being done in rejection of Himself, and that leaders would suffer untold trouble in consequence.

3. They also recognized meaning of parable and Christ's claim to supreme authority, yet feared people and dared not touch Him then because of His popularity.

IV. *Authority Rejected* (20:20-40)

So solemn a warning might well have been heeded, but these men too far gone in callous indifference and bitter hostility towards Christ. So result was other steps taken to entangle Him in hope of bringing Him immediately before Pilate (v.20; cf. 23:1).

1. *Question of Conflict of Loyalties* (vs. 21-26)

a. First attempt made by Pharisees and Herodians (cf. Matt. 22:15,16), ritualists of day, in connection with tribute money: Was it lawful to pay taxes to Caesar or not? Note clever method of approach, calculated to lead Christ into trouble whatever His answer:

(1) If He should say yes, Jews with intense national hostility to Romans, would be aroused against Him;

(2) If He should say no, leaders would report Him to Roman authorities for disloyalty.

b. Answer given was indicative of wonderful balance and of Divine logic:

     (1) They could not deny tribute to Caesar in face of coin in current use;

     (2) Duty to God just as obvious because of spiritual relationship and obligation.

  c. Enemies were thus given far more than expected—statement of relative claims of God and of State.

  d. We, like them, are thus reminded of loyalty to those in authority in response to protection given us by State—no better proof of true religion (Cf. Rom. 13:1-7). But we are to put God first, doing everything to His glory (cf. 1 Cor. 10:31), and in Name of the Lord Jesus (cf. Col. 3:17).

  e. No wonder (v.26) Jewish leaders—
     (1) Felt themselves once more thwarted;
     (2) Marvelled at Christ's wonderful reply; and
     (3) Were silenced.

2. *Question of Nature of Resurrection* (vs. 27-40)

  a. Second attempt made by Sadducees, rationalists of day, in connection with doctrine of resurrection which they denied. Evidently thought problem brought out of unusual, if not grotesque, incident, whether true or not, would be too much for Him: Whose wife would much-married woman be in resurrection?

  b. Yet Jesus answered with dignity and fearlessness—
     (1) By showing it to be altogether outside realm of future life, where earthly conditions do not obtain (vs. 34-36); but, far more,
     (2) By showing God called in Old Testament God of living people, not of dead, thereby proving patriarchs still alive (vs. 37,38).

  c. Enemies again given more than expected—positive statement on immortality of soul. No wonder (vs. 39,40) they—
     (1) Commended Christ, albeit reluctantly, and—
     (2) Dared not continue questioning Him.

V. *Authority Reiterated* (20:41 to 21:4)
   1. *Christ's Claim to Messiahship* (vs. 41-44)
      a. Now our Lord's turn to question, and His is remarkable problem: If David called Messiah Lord (Psa. 110:1), how was it possible, at the same time, for Messiah to be David's Son?
      b. While He does not state answer, nor could enemies (cf. Matt. 22:46), it is self-evident because we know Christ as God and man—of David's line "according to the flesh" (Acts 2:30), and yet "God over all, blessed forever" (Rom. 9:5), something Jews evidently had never before contemplated. Instance of how Christ, in references to Old Testament, separated Himself when necessary from contemporary Jewish belief.
      c. Here is further striking testimony to His claim of authority—He is Messiah.

   2. *Christ's Condemnation of Hypocrisy* (vs. 45-47)
      a. Turned to His disciples and warned of scribes, who—
         (1) Professed to be so religious that they were to receive preferred treatment, but who—
         (2) Lived lives absolutely opposite, robbing widows and orphans, as we should say today.
      b. Pronounced doom upon all such.
      c. Another striking testimony to claim of Christ's authority—He is to be Judge.

   3. *Christ's Commendation of Generosity* (21:1-4)
      a. Without break in continuity (since chapter division is arbitrary and verse 1 begins "And"), Christ noted and expressed another contrast:
         (1) Rich men casting gifts into treasury, and—
         (2) Poor widow casting "two mites" (v.2)—approximately two-eights of cent.

      b. Declared it her entire substance and thus more in sight of God than all gifts of rich, who doubtless were giving only proportion of income. So "widow's mite" not, as so often used, descriptive of small part of small income, but whole principal.

c. A third striking testimony to claim of Christ to supreme authority—He reads human hearts.

4. *Christ's Cautions about the Future* (21:5-38)

a. Remainder of chapter 21 contains our Lord's "Olivet Discourse" to His disciples. It includes much that is deeply interesting, vitally important and very far-reaching, and should be studied in more detail. It gives—

   (1) Warnings as to destruction of Jerusalem in A. D. 70.

   (2) Wider outlook of Christ's own Second Coming at end of age.

b. But main practical thought is that of watchfulness (vs. 8, 28,31,34-36).

c. A fourth striking testimony to claim of Christ's authority—He knows future.

Conclusion

Contemplating this matter of authority, we see—

1. The secret of blessedness is submission to Christ, and—
2. The sadness there is in opposition from sinful hearts. All insubordination is futile, for the "stone which the builders rejected" is certain to "become the head of the corner." Christ is either a "stone of stumbling" (1 Pet. 2:8), or a "chief corner-stone" (v.6). We as "living stones" (v.5, R.V.) may rise on Him to higher things, or else, as did unbelieving Israel, we may stumble over Him; and in the future, if the Stone falls upon us, the result will be permanent disaster indeed. Which is He to be to you?

> "What I have, He claims;
> What He claims, I yield;
> What I yield, He takes;
> What He takes, He fills;
> What He fills, He uses;
> What He uses, He keeps;
> What He keeps, He satisfies."

79

THE LAST PASSOVER AND THE FIRST LORD'S SUPPER

(Luke 22:7-20)

AFTER the events of Passion Week—the parable of the vineyard, the plotting of Christ's enemies, His discourses, and His benedictions, comes a short, beautiful interval of peace—peace before the greatest storm of all.

I. *Preparing Passover* (vs. 7-13)

   1. *The Feast of Passover*
   For origin, ceremonial, and significance, see Exodus 12: 1-28.

   2. *The Need of Preparation*
   Command to Peter and John—their willingness—request to householder under indicated conditions.

     a. Note Christ's knowledge of details—knew at distance what would be instrumental for His purpose, and directed each move and incident, step by step.

     b. His Humanity in observing rite is precious, and His Divinity is shown by His knowledge.

   3. *The Promptness of Obedience*
   Direction—action—completion.

II. *Observing Passover* (vs. 14-18)

   1. *The Hour*
   Memorable—necessary—important.

   2. *The Desire*
   Fulfilment present support to His soul, and retrospect would be comfort to disciples' hearts.

3. *The Anticipation*

This last Passover looked forward to coming Kingdom, when they would be His companions, as now.

a. Showed brotherhood in shrinking from parting and treasuring last moments.

b. Jesus' desire now same—to "open the Kingdom of God to all believers."

III. *Superseding Passover* (vs. 19,20)

1. *The Bread*

Symbolized His Body—breaking and taking.

2. *The Cup*

Symbolized His Blood—covenant-making.

N.B. He did not take Passover lamb, but bread and wine, thus showing He was instituting feast, not sacrifice—a meal connected with a sacrifice, but sacrifice one thing, meal quite another. Cf. distinction in 1 Cor. 5:7. He *was* Passover—*we* keep feast.

3. *The Remembrance*

Cf. verse 19 with Exodus 12:14,27.

IV. *Some Questions*

1. Who is this who claims remembrance on part of world?

a. It is One who dares set aside national observance ordained by God.

b. It is One who in His death commands remembrance—not as in case of ordinary human beings, who usually celebrate births, not deaths, which are often difficult to remember, especially as during more than nineteen centuries millions have passed away.

N.B. Creed of Christian Church has Christ's death, not His birth, as center.

2. What does Christ mean by "remembrance"?
He intends us to—
a. Recall Him as a Good Man.

    b. Accept Him as a Great Saviour.

    c. Appreciate Him as a Loving Friend.

    d. Proclaim Him as a Living Hope.

    e. Expect Him as a Coming Lord.

3. How does the Lord's Supper help us to remember Him?

    a. It makes restful halt in week's or month's pilgrimage.

    b. It becomes helpful sign of satisfaction.

    c. It gives graphic picture of salvation.

    d. It constitutes reassuring promise of grace.

    e. It remains clear prophecy of future.

Conclusion

The Lord's Supper is—

1. *A Retrospect*
   Christ for us—for deliverance—we take the Bread.

2. *An Introspect*
   Christ in us—for life—we drink the Cup.

3. *A Prospect*
   Christ coming—for hope—we do both of these "till He come."

Do we know all this experimentally? We may test ourselves each time we come to His Table by meditating upon Union, Communion, Reunion.

80

THE LORD'S SUPPER
(Luke 22:19,20)

At the time of the institution of the Jewish passover, the Israelites were told not only to observe it "for ever," but also what to say when their children asked them, "What mean ye by this service?" (Exod. 12:26). Even so we, who have been given an ordinance to take the place of the Jewish passover, should be able to answer when asked, "What mean *ye* by *this* service?" It has been given many names:—the Breaking of Bread, the Lord's Supper, the Holy Communion, the Sacrament, the Eucharist. But what does it mean?

I. *Some Answers*

It is—

1. *A Representation*—"This is My Body which is given for you"—also "This is My Blood . . . which is shed for many" (Matt. 26:28)

   a. Phrase must be taken in entirety (not simply "This is my Body . . . This is My Blood"), in order to associate ordinance definitely and solely with Christ's coming death.

   b. Therefore, our spiritual perception of His sacrifice.

2. *An Ordinance*—"This do"

   a. Ordained for perpetual observance.

   b. Therefore, our obedience to His expressed will.

3. *A Commemoration*—"In remembrance of Me"

   a. Remembering His death, its fact and meaning.

   b. Therefore, our memory of Him while absent.

4. *A Covenant—"The new covenant"* (R.V.)
   a. Sacred, binding contract (cf. Jer. 31:31-34).
   b. Therefore, our trust for His redemption.

5. *A Eucharist—*"Gave thanks" (Gr., *eucharisteo*)
   a. To God, while dedicating elements—cf. "cup of blessing which we bless" (1 Cor. 10:16). Word when used with material object, according to Bishop Westcott, must be understood as meaning that our Lord blessed God the Giver for it, not that element itself was blessed.
   b. Therefore, our praise and thanksgiving for His spiritual blessings.

6. *A Communion—*"Gave unto them"
   a. Breaking bread, eating, and drinking signs of fellowship—cf. "the communion of the blood of Christ" (1 Cor. 10:16); "we being many . . ." (1 Cor. 10:17).
      (1) Bread broken—Christ for us.
      (2) Bread eaten—Christ in us.
      (3) Bread partaken together—Christ among us.
   b. Therefore, our hope of His appearing.

7. *A Sacrament—*"Ye do shew the Lord's death" (1 Cor. 11:26)
   a. *"Sacramentum,"* Roman soldier's oath of fealty on enlistment. N.B. not sacri*fice*—cf. Jude 3, R.V. Proclaiming by words rather than by deeds.
   b. Therefore, our confession of loyalty to Him.

8. *An Earnest—*"Till He come" (1 Cor. 11:26)
   a. Anticipation of Second Coming and continuation of rite until "that day."
   b. Therefore, our hope of His appearing.

II. *Some Further Questions Regarding the Lord's Supper*
   1. *Is there not need of proportion?*
      Since there is indeed "the proportion of faith," neither exaltation of sacrament nor depreciation of ordinance is

fitting. Commandment binding, but no more important than others—fact that it was "dying request" sen-
timent only. Remarkable that allusions to it in New
Testament are few—doctrinal Romans and Hebrews, and
Pastoral Epistles silent. Scripture content to state duty
and privilege of obedience to Christ's command.

2. *Is there any unique grace in it?*

If so, we should partake as often as possible. But Scripture contains no proof of this—"as often as ye eat . . . and
drink" is all said as to times or intervals, save what may
be deduced from accounts of early Church practice (Acts
2:42,46; 20:7; 1 Cor. 11:20-34).

3. *Is it the highest act of Christian worship?*

Not in modern sense of comparison. Best to call it,
rather, *central* act of fellowship with Christ and with
other Christians. Primarily, it is not "worship," but
commemoration. Only "acts" ordained by Christ are
"take," "eat," "drink," "do"—not in themselves acts of
worship. Worship is giving, rendering, ascribing, while
these other "acts" imply receiving, appropriating, feast-
ing. However, such a privilege is opportunity and occasion for glorious, precious worship as *result* of our
appropriation of Christ's atoning sacrifice as typified by
sacrament. N.B. "Eucharistic adoration," if it means
adoration of Christ at time of Eucharist, differs in no
wise from worship of Him at all other times; but unfor-
tunately it often has a different connotation.

4. *Does John 6 refer to it?*

Not primarily—addressed mainly to multitude, while Supper was instituted for disciples. Relation is only that of
universal truth (Christ the Bread of Life) to particular
application (Lord's Supper); Christ for world as Sacrifice, Supper for Church, as Sacrament. Instead of discourse referring to Supper, Supper refers to and ampli-

fies discourse, or, better, both refer to same glorious fact, the Cross.

5. *Who are to partake of it?*

Intended for disciples only—whole revelation pre-supposes and is founded on discipleship. Only disciples can "remember," for remembrance implies knowledge, and it is only disciples who "know" their master (cf. John 17:3). Yet each person must decide that for himself and, except in case of flagrant sin, we are not to exclude anyone from the Lord's Table. It is not the Episcopal Table, nor the Baptist Table, nor the Brethren Table—it is the *Lord's* Table.

Conclusion

1. *Remember!* The Past—Christ's Death—with Faith.
   Retrospect: Looking backward to the Cross.
2. *Realize!* The Present—Christ's Life—with Love.
   Aspect: a. Looking inward to our own souls.
   b. Looking outward to souls of others.
3. *Rejoice!* The Future—Christ's Coming—with Hope.
   Prospect: Looking onward to "that Day."

81

TRUE HUMILITY
(Luke 22:25-27)

T HESE verses record our Lord's rejoinder to the dispute among His disciples as to who should be greatest.

I. *A Fact Known* (v.25) —"lordship"
   1. Principle of lordship then familiar, and illustrated by—
      a. Tremendous hierarchy of Jewish religion;
      b. Dominating aristocracy of Roman government.
   2. Conditions same today if human nature left to itself:
      a. Systems centralized, monarchical, dictatorial.
      b. People dominated by superiors or monopolies: e.g., Roman and Greek Churches. *pg 27 improve*

   N.B. Like pyramid—with people as lowest layer, and aristocrats and monopolists in successive layers to pinnacle.

II. *A Counsel Given* (v.26) —"not so" *279 Berkl*
   1. Lordship to be relinquished and authority disclaimed.
      a. Ambition not forbidden as motive, but its exercise directed.
      b. To be chief not wrong if sought aright.
      pg 35 imp
   2. Humblest service to be considered highest dignity:
      a. E.g., that of waiter; *Hum 553* *after Lordsapper*
      b. That of slave.

   N.B. Notion of pyramid completely reversed—as though turned on apex, with social and ecclesiastical authorities beneath people, supporting them. Real question not what supports man, but what man supports—strongest should be at bottom.

III. *A Motive Urged* (v.27) —"he that sitteth . . . he that serv-eth"

  1. The plain fact—"I am . . . he that serveth" (cf. 2 Cor. 8:9). Jesus at bottom of "pyramid." *pg 19 serve*

  2. The clear illustration:

    a. "Chief cornerstone" (Eph. 2:20). If pyramid invert-ed, chief at base—Christ.

    b. New ideal of greatness. Formerly it was either the wise, the rich, the strong; now it is Christ from heav-en, who is God and needs nothing—only gives Him-self to us and for us. We are to be like Him.

Swindoll 58

  3. The final force:

    a. Commence life by stepping down—conviction of sin.

    b. Continue in self-sacrifice, with self-seeking buried:
      (1) Much yet to learn—e.g., menial work necessary.
      (2) Words beautiful, but deeds more so.

    c. Find in it all possible scope—as one stone holds next, so we must try to save our nearest.

    d. Earn surprisingly glorious rewards:
      (1) Painful experience and hard process first.
      (2) Then grand victory over self.

Conclusion

> "For the clear bells of triumph — a knell,
> For the sweet kiss of meeting —farewell
> For the height of the mountain — the steep,
> For the waking in Heaven — death's sleep."

82

SELFLESSNESS
(Luke 22:24-37)

To the shame of the professing Church, from the twelve disciples down, the Lord's Supper has always been associated with strife: at the outset, around the Table, and since then, about the Table. The strife mentioned in these verses may have been as to precedence at the Table, or it may have had to do with the washing of the disciples' feet (John 13:2-20). At any rate, it was noted by Jesus and brought to an end by His gracious yet searching words. In them are shown the imperfection of the disciples' sympathy with Him and His own unconquerable patience. And so He taught one of life's greatest lessons, that of true selflessness.

I. *Selflessness Enjoined* (vs. 24-26)

1. *Selflessness Overlooked* (v.24)
   a. Contending parties at solemn time—imperfect perception.
   b. Disputed topic after three years—slow students.
   c. Unseemly quarrel among brethren—no unity.

2. *Selflessness Rejected* (v.25)
   Gentile leaders—
   a. Clamored for place—"kings"
   b. Exercised lordship—or "authority"
   c. Arrogated to themselves honors—called "benefactors" by those who would flatter their tyrants.

3. *Selflessness Commended* (v.26)
   a. Difference from others because of humility—"not be so"

    b. Brotherhood—"younger" rather than "greatest."

    c. Service—"chief" and yet "doth serve"—service is great-
ness, and doing good a royal crown.

II. *Selflessness Exemplified* (vs. 27-30)

  1. *In Serving* (v.27)

    a. Paradox of servant and master—master greater than
servant—but Christ was "Servant of Jehovah" (cf. Isa.
42:1; 52:13)—so servant from then on more truly
great.

    b. To win love, even He had to show love (cf. 1 John
4:19).

  2. *In Enduring* (v.28)

  Glimpse into heart of Christ:

    a. Tempted and tried all through earthly life, but sin-
less, strong, sympathetic.

    b. Lonely and longing for sympathy—real pain.

    c. Grateful and appreciative—recognizing fidelity, even
though limited.

  3. *In Triumphing* (vs. 29,30)

    a. The Promiser:

      (1) Extroadinary promises from One near death.

      (2) Assertion of own authority as distinct from Fa-
ther's.

      (3) Claim on destiny of others.

    b. The Promise:

    Kingdom appointed like His own, including:—

      (1) Table—satisfaction, repose, fellowship, joy.

      (2) Thrones—victory, dominion, authority, power.

    c. The Recipients

      (1) Told it was to be all of grace—from Christ alone.

      (2) Low motive to be seeking reward? Yet Christ rec-
ognized human desire and provided for its fulfilment.

III. *Selflessness Emphasized* (vs. 31-37)
1. *Because of Coming Danger* (vs. 31,32)
   a. Individual disciple's peril—"you" and "thee"
   b. Satan's demand—to "sift," not to kill—perhaps he had learned his lesson from case of Job (cf. Job 1:12; 2:6).
2. *Because of Certain Disaster* (vs. 33,34)
   a. Simon Peter's rash self-confidence—volunteered not only "sifting" of prison, but death—brave in hopes and plans, but cowardly in actual testing (cf. vs. 54-62).
   b. Christ's clear prediction in face of protestation—knew Peter not only unready for sacrifice, but even unwilling to acknowledge acquaintance (cf. vs. 57,58, 60).
3. *Because of Consequent Difficulty* (vs. 35-37)
   a. Old rule recalled (cf. 10:4) of depending on hospitality.
   b. New rule given—now take all necessities for life and safety.
   c. Great principle suggested—disciples to be, like Christ, objects of world's hostility and so must exercise common sense, even to extent of self-defense—"sword" as well as "purse" and "scrip."

Conclusion

1. "He was a good man" highest tribute possible (cf. "fruit of Spirit . . . goodness," Gal. 5:22).
2. Nothing can take place of this all-embracing element—orthodox, privilege, opportunity, all intended as means toward goodness.
3. Example of our Lord standing testimony to demand for, possibility of, and power for holiness of life, goodness of character, humility of service.

Let us recognize two great reasons for a selfless life: our powerless selves, and our all-powerful Saviour.

83

OUR PATTERN OF SERVICE
(Luke 22:27)

THERE are several very remarkable facts about the day we call Palm Sunday in relation to the Book of Common Prayer. The Collect, Epistle, and Gospel appointed for it are found not under the heading "Palm Sunday," but under "The Sunday next before Easter." Palm Sunday was a day of honor for our Lord, and on it He was nearing the Cross as Saviour of the world. But neither of these elements is in the Prayer Book view here—it is Christ as our Example who is shown forth as we are led by the Collect to pray that we may "follow the example of His patience." Then comes the Epistle, taken from Philippians 2:5-11, which emphasizes the self-humbling of the Son of God. Compare Hebrews 12:2, and First Peter 2:21, where Christ's death, not as atonement, but as example is stressed. The Gospel for the day is not taken from the story of the "Triumphal Entry," as we might expect, but from Matthew's account of the Trial. Thus it strikes immediately, on this first day of Holy Week, the keynote of the events celebrated all through the week and culminating with Good Friday and Easter Day.

Let us therefore use our text as symbolic of all Christ did while on earth—Christ our Example, our Pattern of service.

1. *Service at a Time of Conscious Glory*

    A. *Christ*

    1. Cf. John 13:1 and chapters 14:17—not so much thought of death as of glory beyond (cf. also Heb. 12:2).

2. Cf. John 13:3—hour of supreme consciousness of mystery of Incarnation—knew Who and Whence and Whither.

3. What should He do? Take wings? Show diadem? Confound enemies?

4. No! "Jesus knowing . . . began to wash the disciples' feet" (John 13:3-5). Service and glory (cf. John 8:6,8, "stooped," as He must have done here). Hard to serve in such a moment, but He did.

B. *Ourselves*

1. Should be spirit of our service also—we have some such moments of consciousness of glory in grace—special seasons when we desire to do great things.

2. Then is time for stooping low—such feelings given not for selves, but for others.
   Illus.: Heir, having just come of age, serving as lowest employee.

3. So Christ then, and so must we—true glory in grace.

II. *Service in an Atmosphere Tainted with Selfishness*

A. *Christ*

1. After "dispute" of verse 24—carnal, self-seeking.

2. Picture Him aglow—others thinking of self only.

3. Cf. Paul's experience (Phil. 2:21)—how chilling, depressing, repelling, heartbreaking!

4. But service implies self-forgetfulness, thinking only of others.

B. *Ourselves*

1. Serving even with no return—cf. mother slaving for child, sister or brother helping the other.

2. Life looked at from standpoint of others. Hard? Yes, but Christlike.

3. Someone has called it "life of self-renouncing love"—self displaced and Christ on throne.

III. *Service to Men of Differing Character*
  A. *Christ*
    1. Note circumstances: three years and scarcely any result. Cf. questions in John 14:5,8,22; dispute in present passage; Peter's denial (vs. 54-62); Judas' betrayal (vs. 47,48); and forsaking of Christ by "all" (Matt. 26:56).
    2. Christ unappreciated—no response, no thrill of sympathy apparent.
    3. Yet capabilities in them—so Master went on serving them and never gave up hope.

  B. *Ourselves*
    1. Our lot often cast so—working with no result cause of much grief—sometimes best prospects turn out badly.
    2. Others appreciated, not we—yet go on.
    3. Possibilities yet—grace can as grace has.

IV. *Service Perfect in Every Detail*
  A. *Christ*
    1. Cf. John 13:1-20—rose, laid aside, girded, poured, washed, wiped—neither perfunctory nor hurried.
    2. Consider thoughts then: Gethsemane, betrayal, trial, Calvary—yet time for service because self-controlled and self-possessed.
  B. *Ourselves*
    1. Service—thorough, complete, depending much on manner—no skimping.
    2. Care of least detail—self-possession—faithfulness in little things because nothing trivial.

Conclusion
  Learn—
  1. *"The example of His great humility"*
    a. Cf. Phil. 2:7, R.V.—"emptied Himself"—for others.

b. We often on dignity, hurt—self-esteem easily wounded. We let people know by tongue and actions.

c. Yet Christ endured in "unconscious self-forgetfulness."

2. *"The example of His patience"*

a. Humble not only once, but continually.

b. Not an act, but an attitude—cf. Heb. 12:3.

c. If troubled, we are told by Christ: "In your patience possess ye your souls" (21:19); so "let us run with patience" (Heb. 12:1).

3. *The reason of both humility and patience*

"For your sakes" (2 Cor. 8:9); "by His stripes ye are healed" (Isa. 53:5).

What is your Response?

> "Love so amazing, so Divine
> Demands my soul, my life, my all!"

84

FRIEND AND FOE
(Luke 22:31,32)

IN THESE two verses, Christ makes a twofold revelation
of the unseen world. He very seldom drew aside the veil between that world and this, but did so now, after an experience
of great privilege for the disciples. He revealed that there are
two realms—heaven and hell—and the two beings who preside
over them are both superhuman and both intensely interested
in the value of the individual soul.

I. *The Christian's Great Foe* (v.31)

A being—

1. Superhuman in intelligence and skill.
2. Intensely real.
3. Continually active in spite of human unconsciousness of
   danger.
4. Deeply malignant—destroyer of faith, usefulness, and life
   itself.
5. Anxious for control—"earnestly asked for you that he
   might toss you about—cause friction in your life."

II. *The Christian's Greater Friend* (v.32)

1. Has perfect knowledge—foresees.
2. Has perfect power—forearms.
3. Has perfect love—forewarns.

   a. Personal—saw it would go hardest with Peter, most
      liable, weak in spite of leadership.
   b. Anticipating—beyond human ken.

c. Protecting—in, not from, sifting, which is intended to—

(1) Prove firmness.

(2) Break down pride.

(3) Produce gentleness.

(4) Tame temper.

d. Blessing—covering shame and weakness with grace, and making believer wiser, stronger, more sympathetic.

Conclusion

Note—

1. *The great value of Christ's prayer.*

   a. Not miracle, but intercession.

   b. Is that all? Yes, because it was greatest possible service.

   c. Intercession costs—ever associated with service and sacrifice. Cf. Lev. 16:11-13, Num. 16:46, incense placed on coals of burnt offering. Prayer thus based on sacrifice. Cf. also Acts 10:2, almsgiving and prayer.

2. *The powerful petition in Christ's prayer.*
   "That thy faith fail not"—faith our most precious treasure and strongest weapon.

3. *The expected answer to Christ's prayer*
   "When thou art converted"—not "if"—Christ made definite statement beforehand to encourage Peter and keep him from dispair. Cf. John 17:20; Rom. 8:26; Heb. 7:25.

   Therefore—Listen, for His voice will speak. Lean, for He will never fail.

85

THE AGONY AND THE ARREST
(Luke 29:39-53)

Before the mystery of Gethsemane we are confronted with the necessity for profound reverence. As we try to grasp something of the depth of Christ's sorrow and suffering on our behalf, we must heed the words spoken to Moses: "Put off thy shoes from thy feet, for the place whereon thou standest is holy ground" (Exod. 2:5). Luke's account is condensed, but it contains points peculiar to his Gospel and may be divided into two fivefold pictures of the Suffering Saviour.

I. *The Agony* (vs. 39-44)

  A. *The Thoughtful Christ* (vs. 39,40)

    1. Shows loving care, in midst of own trial, for disciples' coming temptation—oblivious of self even in darkest sorrow.

    2. Urges prayer not for Him, but for themselves.

  B. *The Solitary Christ* (v.41)

    1. Cf. revelry of city and sadness in garden.

    2. Christ's feelings full of conflicting elements—desire for sympathy, but also yearning for solitude.

    3. So "He was withdrawn from them"—for there is a point where deepest human sympathy naturally fails.

  C. *The Praying Christ* (v.42)

    1. His firm grasp of Divine Fatherhood evident—appeal, yet equal submission.

    2. "Cup" refers to suffering of mind, body, and soul, either—

      a. On Cross, which He was already anticipating, or—
      b. Fear of premature death in garden before He could reach Cross.

   3. No faltering of resolve or wavering of will—but natural recoil of perfect human nature to sin and death.
      a. If no dread of Cross felt—no sacrifice—yet—
      b. If shrinking away from Cross—no Saviour.

   4. Full acceptance of Divine purpose and anticipation of Divine path.
      a. Prayer of faith showed repose in God's will as best —so we also may safely put it above own wishes.
      b. Coincidence of human will with God's always highest blessing of prayer.

D. *The Strengthened Christ* (v.43)
   1. Utter physical prostration of Christ's manhood required Divine help, as ours does.
   2. True answer to His prayer was not removal of load, but strength to bear it (cf. Heb. 5:7,8).

E. *The Agonizing Christ* (v.44)
   1. Increased strength brought increased conflict, and then increased earnestness.
   2. Why this agony of apprehension? More than physical fear, or Christ would have been below many ordinary men in courage. Consider—
      a. Perfection of His human nature.

         (1) We steel ourselves, by callousness or by anodynes; but He perfectly apprehended, so perfectly overcame.
         (2) We ignore or deny pain; but He absolutely recognized, so absolutely mastered it.
         (3) Our bodies are imperfect, sinful, defiled; His was undegraded by heritage, unaffected by deviation, undrugged by excess—and so capable of profoundest feeling.

(4) We often lose control or waver in loyalty; He ever combined deep emotion with complete self-control. Cf. three times returning to disciples and going back alone (Matt. 26:40-46).

Thus, while it complicates problems Christ's perfection is one of solutions. Now add—

b. Awful mass of human sin which Christ was already beginning to experience (cf. 2 Cor. 5:21).

(1) His holy soul shrank from contact of sin and horror of being abandoned by God.

(2) His prayer was as to possibility of fulfilling God's will without this.

(3) But, though recoiling from awful position, He was ready to accomplish Divine purpose at any cost.

Thus we may partially understand Gethsemane.

II. *The Arrest* (vs. 45-53)

A. *The Neglected Christ* (vs. 45,46)

1. Disciples, even Simon Peter (Matt. 26:40), who had promised so much (vs. 33,35), could not watch with Him. How much they missed!

2. Yet His thought even then was for them, not for Himself.

B. *The Majestic Christ* (v.47)

1. In spite of sudden burst of multitude, He was ready and sought to know whom they wanted (John 18:4-8).

2. Unmoved, fearless, because made strong (v.43).

C. *The Loving Christ* (v.48)

1. Kiss of Judas should have been sign of friendship, but instead it was signal of treachery.

2. Tenderness and use of Judas' name shows last pleading of love in attempt to wake deadened conscience.

D. *The Patient Christ* (vs. 39-51)
   1. Peter, accustomed to nets rather than swords, struck out wildly—probably to stun or cut off servant's head, but only removed ear.
   2. Christ interposing remonstrated and healed servant before being taken away—heaping benefits on foes.

E. *The Divine Christ* (vs. 52,53)
   1. Rebukes leaders, maintaining own innocence, asserting utter inadequacy of force against Him, and reminding from past He was no thief.
   2. Reveals self-consciousness—very significant at this moment.
   3. States this was their hour, and power of darkness was in opposition to Him as Light of world—but only for "hour."

Conclusion

Gethsemane was a part of our Lord's work for us, which found its culmination on Calvary. Let us look at it from two standpoints:

1. *Christ for us as our Substitute*
   We see—
   a. What sin is, that caused His suffering, and—
   b. What God is, in His righteousness requiring sacrifice, and in His love providing it.
   c. What we are called upon to do—repent, accept, adore.

2. *Christ for us as our Example*
   We have—
   a. Our "cup" of sorrow, in fellowship with His sufferings.
   b. Pain prominent in world—yet we may always find Christ "a little further" on.
   c. Comfort of prayer, faith, submission—world should see similar calmness, patience, love, power, dignity.

Thus, being *in* Christ, and *with* Christ, we shall become *like* Christ.

86

THE TRIAL OF JESUS
(Luke 22:54-71)

THE Jewish trial of Jesus had three stages. First, He was brought before Annas and Caiaphas (John 18:12-24) in order to extort a confession on which to lay a charge. Balked in their purpose, the Sanhedrin surrounded Him, and only then was a pretext found (Matt. 26:59-66). But no decision could be reached till morning, and so it was daybreak before a sentence was pronounced (Luke 22:66-71). The entire time was a revelation of human sin and Christ's attitude to it. There are here three ways in which He Himself was sinned against.

1. *Jesus Denied* (vs. 54-62)
   A. *Evil Surroundings*
   1. Peter cold, exhausted, shivering, sleepy—glad to creep in near fire.
   2. Maid, with woman's sharp eye and curiosity, blurted out accusation.
   3. Why was Peter among enemies of Jesus? John close to Him, yet unmolested (John 18:15).
   4. Man owes much to surroundings—duty easy when all around agree.
   5. If alone, we know risk, but if not, not one of us should judge Peter.
   6. Warm place indoors tended more to comfort than to courage—ready to fight outside—inside, quailed before mere girl—more comforts, more injury to spiritual life sometimes. Thank God for hardships!

B. *Sad Denial*

  1. First interrogator girl, second another, and probably third a man or men (cf. Matt. 26:73; Mark 14:70; John 18:26), after hour had elapsed. Then cock crew, and Jesus "looked upon Peter" (v.61).

  2. Cause of denial any or all of these three:

    a. Cowardice—usual accusation, but few so courageous, even under compulsion of anxiety "to see the end" (Matt. 26:58), as to enter high priest's hall, though "afar off." Cf. others who "forsook Him and fled"—ànd John was safer because "known unto the high priest" (John 18:15).

    b. Over-confidence—lies deeper, for this strong characteristic of Peter. Cf. offer to walk on water (Matt. 14:28); proposal at Transfiguration (9:33); rebuke at teaching of Cross (Mark 8:32); scruple against feet-washing (John 13:8); denial of denial (Mark 14:31); use of sword (John 18:10).

    c. Eclipse of faith—still deeper, for circumstances do cause doubt. Was Jesus what Peter had thought? Staggered at spectacle of Master bound and in power of enemies. Cf. verse 32—"that thy *faith* fail not"—not courage, but faith in Master, so that he would not drop out of group entirely. Cf. "look" of Christ (v.61)—of sorrow, but also of love, pardon, deep meaning. All came back—Jesus the same still —devotion kindled afresh.

C. *Bitter Repentance*

  1. That "look" came as Jesus was passing from earlier trial.

  2. Brought back loyalty, but also caused bitter tears.

  3. Cf. sin of Peter with that of Judas:

    a. Sudden—premeditated.

    b. Lack of trust—evil passion.

    c. Suppression of loyalty—unreality of profession leading to treason.

4. But are we quite sure we understand Peter?

    a. Blamed for being "afar off"—but others not there at all.

    b. They fell more quickly and lower—all self-confident (cf. Matt. 26:35), yet they denied in deed—never followed at all.

    c. Christ did not misunderstand Peter, but knew his worth and fierce struggle.

    d. Peter soon arrested flight and returned—thus sifted (see v. 31, tossed about, friction caused in life), and "converted." Could not face life without Master—they did for a time.

    e. Then it was he upheld and strengthened his brethren (v.32; cf. John 21:7; Acts 1:15; 2:14, etc.). If he was to "strengthen" them, how could they be in better spiritual condition than he?

    f. Easy to scorn another's failure when we ourselves take no risk for Christ. God forbid!

With frightened lips I shall not ever say,
"I know Him not," for none will question me.
I shall not need to speak a word today
To publish to the world my loyalty.
And yet a hundred times there comes the voice,
"Know you this Man, the Master?" and behold,
A hundred times I make the fateful choice
Today, as the apostle once of old.
And every unkind word or straying thought,
Each deed of hatred or disdain
Say plainly to the world, "I know Him not,"
And then the cock crows — bitter morn of pain!
And would indeed today that they might be —
The times I have denied Him — only three!

                    (Mabel F. Arbuthnot)

5. On other hand, it might be argued that Peter could not help Master by telling truth about himself to those

who had no right to it, but might be of use if "good old-fashioned lie" enabled him to stay nearby! But no, lie never justified.

II. *Jesus Derided* (vs. 63-65)

1. "Seized" violently (v.54,R.V.) and beaten.
2. Reviled—to test His prophetic office, as Roman trial tested kingly office. Why outburst of savagery when He had done no wrong?
   a. Instinct of low natures to trample on fallen.
   b. Rude natures have rude way of showing rudeness.
   c. Result of partisanship.
   d. But not so much brutality of human nature as revenge for fear of Him at time of arrest, when they were prostrated at knowledge of His power.

III. *Jesus Defamed* (vs. 66-71)

A. *The Council* (v.66)

1. Included Caiaphas, high priest, and Annas, his father-in-law (John 18:13).
2. Had already decided Christ guilty, and only needed legal pretext to sentence Him.

B. *The Examination* (vs. 67-70)

1. Jesus declines to recognize *bona fides* of judge or competency of tribunal.
2. Claims participation in Divine glory and power.
3. Other men have examined Him, viz.:—
   a. Renan said He was greatest Teacher ever seen or to be seen.
   b. Mill called Him no bad choice as ideal of humanity.
   c. Strauss remarked His conscience not clouded by memory of sin.

4. Yet this Man died because He said He was Son of God. "If He was not God, He was not good"—He was either mad or bad.

5. But He never unfolded truth to those about to reject Him—only to those who were sincerely inquiring.

6. As Prisoner, He said nothing; as Judge, He will say much (cf. Acts 17:31).

C. *The Result* (v.17)

1. His enemies now had quite enough to convict Him.

2. But it was fitting that Israel hear Christ's full claim and so condemn self by rejection of Him.

3. Now only Pilate could say whether He should be put to death.

Conclusion

1. *Man's Sins*

a. Distrust. Peter robbed Christ of personal sympathy.
   (1) Good man carried away suddenly by doubts.
   (2) One more pang for heart of Jesus.
   (3) Parent grieves more over children's falls than over those of outsiders.

b. Brutality. Servants exposed Christ to personal indignity.
   (1) Love of destruction in ignorant.
   (3) Coarse joy over downfall of superiors.

c. Malice. Rulers trapped Christ in order to get rid of Him.
   (1) Sad when will fails—sadder when ignorance is pleased to destroy good—saddest to see good and deliberately reject it.
   (2) Enemies watching opportunity to commit religious perjury—dead religion worse than none.

2. *God's Attitude*
   a. To the weak—look of recall, meeting with love.
   b. To the brutal—patience, prayer of forgiveness, time for repentance.
   c. To the malicious—appeal to judgment, warning of consequences.

   To all sinners, God offers mercy (Isa. 1:18). Have you listened to His offer?

87

TWO SIGNS OF DISCIPLESHIP*
(Luke 22:56,58)

THOSE in the High Priest's house recognized Peter by two circumstances: he had been in the company of Jesus, and he had been in the company of Jesus' followers. These two marks on a human life have always been indications of Christian discipleship, and are the same today. A Christian is one who is united both to Christ and to other Christians. Hence we have a sure but simple test of a true Christian life.

1. *With Christ*—"This man was also with Him" (v.56) —Why? For—
    1. Salvation.
       Our great need as we review past.
    2. Sanctification.
       Our great need for present.
    3. Satisfaction.
       Our great need for past, present, and future.
    All are found only in Christ.

II. *With Christians*—"Thou art also of them" (v.58) —Why? For—
    1. Oneness of life—in Christ.
       The Spirit animating.
    2. Oneness of love—to Christ.
       The Spirit inspiring.
    3. Oneness of labor—for Christ.
       The Spirit directing.

---

* Also in Sermon Outlines, p. 101

The New Testament connects the ideas of a church and fellowship (cf. Acts 2:42-47; 4:23,32-37; 1 John 1:3,6,7).

Conclusion

1. *Two Simple Tests*

   a. What is Christ to me?

   b. What are my fellow-Christians to me?

   If I am not in their company, I must take heed and examine myself.

2. *Two Simple Secrets*

   a. Abiding in Christ (1 John 2:5,6).

   b. Abounding in love to others (1 John 2:10; 3:10).

   So, abiding in Christ, and abounding in love for His people, I shall show forth Whose I am and Whom I serve.

88

THE TOUCHSTONE
OF HUMAN CHARACTER
(Luke 23:1-12)

T HE aged Simeon had said that Jesus Christ would be the means of revealing the thoughts of many hearts (2:35), and all through His ministry this had proved true. Christ revealed man as he was, and He is still the touchstone of human character. In the present chapter, we have the full revelation of the characters of those associated with Christ's trial.

I. *The Rulers* (vs. 2,5,10)

A. *The Circumstances*

1. Had condemned Christ to death, but could not carry out sentence (John 18:31; cf. Matt. 20:18,19; Luke 20:20), so had to swallow bitter pill and go before Roman governor.

2. Since Pilate would not recognize blasphemy as cause for death, they were compelled to make other charges, hoping he would be impressed by their numbers and unanimity.

3. Tried to induce execution without examination (John 18:30).

4. This being impossible, accusation consisted of two falsehoods and one distortion of truth: that Jesus—

   a. Had perverted nation—which He had not done;

   b. Had forbidden people to pay tribute—which was exact opposite to His counsel and example (cf. Matt. 17:24-27); and—

    c. Had set His Kingship in rivalry to that of Caesar —but His idea of kingship altogether different from theirs (cf. John 18:36).

5. Pilate knew every one of them was rebellious at heart, and was not disposed to single out Jesus, even if He were too.

6. They then increased urgency, and spoke cunningly of sedition, mentioning Galilee, known to be district troublous and disaffected, as well as home of Jesus.

B. *The Character*

1. How terrible their ferocity, turning guardians of justice into vindictive creatures revealed here!

2. Why did they go cringing to man most hated, and do utmost by falsehood and misrepresentation to put Jesus to death?

    a. Because His teaching brushed aside ceremonies of their religion;

    b. Because His life opposed whole order of their life and position;

    c. Because He claimed to be Son of God, which they considered blasphemy—and it was unless true claim —but they never countenanced alternative and were tragically blind to His character and love.

3. How awful the depths of hostility to Christ and lengths to which human nature can go!

II. *The Governor*

A. *The Circumstances*

1. Pilate had earned character of intensely cruel man. During six years of term, had done many rash things to alienate Jewish people and make for mutual hatred.

2. Knew leaders' avowed reason for bringing Jesus to him was not real one, but to get him in trouble with Rome (cf. John 19:12).

3. His condemnation most clearly indicated in John's account—Christ's kingdom "not of this world," and Pilate laid special and repeated emphasis on His Kingship, so he ought to have let Him go.

4. Instead, when he heard word "Galilee" (v.5), endeavored to avoid action by handing Jesus over to jurisdiction of Herod (vs. 6,7).

B. *The Character*

1. Indifference—had enough contact with Christ to find light, but preoccupied through absorption in outward things.

2. Scorn—query about truth shows he thought it "moonshine" while Roman Empire was reality—so all "practical" men.

3. Desire for popularity—afraid of people and wished to make his own position secure by pleasing Herod and crowd.

4. Weakness—saw right, but would not follow—intellect stronger than moral sense—found it easier to go with crowd, even though it was not crowd's right to settle fate of Barabbas or of Christ.

5. Blindness—to Christ's beauty and authority, because entirely engaged with self—near to light and yet led away into darkness.

6. Evasion of responsibility—shirker always suffers. Cf. Adam and Eve (Gen. 3:12,13), Saul (1 Sam. 15:20, 21), etc.

III. *The Tetrarch*

A. *The Circumstances*

1. Galilee his tetrarchy or jurisdiction.

2. Basest of all Herods—cowardly, cruel, sensual.

3. With unhallowed gladness and vulgar curiosity, he welcomed opportunity at last to see Jesus (cf. v.8

with 9:9). Hoped for miracle, like trick of conjurer to tickle satiated taste and vacuous nature.

4. But Jesus had ignored him before (9:10), and now was silent before him, refusing to acknowledge him as authority.

5. This goaded him to resentment and, with his "men of war" (v.11), to mockery of Christ as king.

6. No wonder our Lord was silent—Herod's conscience had been stifled through treatment of John the Baptist (Matt. 14:3-11).

B. *The Character*

1. To neglect conscience is to stifle it—time past for twinges, now silence of death.

2. Ridicule dangerous weapon—inane pleasure in mocking innocent man—exquisite jest now, but later, laugh turned. Note also fate of grandson (Acts 12:21-23).

3. Frivolity, shallowness—during ministry of John the Baptist, "heard him gladly"; when he "saw Jesus, he was exceeding glad"—sinister gladness showed occasional, passing interest, but ended by having part in their deaths.

IV. *The Lord*

Now look at attitude of Jesus Christ to these characters:

A. *To the Rulers*

1. Silent at this point because their opportunity past.

2. Had made position clear, but in inveterate hostility they would not heed.

B. *To Pilate*

1. To ignorant Roman, He speaks and explains, endeavoring to win him.

2. But he, too, went past point of opportunity and determined to sacrifice truth to selfish interest.

C. *To Herod*

    1. To well-taught Jew, Christ is silent because man actuated only by curiosity and not by conscience.

    2. Never indifferent to truth-seekers, but always to triflers.

Thus, in a sense, Christ is to us according to what we are to Him.

Conclusion

    1. *Are we like the Rulers?*

    Vindictive. Wait! "The mills of God grind slowly, but they grind exceeding small." God will take vengeance some day (Psa. 94:1; Isa. 35:4; 63:4; Rom. 10:19).

    2. *Are we like Pilate?*

    Evasive. Once start, never clear. Question inevitably comes: "What shall I do then with Jesus?" (Matt. 27:22)

    3. *Are we like Herod?*

    Contemptuous. But one day, Jesus and Herod will change places.

"What doth it profit a man, if he shall gain the whole world, and lose his own soul?" (Mark 8:36)

"How shall we escape if we neglect so great salvation?" (Heb. 2:3).

"Today if ye will hear His voice, harden not your hearts" (Heb. 3:7).

89

THE REVEALER OF HUMAN NATURE
(Luke 23:13-25)

IN THIS second part of one of the longest chapters in his Gospel, Luke not only gives his version of the trial of Jesus Christ, but continues his character studies of the men, Roman and Jewish, who condemned our Lord to die. We see how they in reality were condemned by Him, through their own evil natures.

I. *The Roman—The Wickedness of Weakness*
  A. *The Narrative*
   1. Back from Herod.
     a. Pilate was face to face with Jesus again.
     b. It would seem that message about wife's dream (Matt. 27:19) came at this point.

   2. Innocence Reaffirmed.
     a. Release attempted, but instead condemnation secured.
     b. Triumph for Jews to make Roman subservient.
     c. They knew Pilate well and his fear of Caesar, so their voices prevailed.

   3. Difficult Circumstances.
     a. Roman government demanded blend of concession and firmness in conquered countries—Jews to be coerced, yet not far enough to appeal often to Rome, as Paul did later.
     b. So we can but pity feeble judge like Pilate.

4. Sterner Emotion Enters.

But if Jesus was innocent, Pilate had—

a. No right to send to Herod;

b. No right to scourge Him;

c. No right to compromise by release of Barabbas.

B. *The Truths*

1. The Viciousness of Compromise.

a. In matters of principle duty to stand out forever if right.

b. "Voice of the people" not always "voice of God"— right is right whether people are for or against it.

2. The Danger of Doubtful Preference.

a. Pilate wanted to do right, yet wanted more to please Jews. *Illus.*: Thief would rather be honest if he gets all he wants, and child would rather obey if he gets own way.

b. Knowledge sufficient, power adequate, yet preference often decides.

3. The Error of Expediency.

a. No concession should be made where right concerned. "Give inch, and he will take all." *Illus.*: Trimming sails to go with wind instead of setting them to harness wind to will.

b. No trifling with obligation.

c. Discussion of doubtful, but never of right.

4. The Value of a Single Act.

a. Act of moment often determines life.

b. Not always unfair to judge man by single act or sudden decision—often reveals character and life of years—nothing isolated, all one and leading up to logical end. We may go back link by link and find clue.

    c. Pilate preparing for this act by life of cruelty and selfishness.

    d. Test sure to come and will find us out—character and life decide, and these not of one moment.

5. The Seriousness of Personal Accountability.

    a. One may divest self of much, such as clothing, etc. —but not of responsibility.

    b. Excuses: "way brought up"—"led into it" But strip self of these also and still find impossibility of evasion.

6. The Loss through Weakness.

    a. Pilate made mistake of life by not standing by Jesus, by seeing right and yet not doing it.

    b. "I wish" not enough—"I will" must be said and meant and carried out.

    c. Nearness to light and yet blindness to Christ's beauty and authority.

    d. Full of fear for own position and power, Pilate sacrificed Jesus to clamor and cruelty of crowd.

II. *The Jews—The Weakness of Wickedness*

  A. *The Narrative*

    1. The Intimidation of Pilate.
      His wish overridden by people's will so as to impress him.

    2. The Hatred of Jesus.
      So deadly as to make them determined to be rid of Him at all costs.

    3. The Choice of Barabbas.
      Inconsistency at its worst—accusing Jesus of sedition, and yet accepting Barabbas who was in prison for same offense and, in addition, for murder and robbery.

    4. The Delivery of Jesus into their Hands.

a. Thought all was over—what weak reasoning!

b. With excuse, "No king but Caesar," accepted anything so that Jesus might be murdered—what wickedness!

B. *The Truths*

1. The Necessity of Decision.

   a. Christ comes bringing light, love, wisdom, peace.

   b. Great question is: "What shall I do then with Jesus which is called Christ?" (Matt. 27:22)

2. The Importance of Decision.

   a. We may appear not to decide—yet we do.

   b. What we love, that we are.

   c. Character seen most clearly not in spasmodic action, but in spirit, motive, supreme desire.

   d. What we wish to be if we can be is test.

3. The Possibilities of Decision.

   a. Far-reaching influence over human nature both spiritual and sensual.

   b. Wickedness useless in face of God's almighty power and will—so today as ever.

N.B. These Jewish rulers were men who made fatal choice by deliberate hostility to Christ.

Conclusion

1. *Jesus calls out real quality of human nature.*

   a. Revealing weakness of Pilate and wickedness of Jews.

   b. Making neutrality and unreality impossible.

   c. Being silent and yet causing sinful man to talk.

   d. Looking into man's soul and compelling manifestation.

2. *We must define our relation to Him.*

    a. Opposing? Then sure defeat—develop weakness and wickedness, and end in ruin.

    b. Obeying? Then certain growth—develop strength and goodness, and end in His presence forever.

Therefore—"Acquaint now thyself with Him, and be at peace: thereby good shall come unto thee" (Job 22:21).

90

THE CRUCIFIXION AND DEATH
OF CHRIST
(Luke 23:33-49)

Much in Luke's account of the Crucifixion is found only in this Gospel, and a careful comparison of his story with the other three is rewarding. After Peter's denial (22:54-62), came the accusation before Pilate (23:1-7), the appearance before Herod (vs. 8-12), and the judgment of Pilate (vs. 13-25). Then followed the crucifixion (vs. 26-43) and the death (vs. 44-49). Luke's account is deeply impressive in the unbroken continuity of its clauses. They are linked together by the simple conjunction "and," giving the impression of sorrows multiplied and protracted. But out of this ocean of griefs stand what have been called "three tall cliffs with lights on their summits"—three of the Seven Last Words of Jesus from the Cross: the first, the second, and the seventh. They suggest three pictures of Christ on which to dwell, so that we shall come to see "Jesus only," with everything else in the story incidental.

I. *The Great High Priest* (vs. 33-38)
   A. *The Crucifixion*
      1. Marked absence of details of physical sufferings (v.33).
         a. The place—"there"
         b. The executioners—"they"
         c. The deed—"crucified"
         d. The victim—"Him"

      2. Jesus regarded as chief malefactor (v.33)—"in the midst" (John 19:18).
         a. Christ's Cross center of human history.

b. Towards it everything converged—all through Old Testament, God working up to it.

c. From it everything flowed—all through New Testament, God working out from it.

3. The prayer of Jesus in this "First Word" (v.34).

a. Address—"Father"—deep consciousness of Sonship to God.

b. Appeal—"forgive them"—authoritative intercession of Priestly work. Word "forgive" contraction of "forth" and "give," or give sin forth that it may go clean away—out of sight and mind (cf. scapegoat of Lev. 16:5-10).

c. Argument—"for they know not what they do"—suggesting blindness which was really guilty (cf. John 15:22-25), yet Christ's love found way to make it basis of plea.

(1) Ignorance may diminish yet cannot destroy sin, and sins of ignorance need forgiveness. God's commands absolute, not conditional on man's knowledge or opinion.

(2) Sin always greater than it seems, because sinner never knows extent of loss involved.

(3) All sin more or less from ignorance, but some ignorance is more culpable than involuntary.

B. *The Onlookers*

1. Who they were (vs. 35,36).
In three classes:

a. Curious crowd, with some indifference and some sympathy;

b. Malicious rulers, with virulent hatred;

c. Mocking soldiers, with sheer brutality.

2. What they said (vs. 35,37).

a. In intense animosity, Christ's foes actually bore witness to His power to save—"He saved others."

b. They were also right in saying further, "Himself He cannot save" (Mark 15:31), for He could not if He was to save others, sacrifice being essential to salvation.

c. Taunt of soldiers also directed at Jews, because of—

C. *The Superscription* (v.38)

1. Drawn up by Pilate probably as taunt to Jews who had once had kings and hoped to have one again—perhaps implied that violent death would be *his* fate also.

2. Protested by Jews, showing how sadly they had disowned Jesus.

3. Overruled by God—taunt turned to truth, for it is gloriously true that the Cross was in reality Throne of Christ, and He was then, as ever—

II. *The Glorious King* (vs. 39-43)

A. *Penitence and Impenitence*

1. Reproach of impenitent robber intended as jeer as well as plea, but in reality fine testimony.

2. Rebuke of other striking, in recognition of justice in regard to themselves and injustice in regard to Christ.

3. Reminder of "same condemnation" for all.

B. *Prayer*

1. Sublime faith.

According to King James Version, addressed Jesus as "Lord," implying that at that time he was only person on earth believing in Christ's Lordship. Joseph Parker, in remarkable sermon on this incident, says: "All the disciples are mean men, intellectually, compared with this dying malefactor. They never discovered, up to the time of the Crucifixion, intellectual vigour enough to conceive a figure like this . . . He saw the Lord in the Victim."

2. Broad outlook.
   a. Believed Jesus had a kingdom.
   b. Believed Jesus had power in it.
3. Humble petition.
   a. Believed being remembered by Jesus would be advantageous.
   b. Believed Jesus would remember him in spite of sin.

C. *Pardon*
   1. Blessedness unexpected—"with Me in Paradise"—not wait for kingdom.
   2. Blessedness assured—"thou shalt be"—Jesus' claim, even when dying, of power over unseen world.
   3. Blessedness immediate—"today"—begun in prison, continued on cross, to be ended in Paradise.

D. *Pattern*
   1. Dying thief often regarded as illustrating salvation at eleventh hour. "One was saved that none should despair, and only that none should presume."
   2. Salvation at death blessed possibility, but soul confronted earlier with Christ's claims must not use dying thief to justify postponement of decision; for we do not know that he ever had earlier opportunity of seeing Christ.
   3. What is really true is, we are assured of salvation for everyone who repents and believes: this is truth of matter, only truth, and nothing more.

III. *The Atoning Sacrifice* (vs. 44-49)
   A. *The Last Hours*
      1. Jesus in agony.
      2. Nature in darkness.
      3. Humanity in awe.

B. *The Last Words*
   1. Consciousness clear—last thought in heart.
   2. Confidence full—"Father" last name on lips.
   3. Sacrifice voluntary—last act of will.

C. *The Last Actions*
   1. The Lord's life surrendered—"yielded" (Matt. 27: 50)—Gr., "dismissed His spirit," implying act of will, and differentiated from all other physical death (cf. John 12:18). God's will fulfilled—Christ's duty done.
   2. The world's life secured—way opened for salvation and welcome. Rending of veil indicated man could now approach God.
   3. The individual life influenced—humanity awed by sight (vs. 48,49), but personal testimony of centurion was striking proof of reality of Christ's character and life—"righteous man" (v.47), "Son of God" (Matt. 27:54).

Conclusion
   1. *The Atonement as a Fact*
      a. Christ as High Priest speaks of love; as King, of power; as Sacrifice, of grace.
      b. His death, resurrection, and ascension inseparable: death as Sacrifice, resurrection as King, ascension as Priest.
      c. From God's standpoint, Christ's death meant—
         (1) Manifestation of His righteousness against sin (cf. Rom. 3:25, R.V.);
         (2) Revelation of His love to man (cf. John 3:16). While His righteousness could not be indifferent to sin, His love could not be indifferent to sinner.
      d. From man's standpoint, Christ's death means—
         (1) Redemption—brought back to God (cf. 1 Pet. 3:18).

(2) Holiness—fitted to dwell with God. (cf. Tit. 2: 14).

2. *The Atonement as a Sacrifice*

   a. The testimony of prophecy (Old Testament)—God preparing salvation for thousands of years and knowing His Son would suffer.

   b. The testimony of history (Gospels)—Christ enduring suffering in life culminating in awful agonies of Cross.

   c. The testimony of doctrine (Epistles)—God "spared not His own Son" (Rom. 8:32); "the precious blood of Christ" (1 Pet. 1:19).

3. *The Atonement as a Power*

   a. Grace procured by Christ and possessed by faith, so there must be—

      (1) Personal surrender—repentance.

      (2) Personal appropriation—faith.

      (3) Personal realization—power.

      (4) Personal manifestation—obedience.

      So Christ and believer one in death and in life.

   b. Greatest proof of Christ's death and resurrection—Christ magnified in believer.

   c. Path brighter and brighter until we enter heaven, where atonement no longer needed as means of salvation, but still remains subject of believer's praise forever.

91

THE WOMEN AT THE SEPULCHRE
(Luke 23:55—24:2)

"THAT the thoughts of many hearts may be revealed" (2:35), said the aged Simeon of the Child Jesus. It was true all through our Lord's life, but especially so of His death and resurrection. By His death enemies were revealed in all their unmasked hatred, and the resurrection disclosed His friends in their love and devotion. Let us consider now the women who had ministered to Him during His lifetime as they followed His sacred body to its resting-place, and see the revelation of their love and to their sight.

I. *Love's Devotion*

1. Women last at Cross (v.49), and first at sepulchre—men evidently absent.

2. Cross represents Christ's love to us. By staying close to it, we draw motive for service: by standing afar off, we are not found in forefront of His army.

3. Love is fact, and force, not mere feeling.

II. *Love's Continuance*

1. Women had been told by Christ of His resurrection, but had not believed, or else had not planned to embalm His Body, indicating end of it.

2. No longer trusted, but still loved—if not as Saviour and King, yet as Friend and Teacher. Memory remained.

3. Faith had failed, but love outlived faith and held fast.

> But dark the shadow of the Cross
> Fell then o'er earth and sky;
> There was an echo in each heart
> To that deriding cry—
> "He saved others." Can it be
> Himself He cannot save?
> Ah! Love lives still, but Faith and Hope
> Lie crushed within His grave.

III. *Love's Sacrifice*

1. Women prepared, purchased, and brought costly gifts.
2. Why this "waste"? Because love will always make sacrifices and find relief in so doing. Cf. Mary's advance anointing (John 12:7).

> A rose to the living is more
> Than sumptuous wreaths to the dead;
> In filling love's infinite store,
> A rose to the living is more
> If graciously given before
> The hungering spirit is fled.
>
> (Nixon Waterman)

3. No, love and prudence do not always dwell together.

IV. *Love's Obedience*

1. In spite of anxiety to honor Christ's Body, women rested on sabbath—would not make even passionate grief excuse for disobedience.
2. Law He used to keep, so they, though hearts set on labor of love—must have found it hard to wait.
3. Love not impulse to run wild or ride above duty, nor affection which moves in violation of law.

V. *Love's Reward*

1. Women first saw empty tomb.
2. Women first saw living Lord.
3. Women first heard loving words.
4. Women first told joyful news.

Conclusion

Thus the light of resurrection reveals them—still shining examples of love for Christ. How does it reveal you?

92

THE RESURRECTION OF CHRIST
(Luke 24:1-12)

I<small>T HAS</small> been said that "the Christian Church is built on an empty grave," and certainly it is impossible to over-estimate the importance of Christ's resurrection. Luke's account of it is short, but it has its own distinctive characteristics, such as the role of the women and the emphasis on the disbelief of the disciples. It is especially interesting to note the gradual preparation of overstrained hearts to receive the marvel of the ages: first, the vacant grave, second, the presence of angels, and then the unmistakable evidence, all leading up to the actual sight of the Risen Lord Himself (vs. 13ff.).

I. *The Empty Tomb* (vs. 1-3)

    A. *The Early Visitors* (v.1)

        1. Their Hopelessness.

            a. Women had come to embalm Body of dead Friend no longer their Hope and Joy, as once He had been.

            b. Preparation for embalming shows absolute despair of all, assuming usual end of Body. Yet—

        2. *Their Love.*

            a. Even if Christ not Saviour and Lord, still their dearest Friend and best Man ever known.

            b. So did not cease to love but did best possible for Body.

            c. Endless love includes undying constancy, yearning desire, and solace of self-sacrifice.

B. *The Displaced Stone* (v.2)

    1. Barrier dreaded.

        a. First thought in women's minds because of great weight for feeble strength (cf. Mark 16:3).

        b. Probably expected men followers of Christ still to be absent.

    2. Barrier Removed.

        a. God works for those He loves and leads.

        b. He goes before, and they find way made ready beyond expectation.

        c. Looking ahead, they think of stone in way, but when they press on God shows it "rolled away."

        d. Why was it removed? Not to enable Him to leave tomb, but to allow others to see He had gone.

C. *The Missing Body* (v.3)

    1. Notwithstanding Cruel Death.

        a. *Question for friends then.*

        b. *Question for foes ever since.*

    2. Notwithstanding Careful Watch.

        a. Consider burial, stone, seal, guard.

        b. Two alternative explanations: human, or supernatural:

            (1) If human, friends or foes:

                (a) If friends—could they?

                (b) If foes—would they?

            (2) Therefore, supernatural power removed **Body of Christ.**

II. *The Angels' Message* (vs. 4-7)

    A. *Visitors Heavenly* (vs. 4,5)

        1. Troubled mortals—man's extremity.

        a. Perplexity (v.4), and fear (v.5).

        b. No hope or expectation of resurrection—minds remote.

    2. Ministering angels—God's opportunity.

        a. Assurance—"in shining garments" (v.4)

        b. Correction—"Why seek ye the living among the dead?" (v.5)

B. *Resurrection Assured* (v.6)

    1. Absence of Body—"not here," as they could see.

    2. Cause—"risen," as they still did not realize.

C. *Instruction Recalled* (v.7)

    1. The Cross inevitable—atoning.

    2. The Resurrection inevitable—exalting.

        a. Forgotten words come back with fresh meaning when circumstances have changed and we have made progress in knowledge and character.

        b. Words spoken need experience to interpret them, to grow up to them—dormant until explained by life.

    Illus.: Lamp in tunnel seems but pinpoint of light until approach shows its true size.

    Illus.: Children's minds stored with truth will be illuminated in later life.

III. *The Clear Evidence* (vs. 8-12)

A. *Credible Witnesses* (v.9)

    1. Good news possessed.

    2. Good news proclaimed—these women first preachers! What joy was theirs!

B. *General Unbelief* (v.11)

    1. Testimony disbelieved—phrase "idle tales" shows minds of disciples not predisposed to faith.

C. *Definite Confirmation* (v.12)

    1. The eager visit.

        a. Peter must have gone on winged feet—possible all was not lost.

        b. But must also have remembered sin of denial—sharpest pang is caused by impossibility of changing past.

        c. So hoped, and showed usual impetuosity.

    2. The wondering return.

        a. Why eager to run and yet not to believe?

        b. Weighted down with great sin, heart slow to hope.

        c. John "believed" (John 20:8) —Peter "departed, wondering" (v.12) .

        d. "Linen clothes laid by themselves"—literally, rolled up and, if raised, would be found like deserted chrysalis, with no body in them.

        e. Cf. John 20:7—"the napkin . . . wrapped together in a place by itself"—separate from rest, to indicate Body had extricated itself without unrolling clothes.   Otherwise removal of Body in natural way would have been plausible explanation.   H. Clay Trumbull called this a "divinely inspired emphasis upon the 'exhibit' of the grave clothes of Jesus as a convincing sign of His resurrection."

Conclusion

The Resurrection of Jesus Christ is the foundation, the pivot, the keynote of Christianity. It is unique in the world's religions, for Confucius, Zoroaster, Buddha, Mohammed, etc., died but did not rise again.

    1. *The Resurrection ratifies Christ's loftiest claims.*

        a. Conclusive testimony to His Word.

        b. Strong vindication to His Character.

"Easter morning was the Father's audible Amen to all

the claims of Jesus Christ." (George Matheson).

2. *The Resurrection declares God's acceptance of Christ's sacrifice.*

   a. Bill for debt of sin had been paid and receipted.

   b. Christ raised because of, not for, justification (see note on Rom. 4:25 in Weymouth).

3. *The Resurrection manifests our pattern of life.*

   a. We are to be dead to sin and living to God, as was Christ Rom. 6:10; Col. 3:1-4).

   b. We are to conquer day by day (Matt. 28:20).

4. *The Resurrection reveals our power for life.*

   a. Christ who died, lives, and therefore God accepts and justifies us—cf. Paul's emphasis in Rom. 8:34—"yea, rather"—on resurrection.

   b. His death and resurrection not to be separated—we are not saved by believing in His death, but by believing on Him—death and life included, as in Rom. 5:10.

   c. "Power of His resurrection" (Phil. 3:10) is His risen life for and in us. "Those that know the power of Christ's resurrection have their feet upon adamant" (W. Robertson Nichol).

5. *The Resurrection assures us of a present Friend.*

   a. Christianity not memory of dead Christ to be cherished.

   b. Christianity is companionship with loving Christ to be shared (Gal. 2:20; Heb. 7:25).

6. *The Resurrection anticipates future glory.*

   a. Our own resurrection involved.

   b. As man raises himself to his feet, so Christ will raise His own Body, the Church.

Are we, being spiritually "risen with Christ" (Col. 3:1), and ready to "reign in life by one, Jesus Christ" (Rom. 5:17), looking forward to that glorious time when our bodies will be either "raised" or "changed" (1 Cor. 15:52)?

> "When Jesus died on Calvary,
>   I, too, was there;
> 'Twas in my place He stood for me,
> And now accepted—even as He,
>   His right I share.
>
> When Jesus rose with life divine,
>   I, too, was there;
> His resurrection power is mine,
> And, as the branches and the vine,
>   His life I share.
>
> When Jesus comes some day for me,
>   I shall be there;
> With Him and like Him I shall be,
> And all His glorious majesty,
>   I, too shall share.
>
> O blessed life, so deep, so high!
>   Lord, keep me there;
> Help me with Christ to live, to die,
> And let me with Him by and by
>   His glory share."

(A. B. Simpson)

93

THE STONE ROLLED AWAY
(Luke 24:2)

Many years ago, there lived in the city of Hannover, Germany, a countess of pronounced infidel opinions who absolutely denied a future resurrection. As though to show her defiance of any Divine power which might possibly exist, she ordered that at her death her body should be laid under a massive and, in her judgment, impregnable structure. Her wishes were carried out, and heavy slabs of granite were cemented together and riveted with steel clamps. On the tomb were carved the words: "This burial plot must never be opened." It seemed quite likely that the structure would remain intact for many generations at least, and that the bones of the sceptical countess would rest in the oblivion she desired. But there was a strange sequel to her plans. A tiny seed had shared the woman's resting-place and with its inherent power had burst its shell and sent its small roots into the ground. Then, slowly gathering strength and proportions with the years, it wrenched open its prison doors and severed in twain the granite slabs. Having reached the daylight, the plant spread itself heavenward, until it became a great tree. And there in the cemetery in Hannover today* lie the huge stones divided and fallen over, forced by the power of Nature to give the tree room for its expanding girth.

This is a faint illustration of what happened to the Lord Jesus. His enemies could not leave even His grave alone, but

---

* 1890 is the first date which appears on this sermon.

must needs make it secure by means of stone, seal, and soldiers, because they remembered some words of His about rising the third day. Although their expressed reason for all these precautions was the fear lest His disciples should come and seize the body, it is evident that they had given some thought to the bare possibility that the great Miracle-Worker of Nazareth might baffle them by a resurrection. Be this as it may, the Seed that fell into the earth by that death brought forth much fruit. "Vain the watch, the stone, the seal"—and in the might of His Resurrection the Lord arose and overcame them all. When the women came in the early morning of the first Lord's Day, "they found the stone rolled away from the sepulchre." That stone rolled away tells of the mighty Resurrection by which Christ burst the granite-like opposition of sin, sinners, and Satan, and the "Seed of the woman" showed Himself to be also the Seed of that tree of Christianity which has its roots firmly fixed in the everlasting hills. Nourished by the sunshine and dew of the Spirit of God, it has spread forth its branches throughout the whole world.

What, then, can this stone rolled away teach us?

I. *The Stone was rolled Away from the Tomb of Christ*
   What was the Resurrection to Him? We are apt to think of it solely in relation to ourselves, or to the world, but what about its effect on Him as Man and as Servant of God? By it—

   1. *His ministry was resumed.*

      a. Throughout His life His one desire was to do His Father's will. At age of twelve He said: "I must be about My Father's business" (2:49); and early in ministry, while teaching, He had declared: "My meat is to do the will of Him that sent Me, and to finish His work" (John 4:34).

      b. Training of Twelve, blessing of young, healing of sick, preaching glad tidings, filled His life.

    c. But Cross interrupted.

    d. Now stone is rolled away from tomb and He is at work again, on that same Resurrection day, expounding Word (24:27), and during next forty days was to speak often with disciples on spiritual themes. Cf. Psa. 40:7,8.

2. *His higher life was begun.*

    a. Three years of weakness, pain, want, disappointment, opposition, suffering, death.

    b. Now all that at end and new life begun. Closed doors, words to Mary Magdalene, different form, showing higher life commenced and henceforward no sorrow or death (Cf. Rom. 6:9).

    c. What that meant, only He could have told, but perhaps glimpse in Rev. 1:18 and Heb. 12:2.

    d. We may rejoice that Resurrection for Him marked beginning of life of peace, power, and glory. But, above all,

3. *His claims were justified.*

    a. For three years under cloud of misconception, calumny, enmity.

    b. Claim to be Son of God met by strong denial.

    c. Called deceiver, blasphemer, and yet all while knew claims true.

    d. Hard to rest for years under stigma which He knew false and wait patiently, without attempting to disprove calumnies.

    e. Yet that sensitive spirit, that holy nature, that loving heart, bore these day after day, knowing well that one day everything would be made clear. And so it was, by Resurrection—"declared to be the Son of God with power" (Rom. 1:4).

Illus.: Just as room lit by skylight darkened by fall of snow, and then snow melted by rays of sun, so Christ's life darkened by aspersions of enemies, and then rays of Truth, chasing darkness, showed Him in glory and majesty by "power of resurrection" (Phil. 3:10).

f. God showed His thought of Christ by raising Him from dead and giving Him glory.

g. We can imagine joy and peace that filled Christ's heart as He stepped out of tomb, with light of God in soul, and in His ears words: "Thou art My Son . . . Thy throne, O God, is for ever and ever . . . Thou hast loved righteousness and hated iniquity . . . Thou, Lord, in the beginning hast laid the foundation of the earth . . . Sit on My right hand" (Heb. 1:5,8,9,10,13).

II. *The Stone was Rolled Away from the Hearts of the Disciples*

1. *Joy was restored.*

a. During three years of happy fellowship, hopes kindled, but death seemed to end all. "We trusted that it should have been He which should have redeemed Israel" (24:21).

b. Yet could not leave spot—spent three days in Jerusalem where hopes lay buried.

c. Deep gloom settled down and they never expected to see Master again.

d. But when He rose, doubts removed, mists rolled away, and from that day never lost joy.

e. Even at Ascension there was joy (24:52,53), because Christ more real than ever; and joy prominent in Acts (2:46, etc,; Cf. John 16:22; 1 Pet. 1:8).

2. *Salvation was completed*

a. Christ had come to die for sinners, but not till Resurrection could it be known.

    b. Hence 1 Cor. 15:7—no such thing as confidence in dead for help or salvation.

    c. But now debt cancelled, sin blotted out, God's receipt issued by raising and glorifying His Son.

3. *Holiness was assured*

    a. One has sins forgiven—another enabled to live holy life, having past blotted out and told to sin no more.

    b. But same Lord who made peace gives holiness by resurrection life.

    c. Note Rom. 6:9,14: "Death hath no more dominion over Him . . . sin shall not have dominion over you."

III. *The Stone was Rolled Away from Graves of Our Dear Ones*
Few families into which death has not entered—so many are larger on other side.

1. *The sting of death was removed.*

    a. Remember first experience of death in household—solitariness, stillness, blinds drawn in darkened room where lay covered, pale form, sobs and tears, children bewildered. Faint picture of what life would be with no Resurrection.

    b. But now Christ has removed sting.

    c. Some are afraid to die and fear is bondage. No need —Christ died, but rose, and victory over sin meant victory over fear.

2. *The future life was assured.*

    a. Up to then none had come back except those raised by Christ, and what they told, if anything, is unrecorded.

    b. Christ not only came back, but showed way through death to everlasting life and light.

    c. His pledge—"Because I live, ye shall live also" (John 14:19).

    d. Gloom illumined—Cf. 2 Cor. 5:1-9.

3. *The reunion with loved ones was guaranteed.*

   a. Not lost, but gone before.

   b. By and by, mother and babe, husband and wife, father and child, mother and son, will be together again. "For if we believe that Jesus died and rose . . . then we . . . shall be caught up together with them . . . Wherefore comfort one another with these words" (1 Thess. 4:14-18).

Conclusion

What is the Resurrection of Christ to us personally?

1. If we are "dead in sins"—

   a. Stone still there, but Christ ready to say "Come forth" (John 11:43)

   b. Resurrection both future and present (Cf. John 5:25).

   c. If so, it will be real Easter at Christ's sepulchre which opened from inside by His life and power.

   d. For sin there will be salvation; for death there will be life.

2. If we are already "alive from the dead"—

   a. Let us rejoice in everything brought us by our Lord on this day.

   b. Let us thank God for Christmas—it is indeed precious —but the Lord is not in the manger; let us thank God for Lent—it is undoubtedly helpful—but the Lord is not in the wilderness; let us thank God for Good Friday and Easter Even—they are truly heart-stirring—but the Lord is not on the Cross nor in the grave.

   c. He is on the Throne; and now it is always Easter— and always Pentecost—to the disciples of Christ—even on Good Friday and Easter Eve, when merely "religious" people are gloomy and sad (cf. Rom. 6:9,10).

   d. We need simple faith of New Testament Christians.

    3. If we have special difficulty or sorrow, let it not rob us of Resurrection joy.

       a. Let us cast off grave clothes, as He did, and stand upright.

       b. Let us look up with fervent love, full confidence, living hope.

       c. Let us receive His life, go forth to tell others, and manifest in our lives the blessed truth that Christ is "alive forevermore" (Rev. 1:18).

94

LIVING OR DEAD?
(Luke 24:5)

T HE faithful women who came early to the sepulchre were looking for a dead Christ, and so, of course, they did not find Him. "It was not possible," we are told. "that He should be holden of it"—death (Acts 2:24). Before these women lay—

I. *A Great Mystery*
1. His perfect oneness with human life—even to death.
2. His perfect atonement for human sin—through death.

II. *A Great Marvel*
1. His work accomplished—the atonement accepted.
2. His salvation available—past, present, future—making trust in the dead impossible.

But the women were making—

III. *A Great Mistake*
1. They showed right spirit, but in wrong way—love and respect to Christ's memory, but forgetfulness of His words.
2. This mistake being repeated today—by looking back only to death of Christ and dead past (instead of up as well —to living Christ above), such as those who advocate "ten minutes' colloquy with Christ before a Crucifix" (Furse). Cf. these words: "There is no such Christ; He is not here, He is risen. The crucifix is not the true symbol of redemption . . . Rather the cross shining in the halo of the glory beyond and the crown above" (A.B. Simpson).

Conclusion

Christianity, therefore, is—

1. Trust in a Person.
2. Trust in a Living Person.
3. Trust in a Present Person.
4. Trust in a Powerful Person.

Yes, Christ is a personal, living, present, powerful Saviour. Is He yours?

> 'Tis Easter morn! No more the world
>   Lies hushed in silent gloom,
> No more the sepulchre's dread walls
>   The living Lord entomb.
> Rejoice—the stone is rolled away,
>   The Lord is risen—'tis Easter day.
>
> O sorrowing soul! that long has kept
>   Thy weary watch with sin,
> Throw wide thy darkened doors today,
>   And let the sunlight in;
> Be sad no more; lift up thine eye,
>   The Lord is risen, He reigns on high.
>
> The Lord is risen! O earth, rejoice,
>   Thy myriad voices raise,
> Till heaven's blue arches ring again
>   With songs of solemn praise,
> And far resounds the exultant cry,
>   The Lord is risen, He reigns on high.

95

THE WITNESS OF THE GOSPELS
TO THE RESURRECTION
(Luke 24:6)

T HERE was one point on the battlefield at Waterloo which was taken and re-taken three times during that memorable day. Both Napoleon and Wellington realized the strategic importance of its position, and so concentrated attention on it. Its ultimate possession and retention by British troops doubtless contributed largely to the final result of the battle.

One point in connection with Christianity has been felt from the first to be the vital center of everything, and that is the Resurrection of Christ. Consequently, the enemies of Christianity have concentrated their attacks and its defenders have centered their defense on it. All have realized how essential, how fundamental the Resurrection is to the whole structure of Christianity. With this uncertain, all else is uncertain too, but with this safe, all is safe. Christianity is either based on fact or it is useless.

Among the lines of evidence on which we invite the fullest expression and welcome all possible light is the witness of the Gospels to the Resurrection. Take these records as they stand, in all their simplicity, sincerity and directness. Admittedly, first century documents and most recent criticism tend to push the Gospels back to dates nearer to the events recorded than had once been considered possible. Modern man may be assured beyond the shadow of a doubt that the Resurrection is a historical fact.

I. *The Fact of the Empty Grave.*

These historic occurrences have never been challenged to this day:

1. Christ died.
2. Christ was buried.
3. On third day, tomb empty.

These events were entirely in accord with His miraculous life and Divine character. "It behoved Christ to suffer, and to rise from the dead the third day" (v.46).

II. *The Disappearance of the Body*

1. Consider burial, stone, seal, guard—and yet, no Body!
2. There are two alternative explanations: human or supernatural.

   a. If human, friends or foes:

   (1) If friends, could they?
   Chrysostom points out if Body stolen would not have been stolen naked, because of delay in stripping and removing drugs adhering to it.

   (2) If foes, would they?
   How account for Jews' failure to disprove resurrection? Fairbairn says: "The silence of the Jews is as significant as the speech of the Christians."

III. *The Record of the Appearances*

1. There were two series: at Jerusalem, in Galilee.
2. Evidence of personal testimony—e.g., Emmaus story (vs. 13-35), visit of Peter and John to sepulchre (John 20: 3-10).
3. But what of alleged discrepancies?

   a. None sufficient to invalidate testimony to—

   (1) Empty grave;
   (2) Appearances.

   b. Very existence of variations for nineteen centuries testimony to conviction of truth.

Illus.: Records by eyewitnesses as to events of, e.g., Indian Mutiny, Battle of Sedan, vary in details; yet no question as to historic fact itself.

c. If everything fitted exactly, very fact would be raised as objection and termed collusion.

d. Therefore Church not afraid to leave them as they are because of main fact. Ramsay shows entire compatibility of practical certainty as to main fact with great uncertainty as to precise details. Trustworthiness of whole not affected by any uncertainty as to parts (*St. Paul The Traveler*, p.29).

IV. *The Transformation of the Disciples*

1. After Crucifixion, there was—

   a. On first and second days, sadness—on third day, gladness.

   b. On first and second days, hopelessness—on third day, certain hope.

2. Disciples were incredulous at first and had themselves to be convinced—not eager to "hope against hope" or indulge in "wishful thinking."

3. Nothing else could account for change—mere removal of Body certainly could not, nor can it be dismissed as purely psychological problem.

4. Three days not long enough for legend to develop—needs time.

5. Spiritual efficacy of Resurrection unchallenged—opponents through centuries unable to produce fruit equal to that of Christian Church.

Conclusion

These four Gospels—

1. Have been instruction of Church for ages;
2. Have never been more valued than today;

    3. Welcome all possible tests and use, for they are—
      a. Pure (Psa. 119:140);
      b. Tried (Psa. 18:30).

Therefore, what they say of the Resurrection of Christ is credible, authentic, and to be included in what Luke in his preface calls "those things which are most surely believed among us" (1:1).

96

A PERSONAL EXPERIENCE
(Luke 24:13-32)

T HE STORY of the walk to Emmaus gives us one of the fullest and most beautiful of the Resurrection appearances of Christ. If it were possible to think that Luke himself might have been one of the two travelers, the other being Cleopas (v.18; cf.John 19:25), it would mean that this story was an eyewitness account. It is very doubtful, however, whether Luke was or could have been an eyewitness of any part of our Lord's earthly life, especially in view of what he says in his Introduction (1:2).

But that Luke had sources of information not open either to Matthew or to Mark it is impossible to doubt. Dr. Plummer says: "This narrative is peculiar to Luke, and is among the most beautiful of the treasures which he alone has preserved for us. He almost certainly obtained his information from one of the two disciples, and probably in writing. The account has all the effect of personal experience."

The value of the story is (1) Evidential—a proof of Christ's Resurrection is furnished by the hours of intercourse between the Risen Saviour and these two disciples; (2) Preparatory—such an experience may be considered part of their apprenticeship, as our Lord prepared His followers for His complete bodily absence, and permitted them, as it were, a transition between the old days of sight and the new days of faith; and (3) Symbolic—for when two talk together with Christ as their theme, He draws near, especially if their hearts are troubled, lifting their despondency and enlightening their darkness.

I. *The Sorrowful Walk* (vs. 13-24)

A. *The Conversation*

1. The Day—"that same day" (v.13) —"the first day of the week" (v.1), "The Day of Resurrection."

2. The Destination—"a village called Emmaus" (v.13), about eight miles from Jerusalem.

3. The Disciples—"two of them" (v.13; Mark 16:12) — "one of them whose name was Cleopas" (v.18).

4. The Despondency—"ye walk, and are sad" (v.17).

5. The Difference—"they . . . reasoned" (v.15, "questioned," R.V.) —seems to indicate some difference of opinion.

B. *The Approach*

1. The Master—"Jesus Himself" (v.15). Stranger who joined them none other than Subject of their talk.

2. The Mistake—"their eyes were holden" (v.16) —"Art thou only a stranger?" (v.18) He chose to remain unrecognized because of purposes other than proof of Resurrection—*vide sup.*, Introd., (2) and (3).

3. The Method—"What manner of communications—?" (v.17) Showed interest, sympathy, love. Knowing facts as did no one else, Christ yet chose to draw out in order to clarify cause of sorrow.

C. *The Recital*

1. The Sorrow—"hast not known—?" (v.18) Sorrowful think their cloud enwraps everyone, anything else impossible.

2. The Story—"concerning . . . and how—" (v.19). Sad outpouring of hearts unlocked by sympathy.

3. The Survivor—"a prophet mighty in deed and word before God and all the people" (v.19). To them He was still Prophet and Miracle-Worker, approved by God and man.

    a. Love thus outlived faith.

    b. Christ still revered, loved, mourned.

    c. But love cannot survive long without faith. If Christ had not risen, love would have drooped and at length failed.

    d. He would then have been regarded as deceiver even by His followers.

D. *The Perplexity*

  1. The Doubt—"but we trusted" (v.21). Had waited till third day, but if longer still all doubts would have been settled.

  2. The Disappointment—"today is the third day" (v.21). Did they mean—

    a. Long time had passed, or—

    b. This was day mentioned by Master, momentarily remembered, then lost sight of?

  3. The Difficulty—"made us astonished" (v.22), because of "report of report" of Body's absence.

    a. Note word "alive" rather than "risen."

    b. Surely enough had been reported to encourage faith.

    c. Shows depth of hopelessness, hope having been aroused, then shattered.

II. *The Wonderful Talk* (vs. 25-27)

The Lord emphasized three truths:

A. *Prophets Proclaiming* (v.25)

Had foretold things these men had failed to believe.

  1. Disciples rebuked in both intellect and heart.

  2. Disciples thus led to faith first and not to sight.

    a. Knowledge gained in time of happiness not so lasting, for we will believe anything then.

    b. Lessons learned in sadness abide, for sorrow clarifies thought and steadies emotion.

B. *Messiah Suffering* (v.26)

Had to fulfill former revelation:

1. Suffering and glory revealed not simply in fact, but in relation to past, giving disciples—

   a. Larger conception of Himself.

   b. Broader basis for faith.

   c. Wider scope for work.

2. Necessity shown for death and resurrection.

   a. Spiritual—stressed by Luke, while other Evangelists emphasize great fact (Mark); glorious manifestation (Matthew); influence on believers (John).

   b. Typical—sacrifices, scapegoat, etc.

   c. Prophetic—Isaiah, Daniel, David.

   d. Doctrinal—Priest and Victim, but also King.

   e. Personal—acknowledgment of Father's test of Son's obedience.

   f. Historical—Christ's own references.

C. *Scripture Unfolding* (v.27)

To prove truth and confirm rebuke.

1. "In the Old Testament the New is enfolded; in the New Testament the Old is unfolded."

2. Cf. grander outlook as Gospel ends and Acts of Apostles begins—latter—

   a. Full of quotations from Jewish Scriptures.

   b. Shows Christ as key of past and future.

III. *The Opened Eyes* (vs. 28-32)

1. Disciples urged Stranger to stay with them, and He accepted.

2. He shared their meal and it became sacrament.

3. They recognized Him—by method of taking, blessing, breaking, giving of bread? Or by marks on His hands as He used them?

Though He talked of the Kingdom and all it would bring,
The disciples knew not that they walked with the King;
At the evening repast, on the home table spread,
He was known unto them in the breaking of bread.

So we wonder, we question, we doubt, and we fear,
Seeking Christ in the distance who liveth so near,
And then back to the hearthstone at eventide led
He is known unto us in the breaking of bread.

Through the swift transformations, the movements sublime
That have startled the ages, and still fashion time,
The Divine hand appears; but its glory is shed
Through the acts we count simple, like breaking of bread.

With the purest emotions our hearts may have burned
When the presence of Christ was but dimly discerned;
Yet the spiritual hunger no other has fed—
He is known to our souls in the breaking of bread.

(Alfred J. Hough)

4. With astonishment and joy, they realized what had been happening all along way.

5. Thus, the Scriptures having been opened (vs. 27,32), the disciples' eyes were opened (v.31), and their lips were opened (v.35).

Conclusion

It is vitally important to remember the truth of the saying: "After Easter, always Easter!" Because Christ our Passover was sacrificed for us, we are to "keep continual festival" (1 Cor. 5:8,Gr.) —not fast, even on Good Friday. The Emmaus story suggests some of the features of our life with the Risen Lord.

1. Christ is always—
   a. Journeying with us.
   b. Sympathizing with us
   c. Expounding the Scriptures to us.
   d. Revealing Himself to us.

2. Let us therefore respond by—
   a. Welcoming Him to abide with us.
   b. Rejoicing in Him with our hearts "burning within" us.
   c. Discerning Him in "the breaking of bread."
   d. Telling of our experience of Him to others.

97

CHRISTIAN FRIENDSHIP
(Luke 24:13-35)

Hɪsᴛᴏʀʏ has been described as "the record of individuals used by God for helping onward progress." From time to time, history has centered in one man, or in a particular group of men, to embody the spirit of the age. But behind the man there are the forces that impel him, causing him to be and do what he is and does. Among these forces a prominent place is occupied by friendship. It can be shown that in government, science, philosophy, art, heroism, friendship is a power. But now our object is to show it in Christianity, where it is always a method as well as a force. "By two and two" the Lord sent forth His disciples (Mark 6:7), and in Acts we see Peter and John, Paul and Barnabas working together. Great religious movements have been led or inspired by such pairs as Luther and Melancthon, Erasmus and Colet, the Wesleys, Moody and Sankey, Torrey and Alexander. Wherever Christianity has gone, there has gone also the highest type of friendship between men, for just as Christianity is the expression of the soul Godward, so friendship is the expression of the soul manward.

Now let us take the story of the walk to Emmaus as illustrating friendship and Christianity: not only Christ and one, but Christ and two on the journey of life; and the relationship of the Friend of sinners to true Christian friendship.

I. *A Good Start* (vs. 13-17)

    A. *Based on Christ* (v.13)

        1. "Two of them"—their walk together due to fact they were Christ's disciples.

      2. "Disciples" means learners—did not know all at first.

  B. *Concerned with Christ* (vs. 14,15)

      1. "They talked"—Christ the subject of thought and conversation.

      2. "They communed together and reasoned '—perhaps indicating differences .of opinion—not see alike, yet not affect friendship.

  C. *Known to Christ* (vs. 15,17)

      1. "Drew near, and went with them"—so now Christ owns friendship of His followers.

      2. Invited confidence—drew near when they were talking of Him.

      N.B. So these two friends kept together—had common interest.

II. *A Dark Passage* (vs. 18-24)

  A. *Sorrow* (vs. 18-20)

      1. Overwhelming—thought of nothing else.

      2. Real—had lost their best Friend and He had suffered death.

  B. *Disappointment* (v. 21)

      1. Hopes raised—"we trusted"—imagine glowing expression on faces as they remembered.

      2. Hopes destroyed—"third day"—so long—imagine swift sadness.

  C. *Perplexity* (vs. 22-24)

      1. The women's story—vision of angels—said Christ alive.

      2. The Saviour's absence—tomb empty—Christ away.

      N.B. Yet these friends kept together—sorrow drew them closer.

III. *A Sure Guide* (vs. 25-27)

  A. *Teaching Truth* (vs. 25-27)

      1. Reproof—"fools and slow of heart"

2. Reminder—"ought not Christ—?"
Christ needed to teach them.

B. *Arousing Interest* (vs. 28,29)
1. Feigning continuation of journey—"made as though—"
2. They constrained Him to tarry—"Abide with us"
Christ needed to test them.

C. *Giving Revelation* (vs. 30,31)
1. The familiar act—"took . . blessed . . brake . . gave"
(cf. Mark 14:22).
2. The living Saviour—"they knew Him"
a. But these were not in upper room (22:19) —must
have been present at feeding of 5000 (cf. 9:16),
or have recognized marks in His hands.
b. Thus He took them back to His Life, Death, Resurrection.
N.B. So these friends were kept together by their vital
interest in Christ and Scriptures—sum and substance of Christian friendship.

IV. *A Blessed Ending* (vs. 32-35)
A. *Acknowledging Enjoyment* (v.32)
1. Hearts burning—"Did not . . . while He talked—?"
2. Lives experiencing—"while He opened to us the
Scriptures," now proved to be true.

B. *Sharing Enjoyment* (vs. 33-35)
1. Realized necessity and made immediate start—"rose
up the same hour."
2. We went back to place and friends they had left—"returned to Jerusalem and found the eleven."
3. Heard what others reported—"saying—"
4. Kept back nothing of their own experience—"told
what things were done . . . and how He was known—"

N.B. So these two friends remained together—united more closely than ever, they rejoiced to have and to share.

Conclusion

1. *The experience of these two disciples may be summed up as follows:*

   a. Christ the Source of Friendship.
      (1) They found friendship, real, true, strong, lasting, in Him.
      (2) They found difficult things smoothed by experience of Christ, both individually and together.

   b. Christ the Strength of Friendship.
      (1) They were diverse, yet friends—because they had in Christ—
         (a) Common interest.
         (b) Common sympathy.
         (c) Common need.
      (2) Their friendship became strong through knowledge of the Scriptures, which lead to Christ.

   c. Christ the Satisfaction of Friendship.
      (1) They found, through revelation of Himself—
         (a) Companionship.
         (b) Confidence.
         (c) Comprehension.
         (d) Contentment.
      (2) They discovered that the indwelling Christ can satisfy social as well as all other needs of man.

2. *The experience of these two disciples may be ours today:*

   a. Christianity gives us as individuals a Friend, One who ends our loneliness and fear by first becoming our Saviour.

   b. Christianity ministers to all those social elements and instincts which form so great a part of daily life.

    c. Christianity knits together the various units of life and makes of human friendship a manifestation of a solidarity which is actual, palpable, permanent.

3. *The experience of worldly friendship is unsatisfactory:*

    a. Based on sin, it soon palls and often ends in antagonism.

    b. Based on self-interest, it lacks reality, for true friendship always puts self last.

    c. Based on neighborliness or congeniality, it cannot always stand strain of clashing interests.

    d. Based on patriotism, it is often flimsy, beginning and ending with sentiment.

    e. Based on blood relationship, it is strongest, but even this, alone, is incomplete.

4. *But the experience of Christian friendship lasts forever, for it is the foundation and completion of everything in life.*

    a. It shrinks from sin and repudiates it as a basis;

    b. It transforms self-interest into self-sacrifice;

    c. It strengthens neighborliness against the storms of life;

    d. It solidifies patriotism for the common good;

    e. It gives blood relationship added strength and permanence.

In Christ, therefore, human friendship finds oneness—real, strong, loving, lasting:

    a. Oneness of origin in Christ.

    b. Oneness of nature through Christ.

    c. Oneness of suffering for Christ.

    d. Oneness of grace from Christ.

    e. Oneness of purpose towards Christ, and afterwards—

    f. Oneness of Home with Christ.

Have we experienced friendship like this?

98

EMMAUS AND AFTER
(Luke 24:28-43)

THE appearances of our Lord after His Resurrection served a number of purposes at the time. They assured the faith and hope of His disciples; by them the followers of Christ were trained gradually for His absence; and the transition from knowing Him in His earthly form to losing that bodily presence altogether was made more easily through acquaintance with His spiritual body. For us, in our time, to read of the appearances of Christ confirms our faith in the reality of His Resurrection, teaches us about His present state, and suggests something of the future life of the believer after his own resurrection experience. Two of these appearances are recorded in the present passage. Let us look, first, at—

I. *The Momentary Manifestation* (vs. 28-32)

    A. *Jesus Journeying* (v. 28)

        1. Testing interest.

            a. Acted as any "stranger" would under circumstances.

            b. Would have gone on had not disciples "constrained" Him.

        2. Awakening desire.

            a. Conversation impressed them, evoking invitation.

            b. Made them realize experience, like everything of value, needs effort to retain it.

    B. *Jesus Staying* (v.29)

        1. The hosts—moved by lateness of hour and reluctance to let Stranger go.

2. The invitation—perhaps by restraining hands as well as constraining words.

3. The Guest—invited to lodge all night and share meal.

C. *Jesus Revealing* (vs. 30-32)

　　1. The familiar actions.

　　　　a. But not as of Last Supper—these two not present—perhaps mindful of miracles of feeding multitudes (cf. 9:16; Matt. 15:36).

　　　　b. Or recognized "prints" in hands.

　　2. The opened eyes.

　　　　a. Revelation to sense only after revelation to faith—did not believe because saw, but saw because believed in Resurrection (cf. John 20:29).

　　　　b. Talk had done its work—they saw from Scripture necessity of Resurrection (cf. "must," v.44; John 20:9; also "ought," v.26).

　　　　c. Thus recognition consequence of renewed faith, and not only reason for deepening of faith.

　　3. The glowing hearts.

　　　　a. Words rekindled flame "by the way."

　　　　b. Faith perfected by recognition and sealed by experience.

　　　　c. If Luke one of them, what remembrance as he wrote! (Cf. John 2:22)

　　4. The expressed feelings

　　　　a. Not of wonder at Resurrection, nor of sorrow at disappearance; simply of recalled glow of hearts.

　　　　b. Faith grasped Resurrection as predicted and necessary fact, and this uppermost in thoughts and words.

　　　　c. Thus wider scope opening up—not only return of Friend, but revelation of Lamb of God (cf. John 1:29).

D. *Jesus Withdrawing*
  1. Vanished because purpose of visit accomplished.
  2. Taught them to bear absence instead of enjoying bodily presence.
  3. Accustomed them to trust without sight.

II. *The Expectant Gathering* (vs. 33-35)
  A. *The Return* (v.33)
    1. Animated with new assurance.
      a. Did not wait even till morning.
      b. Silent Christian is anomaly.
    2. Bearing glad message.
      a. Full of joy.
      b. Eager to tell all.
    3. Seeking congenial company.
      a. Willing ears make all the difference.
      b. Returned to their own company (cf. Acts 4:23).

  B. The Reception (v.34)
    1. The Eleven—"gathered together" by Resurrection, as they had been dispersed by Death.
    2. The tidings—"indeed"—definite fact, assuring selves and others—no longer mere reported "vision" (v.23), or even empty tomb only.
    3. The appearance—"to Simon"—first apostle to see Him (cf. 1 Cor. 15:5). Penitence brought pardon and privilege.

  C. *The Report* (v.35)
    1. The weary walk.
    2. The strange Companion.
    3. The marvellous revelation.

III. *The Risen Christ* (vs. 36-43)
  A. *Appearing* (v.36)
    1. The Person—"Jesus Himself"

2. The Place—"in the midst of them"
3. The "Peace"—usual greeting as if after ordinary separation (cf. 10:5; Dan. 4:1, etc.)

B. *Dispelling Fears* (vs. 37-39)
1. The familiar tones—"He said"
2. The earnest questions—no reason to be "troubled" nor to have "reasonings" (R.V.).
3. The comforting assurance—"I myself"

C. *Granting Proofs* (vs. 39-43)
1. Identity—seeing Him.
2. Corporeity—handling Him.
3. Reality—watching Him eat.

Body glorified then—no change revealed afterwards—still "flesh and bones"—"a Man in the Glory."

Conclusion

"Abide with us" (v.29)

1. What are the conditions?
   a. On His side, He must be—
      (1) Teacher (v.27) —not Stranger (v.18).
      (2) Host (v.30) —not Guest (v.29).
      (3) Lord (v.34) —not merely Jesus of Nazareth (v.19).

   b. On our side, there must be—
      (1) Teachableness (v.27).
      (2) Receptiveness (v.29).
      (3) Responsiveness (v.32).

2. What are the results?
   a. Redemption and reconciliation.
   b. Light and love.
   c. Salvation and satisfaction.
   d. Peace and power.

99

THE WAY TO FAITH

(Luke 24:32)

T HE WAY to faith is to have a personal experience of the living Christ through the sacred Scriptures.

I. *Experience alone is unreliable.*

Cf. these men and their—

1. Doubt.
2. Despondency.
3. Despair.

II. *Experience must be illumined by the Bible.*

1. Christ's method was to send them to God's Word.
2. Suffering Messiah was new clew to maze.
3. From Scriptures they passed to Christ Himself.

III. *Experience plus knowledge of the Bible is the great source of power.*

1. Weak Christians show too little Bible study.
2. Much ignorance needs correcting—much life needs replenishing.
3. Experience alone weak at best—often becomes dangerous.
4. Contact with Living Word day by day essential.
5. Faith comes by hearing—Bible is faith's—
   a. Food.
   b. Purifier.
   c. Strengthener.
   d. Guide.
   e. Test.

And so—

"In Thy light shall we see light" (Psa. 36:9) .

100

THE ASCENSION
(Luke 24:44-53)

THE FORTY days between the Resurrection and the Ascension were full of blessing for the disciples. The Ascension was the crown of Christ's earthly experience (cf. Heb. 1:3; Rom. 8:18). It seems to some of us that churches which do not observe this holy day miss the culmination of our Lord's life on earth and the initiation of His life in heaven. As the Anglican Collect for Ascension Day expresses it: "Like as we do believe Thy only-begotten Son our Lord Jesus Christ to have ascended into the heavens; so we may also in heart and mind thither ascend, and with Him continually dwell."

An editorial in *The Christian,* some years ago, has this to say: "The Ascension marks the commencement of the evangelical era, for then the Lord gave to His Church the gifts of apostles, pastors, prophets, evangelists, and teachers (Eph. 4:11) 'unto the work of ministering.' . . . These gifts ended for ever the epoch of a special priesthood and introduced a brotherhood in which 'every joint' supplies something to the Body . . . the brotherhood of which He is the living soul. The Ascension carries within itself the guarantee of this new order, since He who passed within the veil "fills all things' (Eph. 4:10)."

But first our Lord had much to share with the Eleven. Verses 44-49 of this chapter are not in immediate continuation of the preceding section, but a summary of the post-Resurrection teaching of Christ.

I. *The Final Lessons* (vs. 44-48)

A. *Christ and the Scriptures* (vs. 44-46)

1. Things written and spoken.
   (a) Suffering Christ anticipated.
   (b) Risen Christ foretold.

2. Things endured and fulfilled.
   (a) Suffering Christ seen.
   (b) Perfected Christ displayed (cf. vs. 32,45).

3. Things learned and understood.
   (a) To see Jesus is to understand Scriptures—this part of Christ's work.

   (b) Then to see Christ in Scriptures—moral and spiritual preparation necessary to cultivate faculty of observation and interpretation.

N.B. "While I was yet with you" (v.44) —reminder that things no longer same—new intercourse begun.

B. *Christ and the World* (v.47)

1. The Work.
   a. "Repentance"—man's part.
   b. "Remission"—God's part.

2. The Sphere.
   a. "All nations"—both universality and individuality glory of message.
   b. "Beginning at Jerusalem"—mercy magnified, efficacy illustrated, principle established.

3. The Power.
   a. "In His name"—based on His nature.
   b. Also depending on His might and wielded on His authority.

C. *Christ and the Disciples* (v.48)

1. The Work.
   a. "These things"—testimony witnessed.
   b. "Ye"—poor, weak, ignorant ones!

2. The Qualification.

   a. Sight and knowledge—not theory, reasoning, etc.

   b. Facts as foundation.

3. The Force.

   a. Nothing would withstand such testimony.

   b. No new philosophy, but new facts.

N.B. We have not seen, but we have felt and known. Are we witnessing?

II. *The Promised Power* (v.49)

   A. *The Promise of the Father*

   1. Real blessing—"upon you."

   2. Abundant blessing (cf. John 15 and 16).

   3. Assured blessing—"promise."

   B. *The Power from on High*

   1. Divine—"from on high."

   2. Effectual—for speaking, working, enduring.

   3. Complete—"endued," or "clothed" (R.V.) —self to be covered. "The ideas of abundant fulness of qualities, of a gift that is visible on the outside, and of something that wraps and veils and dignifies the naked humanity, lie in that great word 'clothed with power from on high.' " (Alexander Maclaren)

   C. *The Condition of Reception*

   1. "Tarry ye in the city of Jerusalem"—wait just where you are!

   2. Wait—in trust, expectation, self-distrust. But one might question:

   a. Why not go now? Wait—grace!

   b. Have had all necessary teaching? Wait—power!

   c. Ridiculous waiting for nothing? Wait—testing.

   d. Souls perishing? Wait—experience and desire not

lost by waiting, if it will mean more powerful witnessing.

N.B. The Word of God is to be preached by the servants through the Spirit of God.

III. *The Glorious Ascension* (vs. 50-53)

A. *The Great Leader* (v.50)

Significant picture—

1. Christ at head, calm, quiet.

2. Disciples following, ready, expectant.

B. *The Gracious Blessing* (v.51)

Beautiful attitude—standing on Mount of Olives near Bethany.

1. The Master—hands lifted, blessing.

2. The Disciples—heads bowed, receiving.

C. *The Majestic Departure* (v.51)

1. "Parted from them"—to complete His work:

   a. His redemptive sacrifice accepted.

   b. His representative position taken.

2. "Carried up into heaven"—to send the Spirit:

   a. The Father's promise kept to give Comforter (cf. John 14:16).

   b. The Son's promise kept to endue disciples with power (cf. v.49).

N.B. We are assured we shall be where He is, and as He is.

IV. *The True Disciples* (vs. 52,53)

1. "Worshipped"—adoration, dedication.

2. "Returned to Jerusalem"—obedience, expectation.

3. "Were continually in the temple"—praise, worship.

N.B. When cloud of death came, they lost heart; but when cloud of heaven (Acts 1:9) took Him, there was great joy (v.53).

Conclusion

1. The Ascended Christ is the same to us today:
   a. Working through us, actively interested.
   b. Giving us the Holy Spirit to empower us.
   c. Leading us to victory.
   d. Interceding for us.
   e. Blessing us.

2. The blessings of the Ascension are ours today:
   a. Acceptance—unquestioned.
   b. Righteousness—untarnished.
   c. Life—unending.
   d. Peace—undisturbed.
   e. Relationship—unbroken.
   f. Title—undisputed.
   g. Inheritance—unfading.

3. The joy of the Ascension lies in difference between death and life, in appropriation of teaching received after the Resurrection:
   a. Disciples were afraid when He appeared (v.37), rejoiced when He disappeared (vs. 52,53).
   b. Came to know they received more than they lost.
   c. Thus all life was worship—every place a temple, every act, adoration.
   d. Christ in everything and everything in Christ.
   e. Realized they were "seated with Christ" (cf. Eph. 3:6), not looking up from earth to heaven, but down from heaven to earth.

"Your life is hid with Christ in God. When Christ, who is our life shall appear, then shall ye also appear with Him in glory" (Col. 3:4).

101

DIVINE COMPULSIONS
(Luke 24:46,47)

In christ's life-story one little word stands as a key-note—the four-letter word "must." Small though it is, it is very important because it was so often used by our Lord to indicate the dominating principle of His ministry. His was a life lived under pressure of a great necessity, the compulsion of His love, loyalty and earnestness towards His Father in heaven and His mission on earth.

In particular, there are seven word-pictures painted for us by the Evangelists Luke and John in which the word "must" is emphasized: (1) Luke 2:49: "Wist ye not that I *must* be about my Father's business?" (2) Luke 4:43: "I *must* preach the king-dom of God to other cities also." (3) Luke 13:33: "I *must* walk today, and tomorrow, and the day following." (4) Luke 17:25: "First *must* He suffer many things." (5) John 3:14: "Even so *must* the Son of man be lifted up." (6) John 9:4: "I *must* work the works of Him that sent Me." (7) John 10:16: "Other sheep . . . also I *must* bring."

But this obligation did not cease with His death, for in this post-Resurrection chapter we see a threefold necessity:

I. *Of the Past — The Crucifixion* (v.26)

   1. No death, no salvation—"*ought* not Christ—?"

   2. Necessity twofold:

     a. Divine law.

     b. Divine love.

II. *Of the Present — The Resurrection* (v.44)
   1. No resurrection, no assurance of salvation—"all things *must* be fulfilled"
   2. Necessity twofold:
      a. Definite proof.
      b. Definite right.

III. *Of the Future — The Proclamation* (vs. 46,47)
   A. *The Fact*
      1. No proclaiming, no receiving (cf. Rom. 10:14) —"It *behoved* . . . that repentance and remission of sins should be preached—"
      2. Is it realized that this necessity is on exactly same level as others? Said by Christ in same sentence, and is on grammatical equality.
      3. Why is it necessary?
         a. How else can it be known what Christ did?
         b. How else can Gospel be received personally today?
      4. What precisely is necessary?
         a. Repentance and remission.
         b. In His Name.
         c. Among all nations.

   B. *The Factors*
      1. The Warrant.
         Scripture (v.46; cf. Matt. 28:19,20).
      2. The Message.
         a. Sin (v.47; cf. John 16:8).
         b. Repentance (v.47; Acts 2:38).
         c. Forgiveness (v.47; cf. 1:77).
      3. The Power.
         Christ and His Holy Spirit (v.49; cf. John 14:26).
      4. The Scope.
         All nations: home first, then abroad (v.49; cf. Acts 1:8).

5. The Plan.

To reach the depraved, the condemned (v.47; cf. Rom. 6:23).

6. The Medium.

"Ye"—all believers (v. 48; cf. Acts 2:32).

7. The Result.

a. Souls saved (1 Cor. 15:1,2; Jas. 5:20).

b. God glorified (John 15:8; Eph. 3:21).

Thus will the evidences of Christianity be strengthened at our hands, and the Christian life spread and shared.

Conclusion

1. Have we ever faced the following facts?

   a. Many churches give no attention to missions.

   b. Many churches have few members only who contribute in any way.

   c. Yet real interest in missionary work is mark of living church, as always.

   d. And this is one work given to us by Christ:

      (1) In last chapters of all four Gospels, and in first chapter of Acts, forty days given over to "mission study."

      (2) For sake of world and of Christ, missions essential. "No war was ever yet won by mere defence, least of all a war of conquest, which that of Christianity is" (Mahan).

2. What shall we do about it?

   a. Study Bible with subject in mind—e.g., Psa. 72.

   b. Read missionary literature with care and interest.

   c. Consider duty of Giving, Going, Helping—

   d. But, above all, Praying, in which all may join.

3. What will foreign missions do for the Christian?
   They will be a test of his character in respect to—
   a. Knowledge of Scripture.
   b. Grasp of doctrine.
   c. Prayer of faith.
   d. Consecration of life.

102

THE GIFT OF THE HOLY SPIRIT
(Luke 24:49)

T HE GREAT Forty Days must have been a memorable
time for the Eleven. During this post-Resurrection period their
Master explained the Old Testament, illuminated earthly life,
trained their little band for an invisible fellowship with Himself, and prepared them for their future work of evangelization.

All was summed up in the gift of the Holy Spirit, the promise of which He renewed at this time. In the early days of
Christ's ministry there had been no mention of the Third Person of the Holy Trinity; in the later days the idea was introduced and developed; and on the last night of the Saviour's
earthly life the full teaching was given. Then came the great
experience of Calvary, the marvellous gift of Easter, and the
patient waiting for Pentecost.

I. *The Great Need* — "power from on high"

   1. Power.

      a. For life within.

      b. For labor without.

   2. Personal Power.

      a. "Clothed" (R.V.) — (Cf. Job 8:22; Isa. 59:17; Psa. 93:1;
      contra, Heb. of Judg. 6:34).

      b. From food to philosophy—difference between inside
      and out—subject and object.

   3. Divine Power.

      a. "From on high"—only this effectual.

      b. Cf. words and needs by same men—no power before, all
      power after.

II. *The Great Provision* — "the promise of my Father"
   1. What?
      a. "Promise" means "expectation based on word."
      b. Promise of Father to Son (Acts 2:33).
      c. Promise of Son to disciples (John 15:26; 16:7).

   2. How?
      a. By a gift—Divine, perfect.
      b. By definite endowment and equipment.

   3. Why?
      a. As fire, purifying and energizing (Acts 2:3).
      b. As oil, invigorating and healing (Heb. 1:9).
      c. As water, cleansing and fertilizing (John 7:38,39).
      d. As wind, refreshing and vitalizing (Acts 2:2; John 3:8).

III. *The Great Secret* — "tarry"
   1. Tarrying.
      a. To wait, to sit still.
      b. Solitude, silence, meditation, prayer.
      c. Man so little alone—no man much good without solitude.

   2. Trusting.
      a. With active desire—means, first, expecting and, then, accepting.
      b. Does not mean indolence or complete inactivity.

   3. Testifying.
      a. By word.
      b. By deed.

Conclusion

"Solitude, silence, meditation, expectation, desire—all these have to be united if we do not want to stop the flow to us of the gift of the Divine Spirit" (Alexander Maclaren).

Do what thou canst; and leave the rest to Him
Who bore thy heavy burden on the Cross,
Suffer'd the bitter pangs of death for thee,
Enter'd, for thee, the precincts of the grave,
Ascended thence triumphantly on high:
And now, from His own place at God's right hand,
Show'rs down the Spirit's gifts upon mankind,
Thus sanctifying those He died to save;
Thus leading them unto His Father's throne,
And claiming for them thus adoption there.

(Harriet Rebecca King)

DEVOTIONAL SUMMARY OF
THE GOSPEL OF LUKE

The reader is shown that—

1. *Christianity is the religion of humanity*
   This Gospel full of references to our Lord as Son of man, one who—
   a. Has sympathy with human life.
   b. Is touched with feeling of infirmities.
   c. Shows His tenderness to womanhood and to poor.
   d. Deals continually with sorrow and suffering.

2. *Christianity is the religion of redemption*
   This Gospel—
   a. Speaks of salvation for sinners.
   b. Has special message to be proclaimed all over world—forgiveness of sins.

3. *Christianity is the religion of power*
   This Gospel—
   a. Contains several important references to the Holy Spirit.
   b. Reveals Divine grace providing spiritual force necessary to holy living and effectual service.

4. *Christianity is the religion of personal devotion*
   This Gospel—
   a. Is particularly full of praise and prayer.
   b. Emphasizes these as important features of true Christian life.

5. *Christianity is the religion for all the world*
   This Gospel speaks of—
   a. All classes.
   b. All ages.
   c. All races.

Men, women, and children everywhere are within its scope and opportunity. Hence, since Christianity *is* Christ, there emerges from it as depicted in this Gospel of Luke a portrait of our Lord as our Kinsman-Redeemer, One who is both real Man and Divine Saviour, human, gracious, universal—the Saviour of the world.